Animal, Vegetable, Mineral

Books by Louis Kronenberger

No Whippings, No Gold Watches
The Polished Surface
The Cart and the Horse
A Month of Sundays
Marlborough's Duchess
The Republic of Letters
Company Manners
The Thread of Laughter
Grand Right and Left
Kings and Desperate Men
The Grand Manner

Edited or Translated by Louis Kronenberger

Atlantic Brief Lives
The Cutting Edge
Quality: Its Image in the Arts
The Great World: from Greville's Memoirs
The Viking Book of Aphorisms
(*in collaboration with W. H. Auden*)
Novelists on Novelists
The Maxims of La Rochefoucauld
The Pleasure of Their Company
Anouilh's *Colombe*
Cavalcade of Comedy
The Portable Johnson and Boswell
Selected Works of Alexander Pope
The Plays of Sheridan
The Best Plays of 1952–53 through 1960–61
Shaw: A Critical Survey

Animal, Vegetable, Mineral

A COMMONPLACE BOOK

Louis Kronenberger

A WILLIAM COLE BOOK

New York / *The Viking Press*

To Diana and Lionel Trilling

*Pages 326–328 constitute an extension
of this copyright page*

Contents

Introduction

Let me begin by saying that this book lacks one of the essentials of a commonplace book, since it has for the most part been compiled, not accumulated; and envisioned in print, not copied out with a pen. I ought long ago to have begun cutting out, or copying out, verses and speeches, incidents and anecdotes, examples of passion, humaneness, heroism, genius—shortish things, mainly, that moved or roused, entertained or informed, impressed or surprised me. And, being what I am, I should also have clipped or copied out, and commented on, still other things which—because they were weird or incredible or idiotic, or in keeping with the world's Malaprops, or Munchausens, or Micawbers—I found enjoyable; and which I should want to revert to, from time to time, in the book containing them.

But I possess no such book; I possess not even the beginnings of one, as at the age of seventeen I did possess a briefly kept diary. Whether from soon tiring of the idea, or from being all too conscious of how very self-conscious its entries were, I soon gave up the diary; and when, years later, I came upon it and read it with far more nausea than nostalgia, I forthwith—in the language of the diary itself—consigned it to the flames. But a notebook for poetry and prose that appealed to me I never thought of keeping. My father had kept what might be called a commonplace portfolio, a leather contraption with a number of pockets, some of them filled with "family" clippings—births, weddings, obits, and the like—but several others containing bits of printed verse and prose, of oratory and eulogy, of regional glorification and Republican Party grandiloquence. In its small way this was the true stuff for a commonplace book.

Yet in an inferior fashion I did do something, from adolescence on, not altogether different: I marked up books, wrote comments in their margins, and indicated on their inside covers the page numbers of particularly notable passages. This might have served as an untidy version of a commonplace book had I later not started marking up books and noting particular passages for other reasons: to borrow from in an article, or make use of as research, or include in an anthology. So that just *why* I had checked something became in after years a puzzle, and in some cases a passage seemed singled out to make fun of. Nevertheless a few things that I checked and recently came upon I thought delightful, and they appear, with stout commonplace-book credentials, in this volume.

So much for the virtual nonhistory of the volume. But if only two or three years of searching for material have gone into it, many years of remembering have helped dictate its choices, and constitute what would have lodged in my book had there been one. How often I wished that there had been, for, though I remembered what the things were, I had quite forgotten where I found them, so that instead of having a happy reunion, I had to make up a search party. Still, that had its good side, for while searching for old things I came upon new and often better ones. Indeed, compiling this book has had for me a kind of exploratory zest, has been for me a kind of long-shot browsing: sessions with books I had never heard of, or had long since tired of, or had all my life fled from, in the hope that even aridity might have its oases, or pomposity might provide amusement. The whole pleasant experience of assembling this book has led me into fields—and forests, and caves, and walled cities, and woozy habitations—that I might otherwise have never encountered; and now that I have offered *this* commonplace book to the world, I am tempted to start a private one of my own, on old-fashioned ruled blankbook paper where items will be copied down in pre-faded ink or pasted in with vintage smelly glue.

Despite how many remembered things were conscripted for this book, they were things I knew I still liked, and not a delving back into a misty past, or things admitted on sentimental grounds or to demonstrate the vicissitudes of time. Of course one of the merits and charms of a genuine fifty-year-old common-place book would be its chronicling a person's shifts in interest, variations of mood, alterations of taste; how much or how little he was the child of his era or his environment; how much or how little he matured, or never changed, or declined. Done honestly—and perhaps dishonestly—it would have the makings of a cul-tural autobiography. For a few hours I was tempted to try and reassemble the things that would have graced an adolescent commonplace book had I begun one; but beyond doubting that it would interest anyone but myself, I felt it would be a self-indulgent daguerreotype of Myself When Young, something im-posed on the book, not intrinsic to it. Yet a few things here do go back, as lifelong favorites, to my early college days.

Whether then, as now forty-odd years later, the "principles" that govern this book would have been much the same, I don't know. The principles in any case virtually narrow down to exemplifying my tastes and temperament, or to qualifying for what, by my lights, best fits a book of this kind. It seems to me that for the most part the choices should be short and "striking" —poems and verses; observations, epigrams, anecdotes, oddi-ties; extracts from speeches, from essays, from histories, perhaps even from works of fiction. Although many commonplace books have been kept by well-known people, I am sure that in, say, Victorian days or in remote farmhouse parlors or in frontier-like settlements sentimental verse, didactic prose, childlike humor, and childish jokes were the chief commodities, with newspapers and borrowed books the chief sources of supply. These things, because of their naivety, mediocrity, sentimentality, we would nowadays reject, though there may still be a taste for them.

For myself, having said that the material should be short and striking, I would add that the mood should be vivacious, curious, and light. No doubt in the days when people had limited access to printed matter, they might (lest it be lost to them) have copied out of borrowed books entire essays, orations, or sermons.

But today such a procedure is seldom if ever necessary, and it strikes me that a commonplace book should be composed of self-contained things, whether as wholes or excerpts, and that, by virtue of their eloquence, brilliance, trenchancy; their pathos, protest, exhortation; their charm, wit, or nonsense, they should also be self-sufficient. And though a proper commonplace book should have considerable range and variety, it should not be a book one turns to when in a really serious or contemplative mood or when in search of sustained and solid reading matter: it is the difference between listening to a medley of even the finest tunes, and hearing a full-length string quartet or symphony. Just *so*, a commonplace book, unlike a novel or play, permits—indeed all but requires—your opening it anywhere. Its contents can be as personal as a diary or impersonal as a decree, as simple as a nursery rhyme or complex as a puzzle; can shift quickly from the sordid to the elegant, the ridiculous to the sublime; be striking because eccentric or exotic, but also for being sharp-edged— a retort, a metaphor, an astute comparison of two famous men, an indelible description of one, a sophisticated picture of high life, or of low life a gaunt, graphic sketch. All these things, moreover, should help characterize the compiler of them, as an index to his tastes and an inventory of his interests.

The one big exception to all this is poetry, where I haven't hesitated to include some of the greatest things I know—particularly in Shakespeare and Milton—that are also some of the most familiar. Great poetry, like great music, can assert its greatness at once, can be overpowering or proclamatory as well as insinuating and cumulative. Greatness in other forms of writing is seldom so obliging as to fold itself into a paragraph or fulfill itself in a page; and even where, in a novel or play, it achieves a great climax or confrontation, it often requires what preceded it to certify its greatness. Mere excerpts can on many occasions be mendacities or forms of betrayal: there are, after all, thoughts that do often lie too deep for shears.

Otherwise I am glad to have shears for a colleague—at any rate, so long as they know their place and don't mistake themselves for a pen; so long as they know when to draw back and not take to slicing because half a sentence proves dull or a whole one repetitious. But I am gladder about the many things that can be offered uncut and are both short and satisfying. There are people, to be sure, who dislike anthologies or scorn light reading or sniff at anecdotes; there are even those that resemble the young woman at Cambridge, England, who, when asked by her tutor whether she had enjoyed the book under discussion, answered, "I don't read to enjoy, I read to evaluate." Well, such an anecdote and such an answer can themselves induce evaluation. But as against high priggishness in one reader, there are dozens of readers who like to spend half an hour roaming through or revisiting books like these: it is people at the opposite pole, people who having started a book feel compelled, however bored, to finish it, that I have never quite understood.

Though a half-century-old commonplace book would constitute an autobiography of sorts, its changes of taste in literature and of attitudes toward life might have less to do with the book's compiler than with the five decades that the book has spanned. If things changed for the compiler as he grew older, they very likely became, in themselves, old hat; and often the compiler's attitudes, in changing, simply conformed to prevailing attitudes —or to mere seasonal fashions. How much, even at a high level, can tarnish or perish after fifty years! Thus during the 1920s and for a good while after, a very superior anthology with some of the features and flavor of a commonplace book—*The Week-End Book*—was a mainstay for the bed table of weekend guests, and for the bed table of the host and hostess as well. Not to go into what it contained, but only to speak of something it didn't, *The Week-End Book* offered a "list of great poems" it thought too well known and overanthologized for inclusion. There are thirty-three such poems, listed with author, title, and first line. Yet I not only wonder whether a fair number of them would still be considered "great," but also whether people today would be familiar with the first lines, let alone the authors, of half a dozen.

Go from me. Yet I feel that I shall stand
Day of the cloud in fleets, O day
With proud thanksgiving, the mother of her children
I climbed a hill as light fell short
With all my will, but much against my heart
Art thou poor, yet hast thou golden slumbers?

My own omissions, or very small portions, of certain kinds of writing derive from one of two things, which sometimes join hands: either from a lack of rapport or sufficient understanding on my part, or from a sense of their being too heavy or difficult to be read at odd moments in an untaxing mood. One form that I regret leaving out is philosophy—a realm all vaporous and be-clouded for my too concrete mind. I fear I am even less responsive to mystical writing: though I find the lyrical Blake wonderful, the mystical Blake is a closed book to me. Again, I find most scientific prose baffling, while Clough's "How pleasant it is to have money, heigh-ho" supplies for me all the economics needed in such a book as this.

I too, almost fifty years after *The Week-End Book*, have for the most part omitted things that seemed overfamiliar, from limericks and clerihews to epigrams and rejoinders, from poetic gems to famous prose portraits and perorations. I have included some of the very famous passages of my youth, wondering whether they are still favored or even familiar today, and I need hardly say that *I* favor the mockingbird almost as much as the nightingale. So many glances backward are, of course, at odds with the classic compiling of commonplace books, where what one cut or copied out was oftenest a *discovery*, something valued because up till then unknown. Happily this volume is far from lacking in "discoveries," particularly of short things found in books I had never read before, or had read long before and forgotten; and some of them I merely stumbled on without having a commonplace book in mind. This was the brightest facet of my compiling; and this, of course, most resembles the compiling of commonplace books long ago.

L.K.

Animal, Vegetable, Mineral

Alpha and Omega

✠ It is a writer's born duty to be fascinated by words; though to what extent, and in what direction, may well vary. There is the derivation of words, for many of us one of the chief pleasures of knowing some Latin, hence what *eliminate* or *dilapidate* is derived from, or what stepbrothers *equipage* and *cavalry* are, or what twins are *cavalry* and *chivalry*, and how English *day* and French *jour* are related, and so on. There is the descent of words from a common forefather, far back in Indo-European mists; most obviously, *pater* and *Vater*, and *father* and *padre* and *père*. There are words we find beautiful, words we overuse, words we would never use. This last group I find grows bigger every day—that is, if they are to be accepted as words, for on every side we encounter jargon words and phrases: the hideous products of sociology; the hasty, imperfect creations of science; the pretentious, soon ubiquitous contributions of academic criticism. (One should be required to get a permit to use *subsume* any longer, or *epiphany* or *persona* at all.)

Words of course are sometimes the servant of two masters, as, when someone thought *swallow* particularly beautiful, someone else asked, "Do you mean as a bird or a gulp?" And it is easy to disagree with others about words: George Saintsbury says somewhere that the only beautiful man's name in English is *Eustace*, to me so unattractively sibilant that I needn't even bring in its sounding sissified. About that "blessed word, Mesopotamia" I tend to agree; but in truth each word is an island, etc., and it is not till we come upon phrases or whole sentences of words, or lines or lines and a half of poetry, that they most fully flower, or we are most moved or beguiled. Certainly the great rhythmic

✠ This symbol indicates that the accompanying commentary is by Louis Kronenberger.

effects of poetry, or the greatest stylish effects of prose, have need of a number of words; words perfectly placed; whether, in very few words, John Webster's haunting

> . . . a face folded in sorrow;

or, in eleven monosyllables, Shakespeare's

> Keep up your bright swords, for the dew will rust them.

For liquidity, elegance, and enchantment, I know little to rival Marvell's

> Stumbling on melons, as I pass,
> Ensnared with flowers I fall on grass;

for elegance and stylishness in prose, little to rival Congreve's: "Why, one makes lovers as fast as one pleases, and they live as long as one pleases, and they die as soon as one pleases; and then, if one pleases, one makes more." And for magic, beyond even Keats's casements or Coleridge's demon lovers, I would put Blake's

> The lost traveller's dream under the hill.

But there are less lofty or ravishing or haunting uses of words. Though gestures and drawings greatly help, without words we should be very short on fun or wit. We are all entitled to contribute to the vast pile of words, not least by inventing them. How many Shakespeare invented!—More, I dare believe, than even the sociologists. And where the professors are merely polysyllabic, the Lewis Carrolls and Edward Lears could be playful. At word-making I prefer Lear, as more poetic; though of course Carroll's *chortle* has entered the language where, say, *runcible spoon* merely waits at the door. I wish I had made up a word that entered the language; the most I can claim is to have dredged up a metaphor that was subsequently decapitated. It was a metaphor I found listed somewhere and had never seen in print, whereupon I used it several times in a magazine with a large circulation—"happy as a clam at high tide." Thereafter I began to see it in print and to hear it in speech in the truncated form "happy as a clam." Thus what gave it point it had been robbed of: "happy as a clam" is neither good sense nor good nonsense. (Shortenings, to be justified, must not leave the sense in doubt: "A stitch in time" or "Red sky at night" have centuries of use behind them, and we all can complete the quotation.)

I like most uses of words and language, and by no means least at the level of slang, particular lingoes, and lowborn, often high-voltage phrases from various eras, occupations, and evildoers. One hears racy and pungent language behind those heaviest of closed doors, prison doors, where calling a spade a spade would be incredibly genteel. Pungent too is much tramp slang, which I have drawn from, not sure how much today has become obsolete, or been superseded, and if so, by what. From Grose's *Classical Dictionary of the Vulgar Tongue* you will find samples in harmony with the book's intent, and there are, I think, interesting samples from the English public schools (a collection of American prep and high school and indeed college words and phrases, past and present, might be useful). And, indulging this mild hobby of mine once more, I proffer some Victorian phrases long laid to rest. Actions may speak louder, but words still speak better, and fit better into books.

Americana

The American Credo

✠ First published in 1920, and in a revised and enlarged edition in 1927, George Jean Nathan's and H. L. Mencken's *The American Credo* caught on its hook a good many popular beliefs of Americans. Forty-odd to fifty years later it is rather amusing and instructive to see how many are still current, and how many others have become anachronisms. A number of them, to be sure, not even in their own day had anything approaching national support, and others—such as that you can't make bricks without straw—had merely passed from semi-proverbs to clichés. Here, first, are some that still have life to them:

That when a comedian, just before the rise of the curtain, is handed a telegram announcing the death of his mother or only child, he goes out on the stage and gives a more comic performance than ever.

That all one has to do to gather a large crowd in New York is to stand on the curb a few minutes and gaze intently at the sky.

That the Masonic order goes back to the days of King Solomon.

That whiskey is good for snake-bite.

That it is impossible for a United States ambassador to live on his salary, and that only a very rich man can afford to accept such a post.

That all the best cooks and dressmakers are men.

That if one begins eating peanuts one cannot stop.

That St. Louis in summer is the hottest place in the world.

That farm hands begin each day by eating three dozen pancakes.

That when a bride and groom arrive at an hotel resort they never are able to disguise the fact that they have just been married.

That it is not healthful to keep flowers in one's bedroom at night.

That if a waiter in a restaurant has a grudge against one he will surreptitiously spit into one's food. [See, on page 84, the selection from George Orwell's *Down and Out in Paris and London*.]

That the men who own the hat-checking privileges in New York restaurants are all millionaires.

✠ And here are some that are quite outmoded in one way or another:

That there is something slightly peculiar about a man who wears spats.

That a sepia photograph of the Coliseum, framed, is a work of art.

That fish is a brain food.

That one hour's sleep before midnight is worth two after midnight.

That if one dreams of falling and dreams that one lands, one will never awaken and will be dead.

That one never gets a full night's sleep in a sleeping-car.

That all star intercollegiate sprinters die of enlargement of the heart.

That a few minutes before an atheist dies he usually changes his mind and becomes deeply religious, and that if he fails to do so he dies in great agony. [Though this is no part of the credo today, Nathan, a lifelong agnostic, was received into the Roman Catholic Church a short time before he died.]

That it is almost sure death to eat cucumbers and drink milk at the same meal. [In my family, fifty-odd years ago, it was cucumbers and buttermilk; and I still have qualms.]

✠ There are also a few beliefs reflecting a certain level of culture, such as "That Henry James never wrote a short sentence" or "That there is something the matter with a man who can tell a Louis XV clock from a salt cellar by Benvenuto Cellini."

Navigation

There seemed to be one small hope, however: if we could get through the intricate and dangerous Hat Island crossing before night, we could venture the rest, for we would have plainer sailing and better water. But it would be insanity to attempt Hat Island at night. So there was a deal of looking at watches all the rest of the day, and a constant ciphering upon the speed we were making; Hat Island was the eternal subject; sometimes hope was high and sometimes we were delayed in a bad crossing, and down it went again. For hours all hands lay under the burden of this suppressed excitement; it was even communicated to me, and I got to feeling so solicitous about Hat Island, and under such an awful pressure of responsibility, that I wished I might have five minutes on shore to draw a good, full, relieving breath, and start over again. We were standing no regular watches. Each of our pilots ran such portions of the river as he had run when coming upstream, because of his greater familiarity with it; but both remained in the pilot-house constantly.

An hour before sunset Mr. Bixby took the wheel, and Mr. W. stepped aside. For the next thirty minutes every man held his watch in his hand and was restless, silent, and uneasy. At last somebody said, with a doomful sigh:

"Well, yonder's Hat Island—and we can't make it."

All the watches closed with a snap, everybody sighed and muttered something about its being "too bad, too bad—ah, if we could *only* have got here half an hour sooner!" and the place was thick with the atmosphere of disappointment. Some started to go out, but loitered, hearing no bell-tap to land. The sun dipped behind the horizon, the boat went on. Inquiring looks passed from one guest to another; and one who had his hand on the door-knob and had turned it, waited, then presently took away his hand and let the knob turn back again. We bore steadily down the bend. More looks were exchanged, and nods of surprised admiration—but no words. Insensibly the men drew together behind Mr. Bixby, as the sky darkened and one or two dim stars came out. The dead silence and sense of waiting became oppressive. Mr. Bixby pulled the cord, and two deep, mellow notes from the big bell floated off on the night. Then a pause, and one more note was struck. The watchman's voice followed, from the hurricane-deck:

"Labboard lead, there! Stabboard lead!"

The cries of the leadsmen began to rise out of the distance, and were gruffly repeated by the word-passers on the hurricane-deck.

"M-a-r-k three! M-a-r-k three! Quarter-less-three! Half twain! Quarter twain! M-a-r-k twain! Quarter-less—"

Mr. Bixby pulled two bell-ropes, and was answered by faint jinglings far below in the engine-room, and our speed slackened. The steam began to whistle through the gauge-cocks. The cries of the leadsmen went on—and it is a weird sound, always, in the night. Every pilot in the lot was watching now, with fixed eyes, and talking under his breath. Nobody was calm and easy but Mr. Bixby. He would put his wheel down and stand on a spoke, and as the steamer swung into her (to me) utterly invisible marks—for we seemed to be in the midst of a wide and gloomy sea—he would meet and fasten her there. Out of the murmur of half-audible talk, one caught a coherent sentence now and then—such as: "There; she's over the first reef all right!"

After a pause, another subdued voice:

"Her stern's coming down just *exactly* right, by *George!*"

"Now she's in the marks; over she goes!"

Somebody else muttered:

"Oh, it was done beautiful—*beautiful!*"

Now the engines were stopped altogether, and we drifted with the current. Not that I could see the boat drift, for I could not, the stars being all gone by this time. This drifting was the dismalest work; it held one's heart still. Presently I discovered a blacker gloom than that which surrounded us. It was the head of the island. We were closing right down upon it. We entered its deeper shadow, and so imminent seemed the peril that I was likely to suffocate; and I had the strongest impulse to do *something,* anything, to save the vessel. But still Mr. Bixby stood by his wheel, silent, intent as a cat, and all the pilots stood shoulder to shoulder at his back.

"She'll not make it!" somebody whispered.

The water grew shoaler and shoaler, by the leadsman's cries, till it was down to:

"Eight-and-a-half! E-i-g-h-t feet! E-i-g-h-t feet! Seven-and—"

Mr. Bixby said warningly through his speaking-tube to the engineer:

"Stand by, now!"

"Ay, ay, sir!"

"Seven-and-a-half! Seven feet! *Six*-and—"

We touched bottom! Instantly Mr. Bixby set a lot of bells ringing, shouted through the tube, *"Now,* let her have it—every ounce you've got!" then to his partner, "Put her hard down! snatch her! snatch her!" The boat rasped and ground her way through the sand, hung upon the apex of disaster a single tremendous instant, and then over she went! And such a shout as went up at Mr. Bixby's back never loosened the roof of a pilot-house before!

M ARK T WAIN, Life on the Mississippi

San Francisco Four Months Later

Of all the marvelous phases of the history of the Present, the growth of San Francisco is the one which will most tax the belief of the Future. Its parallel was never known, and shall never be beheld again. I speak only of what I saw with my own eyes. When I landed there, a little more than four months before [in September 1849] I found a scattering town of tents and canvas houses, with a show of frame buildings on one or two streets, and a population of about six thousand. Now, on my last visit, I saw around me an actual metropolis . . . Then, the gold-seeking sojourner lodged in muslin rooms and canvas garrets, with a philosophic lack of furniture, and ate his simple though substantial fare from pine boards. Now, lofty hotels, gaudy with verandas and balconies, were met with in all quarters, furnished with home luxury, and aristocratic restaurants presented daily their long bills of fare, rich with the choicest technicalities of the Parisian cuisine. Then, vessels were coming in day after day, to lie deserted and useless at their anchorage. Now, scarce a day passed, but some cluster of sails, bound *outward* through the Golden Gate, took

their way to all the corners of the Pacific. Like the magic seed of
the Indian juggler, which grew, blossomed, and bore fruit before
the eyes of his spectators, San Francisco seemed to have accomplished in a day the growth of half a century. . . .

Not only was the heaviest part of the business conducted on
cash principles, but all rents, even to lodging in hotels, were required to be paid in advance. A single bowling alley, in the base-
ment story of the Ward House—a new hotel on Portsmouth
Square—prepaid $5,000 monthly. The firm of Findley, Johnson &
Co. sold their real estate, purchased a year previous for $20,000, at
$300,000 . . . This was a fair specimen of the speculations daily
made. Those on a lesser scale were frequently of a very amusing
character, but the claims on one's astonishment were so constant
that the faculty soon wore out, and the most unheard-of opera-
tions were looked upon as matters of course. Among others that
came under my observation was one of a gentleman who purchased a barrel of alum for $6, the price in New York being $9. It
happened to be the only alum in the place, and as there was a
demand for it shortly afterwards, he sold the barrel for $150. . . .
A friend of mine expended $10,000 in purchasing barley, which
in a week brought $20,000. The greatest gains were still made by
the gambling tables and the eating houses. Every device that art
could suggest was used to swell the custom of the former. . . .

For a month or two previous to this time, money had been very
scarce in the market, and from ten to fifteen per cent monthly was
paid, with the addition of good security. Notwithstanding the
quantity of coin brought into the country by emigrants, and the
millions of gold dust used as currency, the actual specie basis was
very small compared with the immense amount of business trans-
acted. Nevertheless, I heard of nothing like a failure; the principal firms were prompt in all their dealings . . . The merchants
had a 'Change and Newsroom, and were beginning to cooperate
in their movements and consolidate their credit. . . .

There had been a vast improvement in the means of living
since my previous visit to San Francisco. Several large hotels had
been opened, which were equal in almost every respect to houses

of the second class in the Atlantic cities. The Ward House, the Graham House—imported bodily from Baltimore—and the St. Francis Hotel completely threw into the shade all former establishments. . . . A room at the Ward House cost $250 monthly, without board. The principal restaurants charged $35 a week for board, and there were lodging houses where a berth or "bunk"—one out of fifty in the same room—might be had for $6 a week. The model of these establishments—which were far from being "model lodging houses"—was that of a ship. A number of state-rooms, containing six berths each, ran around the sides of a large room, or cabin, where the lodgers resorted to read, write, smoke, and drink at their leisure. . . .

The great want of San Francisco was society. Think of a city of thirty thousand inhabitants peopled by men alone! The like of this was never seen before. Every man was his own housekeeper, doing, in many instances, his own sweeping, cooking, washing and mending. Many home arts, learned rather by observation than experience, came conveniently into play. He who cannot make a bed, cook a beefsteak, or sew up his own rips and rents, is unfit to be a citizen of California. . . .

Towards the close of my stay, the city was as dismal a place as could well be imagined. . . . The wind now and then blew a heavy gale, and the cold, steady fall of rain was varied by claps of thunder and sudden blasts of hail. The mud in the streets became little short of fathomless . . . A powerful London dray-horse, a very giant in harness, was the only animal able to pull a good load; and I was told that he earned his master $100 daily. . . . One could not walk any distance without getting at least ankle-deep . . . The universal custom of wearing the pantaloons inside the boots threatened to restore the knee-breeches of our grandfathers' times. Even women were obliged to shorten their skirts and wear high-topped boots. The population seemed to be composed entirely of dismounted hussars. . . .

As the rains drove the deer and other animals down from the mountains, game of all kinds became abundant. Fat elks and splendid black-tailed does hung at the doors of all the butcher shops . . . "Grizzly bear steak" became a choice dish at the eating houses; I had the satisfaction one night of eating a slice of one that had weighed eleven hundred pounds. The flesh was of a bright red color, very solid, sweet, and nutritious; its flavor was preferable to that of the best pork. . . . I may mention that a [middling hotel] dinner for fifteen persons, to which I was invited at the Excelsior, cost the giver of it $225.

The effect of a growing prosperity and some little taste of luxury was readily seen in the appearance of the business community of San Francisco. The slouched felt hats gave way to narrow-brimmed black beavers; flannel shirts were laid aside, and white linen, though indifferently washed, appeared instead; dress and frock coats, of the fashion of the previous year on the Atlantic side, came forth from trunks and sea-chests; in short, a San Francisco merchant was almost as smooth and spruce in his outward appearance as a merchant anywhere else. . . .

The steamers which arrived at this time brought large quantities of newspapers from all parts of the Atlantic States. . . . There was a glut in the market, in consequence whereof newspapers came down to fifty and twenty-five cents apiece. The leading journals of New York, New Orleans and Boston were cried at every street corner. The two papers established [in San Francisco] issued editions "for the Atlantic Coast" at the sailing of every steamer for Panama. The offices were invaded by crowds of purchasers, and the slow hand-presses in use could not keep pace with the demand. The profits of these journals were almost incredible, when contrasted with their size and the amount of their circulation. Neither of them failed to count their gains at the rate of $75,000 a year, clear profit.

BAYARD TAYLOR, *Eldorado* (1850)

✠ No doubt the city was peopled, in a family sense, by men alone; but surely at this stage of easy money and high living, prostitutes, not to speak of brothels, must have made an appearance.

Tramp and Underworld Slang (circa 1930)

Admiral's watch—A good sleep, or chance to rest. (Originally a sailor's phrase.)

Alligator bait—Fried liver.

Artillery—Beans.

Belly robber—A poor cook or mess sergeant.

Biscuit shooter—A waitress or short-order cook.

Bum—The following distinction is made: "Bums loafs and sits. Tramps loafs and walks. But a hobo moves and works, and he's clean."

Buttermilker—A tramp from the "Pittsburgh district." Origin or significance unknown.

California blankets—Newspapers when used as bedding or stuffed inside clothing to keep warm.

Carrying the mail—Traveling fast; said of anyone in a hurry.

Cover with the moon—To sleep in the open.

Cupid's itch—Any venereal disease.

Curbstones—Cigar and cigarette butts picked up from the street or the gutter.

Execution day—Monday, when the washing is "hung."

Exhibition—A meal given a tramp to eat on the steps or back porch, in full view of the neighbors.

Fifty cards in the deck—Two cards short of a full deck, hence not quite all there in the head.

Foolish powder—Originally heroin; later any unbalancing narcotic.

Gadget—In its original Navy-born meaning, an unknown or unfamiliar object. (*Gimick,* so spelled, was a lame person; *gamb,* so spelled, is the technical term in heraldry for a leg.)

Glue neck—A filthy prostitute.

Holding the lady down—Riding—over a rough stretch of track or on a fast train—face down on the "rods" and holding on tight so as not to fall off.

Kneeling at the altar—Committing pederasty.

Magazine—A six-month jail sentence (the time it takes an uneducated man to read a magazine). *Newspaper* is a thirty-day jail sentence.

Mustard shine—Using oil of mustard on shoes to keep dogs from following the scent.

P.P.—A plaster-of-Paris cast on a leg to fake a fracture.

(Drawn from Godfrey Irwin, *American Tramp and Underworld Slang*)

Ancient Rome

Virtus was the quality that distinguished the man, *vir,* from the mere human creature, *homo.* There is no exact word for it; but if we wish to know what a nation admires we can go to its nursery tales, the old stories of Washington and the Cherry Tree, Alfred and the Cakes, Bruce and the Spider. For the Roman, such stories were those Livy tells of the beginnings of the Republic; they are concerned not with truthfulness or democracy or perseverance, but with valor and complete devotion to country. Every Roman schoolboy knew the stories of Horatius at the Bridge, of Quintus Curtius leaping his horse into the gulf, of Lucius Junius Brutus, who commanded and witnessed the execution of his own sons for conspiracy against the city. There was the story of the other Horatius, who supplied the subject of a play by Corneille; in the service of the city, he killed the man his sister loved, and killed his sister because she mourned for him; he was sentenced for the killing of his sister to a purely nominal punishment, that justice might be preserved. There was Gaius Mucius, who slipped into the camp of the besieging Lars Porsena with intent to kill him, but killed one of his followers by mistake and was taken prisoner. He declared to Lars Porsena that though he had failed, there were three hundred men in Rome who had sworn to attempt Porsena's life, one after the other. When Porsena threatened him with torture unless he revealed their names, he smiled and held his own right hand in the brazier until it was burned off. Lars Porsena thought it wiser to come to terms with the Romans, and Mucius was given the name of Scævola, or Left-handed, which was borne by his descendants down to imperial times.

The story is important as showing what the Romans admired, even though I think it is probable that it was invented later to explain a nickname "Lefty" bestowed in the ordinary way. There was a similar story about the name Brutus, which means "Stupid" or "Brutish"—Hamlet's pun to Polonius was better than he knew. The story is that Lucius Junius Brutus, like Hamlet, feigned idiocy to escape the suspicion of his uncle, the last of the kings. Possibly; but the original Lefty and Stupid may have been called so for no such complimentary reason. The Romans had a schoolboyish aptitude for names based on personal peculiarities. Cicero means "Warty"; Caesar probably "Hairy." It is part of the quality in them which led, on the one hand, to the only two art forms they invented, the portrait bust and the satire; and on the other, to the abuse and smut of some of the epigrams. For, as Aristotle says, every virtue is a mean between two vices, one consisting of its defect, the other of its excess, and, it may be added, the virtue and the excess are sometimes present in the same person. It is not hard to see the excess in the stories of Horatius's murder of his sister, and even in Brutus's execution of his sons. To us, the phrase "a Roman father" implies a somewhat doubtful virtue. As the Romans might have said if they could have thought of it, in their anxiety not to be unmanly they became inhuman.

Even in their carefully maintained indifference to death and pain there came to be something almost theatrical, an attitude that reaches its full expression in the epic poets of the Silver Age, and in the tragedies of Seneca, whose characters are the ancestors of all the declamatory seventeenth-century heroes, Corneille's and Dryden's. And from disregarding their own pain they came to disregard that of others, or to enjoy it. Their *virtus* was always liable to be stained by the vice to which the soldier is tempted, ruthlessness and cruelty. Julius Caesar was in general a humane commander, but once he cut off the hands of his prisoners, to teach them not to revolt. The cruelty of the arena, at first occasional, became habitual, so that it could be said of one of the late emperors, "he never dined without human blood."

B A S I L D A V E N P O R T, "Introduction," *The Portable Roman Reader*

Anecdotes

"Oats: in England the food of horses, in Scotland that of men." —Dr. Johnson. . . . But Lord Elibank answered well when he said, "Yes, and they are the best horses and the best men in Europe."

[In] Edinburgh are a set who hawk about oysters for sale, thence called *oyster-wives*. One of them, speaking of . . . a neighbour of hers, said she was but a low-lifed creature, being only in the *mussel* line.

There was one delicate piece of politeness, which I never saw carried so far as in Edinburgh in my younger days, that of never producing children before any lady who had no family or who had lost her children.

[A miser] while he was wiping his hat with his handkerchief, was overheard by a young man . . . to utter the following soliloquy: "Alas! My good new hat! It has not met with such a shower these seven years."

I forget which of our criminal judges it was before whom a man was tried for theft, and made the singular defence that he was born with this propensity and had just got a *habit* of stealing.— "Well, Sir," replied the judge, "and we have a habit of hanging such persons."

[Mr. Lockhart of Carnwath] was a remarkably good horseman, tho' sixteen or seventeen stone weight; and to shew his horsemanship he used to put a sixpenny piece between the sole of his foot and his stirrup-iron, which was never moved during the whole of the chase.

[Of Shafto, a great racer of horses:] His rider came to him, and informed him that he had been offered a large bribe to ride foul.— "And did you take the money?"—"No, Sir . . ."—"Then meet with the person that offered it to you, and take the money; and your honour, even as to him, shall be saved."—The lad acted accordingly, and Shafto's antagonists thought themselves sure of succeeding, and on that assurance raised the bets to a very large sum. Shafto rode up to the starting post and, taking out his pocket book, summed up the bets he had depending on the match, which by this time amounted to eight or ten thousand pounds. "Gentlemen," said he, "there is too much money to trust to any other man's riding; I shall ride my horse myself." He did so, and won the match.

A gentleman told me that he attended once at Dunfermline . . . a sacramental service conducted by Ebenezer Erskine which lasted about sixteen or eighteen hours.

[Of Charles James Fox and his brother Stephen:] Their nonchalance was almost incredible. While their theatre at the family seat in Wilshire was on fire and burning, they were laying bets on the progress of the flames.

[James Balfour, seeking a favor of a bigwig who rather ignorantly collected pictures, and had just bought a very questionable Salvator] obtained the interview he wished, was shewn into the great

man's library, and saw the picture . . . but . . . had forgot the
name *Salvator*. He set himself, however, in an attitude of admiration; the [collector] on his entry into the room took immediate
notice of this. "I see," said he, "Mr. Balfour, you have an eye for
excellence in painting. Whose hand may you take that to be?"—
"I know the hand, I believe," said Balfour with a happy forward-
ness; "it is undoubtedly Melchisedec's."—"Melchisedec's!" replied the great man; "Why, it is Salvator's!"—"I know it is,"
rejoined Balfour, "but Melchisedec was a nick-name given him at
school."—"Indeed, I never knew that anecdote before; allow me to
put it down in my commonplace book."—That was done, and
Balfour obtained the favour he solicited.

The Anecdotes and Egotisms of Henry Mackenzie

✠ A propos the last anecdote, one commonplace book
perhaps deserves another. These quotations of Mackenzie's have
in themselves the quality of a period collector and recollector of
anecdotes, portraits, tidbits, and "egotisms" that have oftener a
pungent local tang than a brilliant cosmopolitan aura, yet at the
same time are not homely yarns or dialect witticisms; Mackenzie
was, after all, so much a part of Edinburgh society as to be called
"the Addison of the North," and is still remembered as the author
of *The Man of Feeling*. The *Anecdotes and Egotisms* is well
worth browsing in.

A lady was awoke in the night with the disagreeable sense of not
being alone in the room, and soon felt a thud upon her bed.
There was no doubt that some one was moving to and fro in the
room, and that hands were constantly moving over her bed. She
was so dreadfully frightened that at last she fainted. When she
came to herself, it was broad daylight, and she found that the
butler had walked in his sleep and had laid the table for fourteen
upon her bed.

AUGUSTUS HARE, *The Story of My Life*

I have heard of a lady, by birth, being reduced to cry "Muffins to sell" for a subsistence. She used to go out a-nights with her face hid up in her cloak, and then she would in the faintest voice utter her cry. Somebody passing by heard her cry—"Muffins to sell, muffins to sell! Oh, I hope nobody hears me."

HENRY CRABB ROBINSON, *Diary* (1838)

Dan Burgess preaching, said, "I have but one whore in my congregation, and I'll fell her"—and making an offer to throw the bible, a great many bowed to shun the book—at which he said, "I gather I have nothing else but whores."

THE REVEREND JOHN THOMLINSON, *Diary* (1718)

I spent a couple of hours with Mr. George Young. I took courage to relate to him an anecdote about himself. Nearly forty years ago, I happened to be in a hackney stage-coach with Young. A stranger came in—it was opposite Lackington's. On a sudden the stranger struck Young a violent blow on the face. Young coolly put his head out of the window and told the coachman to let him out. Not a word passed between the stranger and Young. But the latter having alighted, said in a calm voice, before he shut the door, "Ladies and gentleman, that is my father."

HENRY CRABB ROBINSON, *Diary* (1838)

An Englishman told me that going behind a posada by moonlight he saw one of those hollow pieces of wood with its stone cover, and [took] it for a sort of necessary convenience, the want of which is the great inconvenience our countrymen feel either in Spain or in Edinburgh. . . . He was in the worst trim possible for making a speedy retreat, when he took off the cover, and out came the bees upon him.

ROBERT SOUTHEY

At Madame Tussaud's I made a somewhat unpleasant discovery: either I am quite incapable of reading human faces, or else physiognomies are deceptive. So for example I was at first sight attracted by a seated gentleman with a goatee beard, No. 12. In the catalogue I found: "12. Thomas Neill Cream, hanged in 1892. Poisoned Matilda Glover with strychnine. He was also found guilty of murdering three other women." Really, his face is very suspicious. No. 13, Franz Müller, murdered Mr. Briggs in the train. H'm. No. 20, a clean-shaven gentleman, of almost worthy appearance: Arthur Devereux, hanged 1905, known as the "trunk murderer," because he hid the corpses of his victims in trunks. Horrid. No. 21—no, this worthy priest cannot be "Mrs. Dyer, the Reading baby murderess." I now perceive that I have confused the pages of the catalogue, and I am compelled to correct my impressions: the seated gentleman, No. 12, is merely Bernard Shaw; No. 13 is Louis Blériot, and No. 20 is simply Guglielmo Marconi.

KAREL CAPEK, *Letters from England*

A certain man of pleasure about London received a challenge from a young gentleman of his acquaintance, and they met at the appointed place. Just before the signal for firing was given, the man of pleasure rushed up to his antagonist, embraced him, and vehemently protested that "he could not lift his arm *against his own flesh and blood!*" The young gentleman, though he had never heard any imputation cast upon his mother's character, was so much staggered that (as the ingenious man of pleasure had foreseen) no duel took place.

Humphrey Howarth, the surgeon, was called out, and made his appearance in the field stark naked, to the astonishment of the challenger, who asked him what he meant. "I know," said H., "that if any part of the clothing is carried into the body by a gunshot wound, festering ensues; and therefore I have met you thus." His antagonist declared, that fighting with a man *in puris naturalibus* would be quite ridiculous; and accordingly they parted without further discussion.

S A M U E L R O G E R S , *Table Talk*

On the Friday morning when Hitler invaded Poland, I chanced to be in [the] Long Room at Lord's watching through windows for the last time for years. Though no spectators were present, a match was being continued; there was no legal way of stopping it. Balloon barrages hung over Lord's. As I watched . . . , a beautifully preserved member of Lord's, spats and rolled umbrella, stood near me inspecting the game. We did not speak of course; we had not been introduced. Suddenly two workmen entered the Long Room in green aprons and carrying a bag. They took down the bust of W. G. Grace [the most famous British cricket player], put it into the bag, and departed with it. The noble lord at my side watched their every movement; then he turned to me. "Did you see, sir?" he asked. I told him I had seen. "That means war," he said.

N E V I L L E C A R D U S , *Autobiography*

Here [at a fashionable Edinburgh assembly] were the last remains of the ball-room discipline of the preceding age. Martinet dowagers and venerable beaux . . . made all the preliminary arrangements. No couple could dance unless each party was provided with a ticket prescribing the precise place, in the precise dance. If there was no ticket, the gentleman, or the lady, was dealt with as an intruder, and turned out of the dance. If the ticket had marked upon it—say for a country dance—the figures 3.5, this meant that the holder was to place himself in the 3d dance, and 5th from the top; and if he was anywhere else, he was set right, or excluded. And the partner's ticket must correspond. Woe on the poor girl who with ticket 2.7, was found opposite a youth marked 5.9! It was flirting without a license . . . and would probably be reported . . . to the mother. . . . Tea was sipped in side-rooms; and he was a careless beau who did not present his partner with an orange at the end of each dance; and the oranges and the tea, like everything else, were under exact and positive regulations.

There are few people who now know that so recently as 1799 there were slaves in this country [Scotland]. Twenty-five years before, that is, in 1775, there must have been thousands of them; for this was then the condition of all our colliers and salters. They were literally slaves. They could not be killed nor directly tortured; but they belonged . . . to their respective works, with which they were sold as a part of the gearing. With a few very rigid exceptions, the condition of the head of the family was the condition of the whole house. . . . So that wives, daughters, and sons went on from generation to generation under the system which was the family doom.

I heard him [Lord Eskgrove, a judge], in condemning a tailor to death for murdering a soldier by stabbing him, aggravate the offense thus, "and not only did you murder him, whereby he was berea-ved of his life, but you did thrust or push or pierce, or project, or propell, the le-thall weapon through the belly-band of his regimen-tal breeches, which were his Majes-ty's!"

Sydney Smith, an enormous talker, complains of Macaulay never letting him get in a word. Smith once said to him, "Now, Macaulay, when I am gone you'll be sorry that you never heard me speak."

HENRY THOMAS COCKBURN (1779–1854),
Journals and *Memorials*

Antiwar

War, what other thing else is it than a common manslaughter of many men together, and a robbery, the which, the farther it sprawleth abroad, the more mischievous it is? But many gross gentlemen nowadays laugh merrily at these things, as though they were the dreams and dotings of schoolmen . . . And yet of those beginnings, we see we be run so far in madness, that we do naught else all our life-days. We war continually, city with city, prince with prince, people with people, yea and . . . cousin with cousin, alliance with alliance, brother with brother, the son with the father . . .

But . . . as I have . . . compared man with war, that is to say, the creature most demure with a thing most outrageous, to the intent that cruelty might the better be perceived: so will I compare war and peace together, the thing most wretched, and most mischievous, with the best and most wealthy thing that is. And so at last shall appear, how great madness it is, with so great tumult, with so great labours, with such intolerable expenses, with so many calamities . . . whereas agreement might be bought with a far less price. . . . What in all this world is more sweet or better than amity or love? Truly nothing. And I pray you, what other thing is peace than amity and love among men . . . ? Farther, if the love of one singular person with another be so sweet and delectable, how great should the felicity be if realm with realm, and nation with nation, were coupled together, with the band of amity and love? . . .

But as soon as the cruel tempest of war cometh on us, good Lord, how great a flood of mischiefs occupieth, overfloweth, and drowneth all together. The fair herds of beasts are driven away, the goodly corn is trodden down and destroyed, the good husbandmen are slain, the villages are burned up . . . so much readier and prompter men are to do hurt than good. The good citizens are robbed and spoiled of their goods by cursed thieves and murderers. Every place is full of fear, of wailing, complaining, and lamenting. The craftsmen stand idle; the poor men must either die for hunger, or fall to stealing. . . . Wives, being destitute of their husbands, lie at home without any fruit of children, the laws are laid aside, gentleness is laughed to scorn, right is clean exiled, religion is set at naught, hallowed and unhallowed things all are one . . . Alas, there be . . . already . . . too many mischiefs and evils, with which the wretched life of man

. . . is continually vexed, tormented, and utterly consumed. . . .

We read that in one place whole cities have been destroyed with earthquakes. We read, also, that in another place there have been cities altogether burnt with lightning; . . . I need not here to remember what a great multitude of men are daily destroyed by divers chances. . . . One hath been strangled with drinking of a hair in a draught of milk, another hath been choked with a little grapestone, another with a fishbone sticking in his throat. . . . Besides all this, what mortal pestilence see we in every place. . . . In war if there happen anything luckily . . . it pertaineth to very few, and to them that are unworthy to have it. The prosperity of one is the destruction of another. . . . The triumph of one is the lamentable mourning of another, so that the infelicity is bitter and sharp, the felicity is cruel and bloody. . . . Consider, how loathly a thing the rumour of war is, when it is first spoken of. Then how envious a thing it is unto a prince, while with often tithes and taxes he pillageth his subjects. . . .

What expenses and labours must he make in setting forth his navy of ships, in building and repairing of castles and fortresses, in preparing and apparelling of his tents and pavilions, in framing, making, and carrying of engines, guns, armour, weapons, baggage, carts and victual? What great labour is spent in making of bulwarks, in casting of ditches, in digging of mines, in keeping of watches, in keeping of arrays, and in exercising of weapons? I pass over the fear they be in; I speak not of the imminent danger and peril that hangeth over their heads: for what thing in war is not to be feared? . . . Their meat is so ill that an ox of Cyprus would be loath to eat it; they have but little sleep, nor yet that at their own pleasure. Their tents on every side are open on the wind. What, a tent? No, no; they must all the day long, be it hot or cold, wet or dry, stand in the open air, sleep on the bare ground, stand in their harness. They must suffer hunger, thirst, cold, heat, dust, showers; they must be obedient to their captains; sometimes they be clapped on the pate with a warder or a truncheon: so that there is no bondage so vile as the bondage of soldiers.

Besides all this, at the sorrowful sign given to fight, they must run headlong to death: for either they must slay cruelly, or be slain wretchedly.

ERASMUS, *Against War* (circa 1514)

Boldness

It is a trivial grammar-school text, but yet worthy a wise man's consideration. Question was asked of Demosthenes, *what was the chief part of an orator?* He answered, *action;* what next? *action:* what next again? *action.* He said it that knew it best and had by nature himself no advantage in that he commended. A strange thing, that that part of an orator which is but superficial, and rather the virtue of a player, should be placed so high above those other noble parts of invention, elocution and the rest; nay almost alone, as if it were all in all. But the reason is plain. There is in human nature generally more of the fool than of the wise; and therefore those faculties by which the foolish part of men's minds is taken are most potent. Wonderful like is the case of boldness in civil business; what first? *boldness;* what second and third? *boldness.* And yet boldness is a child of ignorance and baseness, far inferior to other parts; but nevertheless it doth fascinate and bind hand and foot those that are either shallow in judgment or weak in courage, which are the greatest part; yea, and prevaileth with wise men at weak times. Therefore we see it hath done wonders in popular states, but with senates and princes less; and more ever upon the first entrance of bold persons into action than soon after; for boldness is an ill keeper of promise. Surely, as there are mountebanks for the natural body, so are there mountebanks for the politic body; men that undertake great cures and perhaps have been lucky in two or three experiments, but want the grounds of science, and therefore cannot hold out. Nay, you shall see a bold fellow many times do Mahomet's miracle. Mahomet made the people believe that he would call a hill to him, and from the top of it offer up his prayers for the observers of his law. The people assembled; Mahomet called the hill to come to him again and again, and when the hill stood still, he was never a whit abashed, but said, "If the hill will not come to Mahomet, Mahomet will go to the hill." So these men, when they have promised great matters and failed most shamefully, yet (if they have the perfection of boldness) they will but slight it over, and make a turn, and no more ado. Certainly to men of great judgment, bold persons are a sport to behold; nay, and to the vulgar also boldness hath somewhat of the ridiculous. For if absurdity be the subject of laughter, doubt you not but great boldness is seldom without some absurdity. Especially it is a sport to see when a bold fellow is out of countenance, for that puts his face into a most shrunken and wooden posture, as needs it must; for in bashfulness the spirits do a little go and come; but with bold men, upon like occasion, they stand at a stay, like a stale at chess where it is no mate, but yet the game cannot stir. But this last were fitter for a satire than for a serious observation. This is well to be weighed, that boldness is ever blind, for it seeth not dangers and inconveniences: therefore it is ill in counsel, good in execution, so that the right use of bold persons is, that they never command in chief, but be seconds and under the direction of others. For counsel it is good to see dangers, and in execution not to see them, except they be very great.

BACON, *Essays*

A First Round of Poetry

Musée des Beaux Arts

About suffering they were never wrong,
The Old Masters: how well they understood
Its human position; how it takes place

While someone else is eating or opening a window or just
   walking dully along;
How, when the aged are reverently, passionately waiting
For the miraculous birth, there always must be
Children who did not specially want it to happen, skating
On a pond at the edge of the wood:
They never forgot
That even the dreadful martyrdom must run its course
Anyhow in a corner, some untidy spot
Where the dogs go on with their doggy life and the tor-
   turer's horse
Scratches its innocent behind on a tree.

In Brueghel's *Icarus,* for instance: how everything turns
   away
Quite leisurely from the disaster; the ploughman may
Have heard the splash, the forsaken cry,
But for him it was not an important failure; the sun
   shone
As it had to on the white legs disappearing into the green
Water; and the expensive delicate ship that must have
   seen
Something amazing, a boy falling out of the sky,
Had somewhere to get to and sailed calmly on.

W. H.   A U D E N

The Deserted Poet

This part of the country is underpeopled.
Not a word waits in hiding under the ferns
To reach up for my hand and lead me out
Of myself. No words have passed this way this season:
I have forgotten even the sound of their footsteps
Whickering through the leaves at my approach.

Look at my face, never an honest one.
It covers my desertion by pretending
That words have never meant a thing to me.
This face settles for the lie. It puts on
Creases of feigned anger between the eyes,
Furrows of mock surprise across the brow.

I wear the mask of an actor who returns
From a long journey to find his wife and children dead.

PETER DAVISON

From *The Hunting of the Gods*

Stars enamoured with pastimes Olympical
  Stars and planets that beautiful shone,
Would no longer that earthly men only shall
  Swim in pleasure, and they but look on.
Round about hornëd Lucina they swarmëd,
  And her informëd how minded they were,
Each god and goddess, to take human bodies
  As lords and ladies, to follow the hare.

Chaste Diana applauded the motion,
  And pale Proserpina set in her place,
Lights the welkin and governs the ocean,
  While she conducted her nephews in chase . . .
Yellow Apollo the kennel doth follow
  With whoop and hollo, after the hare.

Hymen ushers the ladies: Astraea
  The just, took hands with Minerva the bold,
Ceres the brown, with bright Cytherea,
  With Thetis the wanton, Bellona the old;
Shamefaced Aurora with subtle Pandora
  And Maia with Flora, did company bear:

Juno was stated too high to be mated,
   But yet she hated not hunting the hare.

. . . . . .

Young Amyntas supposed the gods came to breathe
   After some battle, themselves on the ground;
Thyrsis thought the stars came to dwell here beneath,
   And that hereafter the world would go round.
Corydon agëd, with Phyllis engagëd,
   Was much enragëd with jealous despair;
But fury vaded, and he was persuaded,
   While I thus applauded the hunting the hare.

. . . . . .

Three broad bowls to the Olympical Rector
   His Troy-born eagle he brings on his knee;
Jove to Phoebus carouses in nectar,
   And he to Hermes, and Hermes to me;
Wherewith infusëd, I piped and I musëd
   In songs unusëd this sport to declare:
And that the rouse of Jove, round as his sphere may
   move—
Health to all, that love hunting the hare.

ANON.

From *The Ecstasy*

As twixt two equal armies, fate
   Suspends uncertain victory,
Our souls (which to advance their state
   Were gone out) hung twixt her and me.
And whilst our souls negotiate there
   We like sepulchral statues lay;
All day, the same our postures were
   And we said nothing, all the day.

JOHN DONNE

The Quip

The merry world did on a day
   With his train-bands and mates agree
To meet together where I lay,
   And all in sport to jeer at me.

First Beauty crept into a rose;
   Which, when I plucked not, "Sir," said she,
"Tell me, I pray, whose hands are those?"
   But Thou shalt answer, Lord, for me.

Then Money came, and chinking still,
   "What tune is this, poor man?" said he;
"I heard in music you had skill."
   But Thou shalt answer, Lord, for me.

Then came brave Glory puffing by
   In silks that whistled, who but he?
He scarce allowed me half an eye.
   But Thou shalt answer, Lord, for me.

Then came quick Wit and Conversation,
   And he would needs a comfort be,
And, to be short, made an oration.
   But Thou shalt answer, Lord, for me.

Yet when the hour of Thy design
   To answer these fine things shall come,
Speak not at large; say, I am Thine;
   And then they have their answer home.

GEORGE HERBERT

From *The Garden*

What wondrous life in this I lead!
Ripe apples drop about my head;
The luscious clusters of the vine
Upon my mouth do crush their wine;
The nectarine and curious peach
Into my hands themselves do reach;
Stumbling on melons, as I pass,
Ensnared with flowers I fall on grass.

.   .   .   .   .   .

Here at the fountain's sliding foot
Or at some fruit tree's mossy root
Casting the body's vest aside
My soul into the boughs does glide:
There like a bird it sits, and sings,
Then whets and combs its silver wings;
And, till prepared for longer flight,
Waves in its plumes the various light.

ANDREW MARVELL

From *Paradise Lost*

[SATAN]
            But he his wonted pride
Soon recollecting, with high words, that bore
Semblance of worth not substance, gently raised
Their fainting courage and dispelled their fears.
Then straight commands that at the warlike sound
Of trumpets loud and clarions be upreared
His mighty standard; that proud honor claimed
Azazel as his right, a cherub tall:
Who forthwith from the glittering staff unfurled

The imperial ensign, which full high advanced
Shone like a meteor streaming to the wind
With gems and golden lustre rich emblazed,
Seraphic arms and trophies: all the while
Sonorous metal blowing martial sounds
At which the universal host upsent
A shout that tore Hell's conclave, and beyond
Frighted the reign of Chaos and old Night.

.   .   .   .   .   .

Their dread commander: he above the rest
In shape and gesture proudly eminent
Stood like a tower; his form had yet not lost
All her original brightness, nor appeared
Less than archangel ruined, and the excess
Of glory obscured . . .
                              But his face
Deep scars of thunder had intrenched, and care
Sat on his faded cheek, but under brows
Of dauntless courage and considerate pride
Waiting revenge. . . .
                              [Book I]

[LIGHT]
Hail holy light, offspring of Heaven first-born
Or of the eternal co-eternal beam
May I express thee unblamed? . . .
                              Before the sun,
Before the Heavens thou wert, and at the voice
Of God, as with a mantle didst invest
The rising world of waters dark and deep,
Won from the void and formless infinite.
Thee I revisit now with bolder wing,
Escaped the Stygian pool, though long detained
In that obscure sojourn, while in my flight
Through utter and through middle darkness borne,

With other notes than to the Orphean lyre
I sung of chaos and eternal night. . . .
                              Yet not the more
Cease I to wander where the Muses haunt
Clear spring, or shady grove, or sunny hill,
Smit with the love of sacred song; but chief
Thee Sion and the flowering brooks beneath
That wash thy hallowed feet, and warbling flow,
Nightly I visit; nor sometimes forget
Those other two equalled with me in fate,
So were I equalled with them in renown,
Blind Thamyris and blind Mæonides,
And Tiresias and Phineus, prophets old.
Then feed on thoughts that voluntary move
Harmonious numbers, as the wakeful bird
Sings darkling and in shadiest covert hid
Tunes her nocturnal note. Thus with the year
Seasons return, but not to me returns
Day, or the sweet approach of even or morn,
Or sight of vernal bloom, or summer's rose,
Or flocks or herds or human face divine,
But cloud instead, and ever-during dark
Surrounds me. . . .

                              [Book III]

[LOSS OF EDEN]

So spake our mother Eve, and Adam heard
Well pleased but answered not; for now too nigh
The Archangel stood, and from the other hill
To their fixed station all in bright array
The cherubim descended; on the ground
Gliding meteorous, as evening mist
Risen from a river o'er the marish glides
And gathers ground fast at the laborer's heel
Homeward returning. High in front advanced,
The brandished sword of God before them blazed

Fierce as a comet, which with torrid heat
And vapour as the Libyan air adust
Began to parch that temperate clime; whereat
In either hand the hastening angel caught
Our lingering parents, and to the eastern gate
Led them direct and down the cliff as fast
To the subjected plain; then disappeared.
They, looking back, all the eastern side beheld
Of Paradise, so late their happy seat,
Waved over by that flaming brand, the gate
With dreadful faces thronged and fiery arms.
Some natural tears they dropped, but wiped them soon;
The world was all before them, where to choose
Their place of rest, and Providence their guide.
They hand in hand with wandering steps and slow
Through Eden took their solitary way.

[Book XII]

MILTON

Bulgarian Proverbs

✠ Though the proverbs of all countries say much the same thing, here and there they seem more piquant or trenchant, or sharp-tongued or sad-faced, than elsewhere. The Bulgarians, for me, qualify on this count, perhaps in part because they are among the last nations whose proverbs one might seek out, and I, indeed, much less sought them out than came upon them. Here are some that made an impression:

Hunger sees nothing but bread.

In every village is the grave of Christ.

The clean gets dirty more easily.

The devil knows everything except where women sharpen their knives.

Dry pants eat no fish.

Forests have eyes; meadows, ears.

God is not sinless. He created the world.

God's feet are of wool; His hands are of iron.

One guest hates the other, and the host both.

Do not lie for lack of news.

The oversaintly saint is not pleasing even unto God.

The smaller saints will be the ruin of God.

Man is ever self-forgiving.

God does not shave—why should I?

Do not salt other people's food.

Become a sheep and you will see the wolf.

Where there is union a bullet can swim.

The wife carries her husband on her face; the husband carries his wife on his linen.

When a wool merchant speaks of sheep he means cloth.

A long dark night—the year.

Characters Drawn from Life

✠ How many characters in fiction have been drawn, or drawn and quartered, from life is unanswerable, so many having been drawn in part rather than as a whole, or having been ascribed by the readers of novels rather than the writers, or attributed by mere guesswork. In glancing through the lists that have at one time or another been assembled, one is made aware of in how many cases either the novels are all but forgotten, or the prototypes are. Have you read Constance Bridges' *Thin Air* lately? And if so, could you tell us just who John Langdon—the model for a character in the book named David Wendel—was? Melted into air, thin air, indeed. At the other extreme there are a few characters whose prototypes are very famous, and in books that are equally so—such as Robinson Crusoe and Alexander Selkirk (or Selcraig), or Rebecca Gratz and Rebecca in *Ivanhoe*. Herewith some others, some of them conjectural or controversial or both:

Balzac's Eugène de Rastignac, who appears over and over in his novels, was modeled after the famous statesman Adolphe Thiers.

Charlotte Bronte's Shirley, in her novel of that name, was drawn from her sister Emily; her Paul Emanuel in *Villette* from M. Héger, at whose *pensionnat* she studied and with whom she fell in love.

In Dickens' *Bleak House* Mr. Boythorn was suggested by Walter Savage Landor, Harold Skimpole by Leigh Hunt, and something of Mrs. Jellyby by Harriet Martineau. Pecksniff in *Martin Chuzzlewit* derives from S. C. Hall, editor of the *Art Journal;* and in Podsnap, in *Our Mutual Friend,* there are some traces of Dickens' friend and biographer John Forster.

Disraeli's novels abound in characters drawn from life. Lord Monmouth in *Coningsby* is drawn from Lord Hertford, who in Thackeray's *Vanity Fair* is known as Lord Steyne. In *Endymion* Lord Roehampton is based on Palmerston, Zenobia on Lady Jersey, the Neuchatel family on the Rothschilds; St. Barbe is thought to be Thackeray, and Mr. Gushy, Dickens. In *Venetia* Cadurcis is Byron—who will keep cropping up in this list—Lady Monteagle is his mistress Lady Caroline Lamb, and Marmion Herbert is Shelley.

The Clyde Griffiths of Dreiser's *An American Tragedy* is, as is well known, Chester Gillette.

Dostoevski, in *The Possessed,* caricatured Turgenev as Karamazinov.

In Paul Leicester Ford's once-famous *The Honorable Peter Stirling,* the title character was drawn from Grover Cleveland.

In Anatole France's *Red Lily* Choulette is taken from Verlaine.

Maxwell Bodenheim gave rise to Ben Hecht's Count Bruga, in the novel of that name.

In Aldous Huxley's *Point Counter Point,* Mark Rampion is drawn from D. H. Lawrence.

In Madame de La Fayette's *La Princess de Clèves* the Duc de Nemours is La Rochefoucauld.

In D. H. Lawrence's *Women in Love* the egregious Lady Ottoline Morrell, who had befriended and helped Lawrence, saw herself—and very angrily—as Hermione.

Strickland, the hero of Somerset Maugham's *The Moon and Sixpence,* was based on Gauguin; the chief character of his *Cakes and Ale* was said (though Maugham denied it) to be based on Thomas Hardy [and the character of Alroy Kear was more confidently said to be based on Hugh Walpole].

Diana Warwick, the heroine of George Meredith's *Diana of the Crossways,* derives from Sheridan's beautiful granddaughter Caroline Norton; Vernon Whitford in Meredith's *The Egoist* derives from Leslie Stephen.

In *Nightmare Abbey* Thomas Love Peacock drew on Shelley for Scythrop Glowry, on Bryon for Mr. Cypress, and on Coleridge for Flosky.

In Proust of course the prototypes, or attributed ones, are very numerous, but in a good many cases not themselves well known; among minor characters Elstir is said to be Monet, and Bergotte,

Anatole France; the most famous model, Count Robert de Montesquiou, is Proust's Baron de Charlus, as well as the Des Esseintes of Huysmans' *A Rebours*.

François Villon is thought to be Rabelais's model for Panurge.

In Trollope's *Phineas Redux* Mr. Turnbull is a satirized John Bright, and Daubeny is Disraeli.

Carl Van Vechten's *Peter Whiffle* modeled Edith Dale on Mabel Dodge Luhan.

In Thornton Wilder's *Bridge of San Luis Rey* the Marquesa de Montemayor was modeled on Madame de Sévigné.

The Orlando in Virginia's Woolf's book of that name is drawn from V. Sackville-West [Mr. Ramsey, in *To the Lighthouse,* is Mrs. Woolf's father, Leslie Stephen].

H. G. Wells's Oscar and Altiora Bailey, in *The New Machiavelli,* derive from Mr. and Mrs. Sidney Webb.

(Drawn from Earle Walbridge, *Literary Characters Drawn from Life*)

Cities

A city has an unseen history which also forms its aesthetic. A city is not architecture alone, perhaps not even principally.

Cities have noises. There are the shrill engine whistles at the Gare St. Lazare, the chants of the street peddlers of Naples, the bells of the betjaks in Jakarta, the horns in the fogs of San Francisco Bay, the subterranean rumble of the subways of Manhattan, the unmuffled motorcycle engines on the Corso.

Cities have people and people have tongues. Street voices do not sound the same even in a single country. The sharpness of Albany is countered by the softness of New Orleans, the flatness of Omaha by the twang of Portsmouth, New Hampshire. None is like the diapasons of Hamburg, the falsetto upturnings of London, the liquids of Rome or Helsinki, the wails or bleats of Bombay or Cairo. When they stop talking some people in some cities sing, some listen to sidewalk orchestras, some are silent. Thus cities do not sound alike.

Cities have smells. Wood smoke and manure provide the warm full atmosphere of Bourges; coal gas cares for Lille, or Birmingham, or Washington, Pennsylvania; oil for Galveston; fish drying in the sun for Ålesund; coffee roasting for Boston; while, when the wind is in the southwest, Chicago knows the sick sweet odor of drying blood and recently ardent flesh. Mainz is redolent with honeysuckle. . . .

As we think of old—or even new—fine cities we will often think of them in terms of a major approach or gateway: The spire of Chartres across the wheat fields of La Beauce, the towers of lower Manhattan as one steams up toward the Battery, the air approach to Chicago across the false front of the skyscrapers of Michigan Avenue. There are cities of hills and sea: San Francisco, Rio de Janeiro, Lisbon, Sydney, Wellington, Oslo. There are cities that rise from the ocean: Boston, New York, Copenhagen. There are cities of the big rivers or estuaries: London, St. Louis, Rome, Paris, St. Paul, Melbourne, Vienna. There are cities of the plains: Moscow, Salisbury, Lincoln in England or Nebraska. All of these, except perhaps the cities of the plains, have a particular appearance that must be seen from a particular direction, and historically there has been one dominating approach which has established the image of such a city.

Jоны Ely Burchard, "The Urban Aesthetic"

Counting-Out Rhymes

✠ Counting-out rhymes are, or used to be, one of most people's oldest memories, and may be among the oldest tokens of childhood. Who can remember when he first heard "Eeny, meeny, miny, mo"; and who ever forgets it? Can anybody not have responded to the mingling of nonsense and magic in some of the rhymes—in, for example, "One-ery, two-ery, ziccary zan"? As it has into nursery rhymes, a certain amount of mistreated history has gone into counting-out ones, and a certain amount of scrambled geography as well. I would suppose that the youngest players in a game partly learned to count through counting-out rhymes, when "five, six, pick up sticks" or "thirteen, fourteen, girl's a-courting" became the prelude to the game. The book I have quoted from must have been a labor, though one of love, with tentacles that touched at regions all over the world, and that had the assistance of countless former children. We can guess at what inspired many of the rhymes that have fairly concrete meanings, but I am led to wonder just who made them up —parents, teachers, nursemaids, or children themselves? Or did somebody speak a nonsense line and others then add a rhyming one, or complete a stanza? If children tended to make them up, I would think girls did oftener than boys, because they for the most part played counting-out games longer or later. One certainly doubts, however, that children created "All good children go to Heaven"; and one wonders whether they made up "Nobody at home but jumping Joan,/ Father, mother and I": the *I*, if they did, should be *me*. But children may very well have composed the most imaginative and absurd of the rhymes, as the equivalents long ago of the imaginative and funny paintings by children today. And are there "new" counting-out rhymes? Should there be, and should they be up to snuff, it would be nice to add them— should there be future editions—to this book.

Perhaps the three most common starters, with variations even in the first line, are:

(1)

One-ery, two-ery, ziccary zan,
Hollow-bone, crackbone, ninery ten;
Spittery spot it must be done
Twiddleum, twaddleum twenty-one

(2)

One, two, three, four, five, six, seven,
All good children go to Heaven;
One, two, three, four,
All bad children go next door.

✠ A variant, born of Garfield's assassination, concludes:

All bad children go below
To keep company with Guiteau.

(3)

Eeny, meeny, miny, mo,

✠ with many nationalities as well as one race to "catch" in the second line, and with many variations on

Crack a feny, finy, fo.

✠ Other counting-out rhymes:

Inty, minty, tippety, fig
Delia, dilia, dominig;
Otcha, potcha, dominotcha,
Hi, pon, tusk.
Huldy, guldy, boo,
Out goes you. [Hartford, Conn.]

Hackabacker, chew tobacco,
Hackabacker chew;
Hackabacker eat a cracker,
Out goes you. [Newport, R.I.]

Hink, spink, the puddings stink,
The fat begins to fry;

Nobody at home but jumping Joan,
Father, mother and I. [England.]

As I was walking down the lake,
I met a little rattlesnake.
I gave him so much jelly-cake
It made his little belly ache;
One, two, three, out goes she!
   [Hartford, Conn.; Hoboken, N.J.]

A knife and a fork,
A bottle and a cork,
And that's the way
To spell New York. [New York.]

Nebuchadnezzar, king of the Jews,
Slipped off his slippers and slipped on his shoes.
[Second-line variation: Wore six pair of stockings and
   seven pair of shoes.]
                       [New York; New England.]

Queen, Queen Caroline
Dipped her hair in turpentine,
Turpentine made it shine.
Queen, Queen Caroline. [Edinburgh, Scotland.]

Here's a Spanian just from Spain
To court your daughter Mary Jane.
My daughter Jane is far too young
To be controlled by any one. [Washington, D.C.]

Old Dan Tucker
Came home to supper,
And eat the hind leg of a frog;
He peeped over the steeple,
Saw many fine people,
And looked at the mouth of a dog. [Indiana.]

✠ "One, two, buckle my shoe" has a German "equivalent" which is all too wonderfully characteristic:

Eins, zwei, Polizei;
Drei, vier, Offizier . . .

✠ There are also pairing-off rhymes, such as this from New Hampshire:

Daisy Deborah Delilah Dean,
Fresh as a rose and proud as a queen!
Daisy Deborah, drawn from the pool
By Harry and Dick, came dripping to school.
Daisy Deborah, wet as a fish,
Her mother says *bed*
While her father says *pish!*

✠ Those pointed at with "Daisy Deborah" and "Harry and Dick" would pair off; also those pointed at with "bed" and "pish."

Cowboy Songs

✠ The cowboy literature is of course huge, and almost all of it in the form of verse is meant to be sung. Most of the songs and ballads run on and on for fifteen or twenty stanzas or more, partly to get their story told, partly to keep the singing alive. On the printed page many of the songs, or many stanzas in the better songs, fall short. Nor does the subject matter provide the rhythms and beat of the grand old English and Scottish ballads; a good deal of it is sentimentalism, and a palpable part of it smacks of cynicism, such as runs through "Hard Times":

From father to mother, from sister to brother,
From cousin to cousin, they're cheating each other.

. . . . . .

Whatever he sells you, my friend, you are sold;

. . . . . .

But when she gets married she'll cut quite a dash,
She'll give him the reins, and she'll handle the cash.

✠ And there are the cowboy songs to be passed over,
from being too well known, but not quite in silence—

Oh, give me a home where the buffalo roam,
Where the deer and the antelope play. . . .

But that dirty little coward that shot Mr. Howard
Has laid poor Jesse in his grave.

O bury me not on the lone prairie . . .

✠ I have thrown in some extracts from longer works,
less because they have any great superiority than because they
catch the prevailing moods of the songs; and have included
"Westward Ho" because it suggests a rather odd narrator, what
might be called a sensible cowboy who has decided to settle
down, to get rich quick, and doesn't, at least explicitly, include
romance, even a wife-getting domesticity, in his plans. Still, he
has not left adventure out, and his preferring grizzlies and
tarantulas to faro and poker gives him a certain Wild West
stature as well as get-rich sense.

Westward Ho

I love not Colorado
Where the faro table grows,
And down the desperado
The rippling Bourbon flows;

Nor seek I fair Montana
Of bowie-lunging fame;
The pistol ring of fair Wyoming
I leave to nobler game.

Sweet poker-haunted Kansas
In vain allures the eye;
The Nevada rough has charms enough
Yet its blandishments I fly.

Shall Arizona woo me
Where the meek Apache bides?
Or New Mexico where natives grow
With arrow-proof insides?

Nay, 'tis where the grizzlies wander
And the lonely diggers roam,
And the grim Chinese from the squatter flees
That I'll make my humble home.

I'll chase the wild tarantula
And the fierce coyote I'll dare,
And the locust grim, I'll battle him
In his native wildwood lair.

Or I'll seek the gulch deserted
And dream of the wild Red man,
And I'll build a cot on a corner lot
And get rich as soon as I can.

ANON.

From *The Cowboy's Lament*

Let sixteen gamblers come handle my coffin,
Let sixteen cowboys come sing me a song,

Take me to the graveyard and lay the sod o'er me,
For I'm a poor cowboy and I know I've done wrong.

. . . . . .

Get six jolly cowboys to carry my coffin;
Get six pretty maidens to bear up my pall.
Put bunches of roses all over my coffin,
Put roses to deaden the clods as they fall.

ANON.

From *Greer County*

Hurrah for Greer County!
The land of the free,
The land of the bed-bug,
Grass-hopper and flea;
I'll sing of its praises
And tell of its fame,
While starving to death
On my government claim.

ANON.

Tail Piece

Oh, the cow-puncher loves the whistle of his rope,
As he races over the plains;
And the stage-driver loves the popper of his whip,
And the rattle of his concord chains;
And we'll all pray the Lord that we will be saved,
And we'll keep the golden rule;
But I'd rather be home with the girl I love
Than to monkey with this goddamn'd mule.

ANON.

Curiouser and Curiouser

Most things move the under-jaw, the crocodile not;
Most things sleep lying, the elephant leans or stands.

GEORGE HERBERT

A time there is for all, my mother often says,
When she with skirts tucked very high with girls at stool-
ball plays.

Attributed to SIR PHILIP SIDNEY

I know no happier-looking woman of the tranquilly happy sort
than Mrs. J. since she took to make Dresden china of leather for
the Roman Catholic bazaars.

JANE WELSH

The face must needs be plain that wants a nose.

JOHN BULWER

The parliament intended to have hanged him [David Jenkins],
and he expected no less, but resolved to be hanged with the Bible
under one arm and Magna Carta under the other.

I have heard Mr. [Thomas] Hobbes say that he was wont to draw
lines on his thigh and on the sheets, abed, and also multiply and
divide.

[Thomas Chaloner] had a trick sometimes to go into Westminster Hall in a morning in term time, and tell some strange story
(sham) and would come thither again about 11 or 12 to have the
pleasure to hear how it spread; and sometimes it would be al-
tered, with additions, he could scarce know it to be his own.

Aubrey's Brief Lives

Dr. Swift lies a-bed till eleven o'clock, and thinks of wit for the day.

JOSEPH SPENCE

I have known a gentleman at a feast receive an affront, disguise his rage, step home, vent it all upon his wife, return to his companions, and be as good company as if nothing had happened.

ELIZABETH INCHBALD

And I will report of all heroism from an American point of view.

WALT WHITMAN

We will now discuss in a little more detail the Struggle for Existence.

CHARLES DARWIN

Ann Moore, aged 48, now living at Tutbury, in Staffordshire, has swallowed no kind of food whatever, either solid or fluid, for the last two years and a half. Her appetite began to decline about seven years ago, in consequence of a weak digestion, and in March, 1807, the passage to her stomach became completely closed, so as not to admit of her swallowing even a drop of water; from the pit of her stomach downward she is a mere skeleton, notwithstanding which her countenance is perfectly cheerful, and has the appearance of good health. So late as last Friday she was visited by the writer of this article, and was then in excellent spirits, and felt no pain whatever except a slight shooting across her forehead; she has been offered £1,000 to visit the metropolis, and though poor, she declines leaving her home and friends. She never sleeps, but amuses herself by reading all night, and receiving the visits of vast numbers who daily flock to her humble roof. Her memory is amazingly retentive and she feels no inconvenience but from the approach of persons who have been drinking spirits, which affects her much. Numerous medical men have gone from London to behold this wonderful phenomenon, and on examination, are fully convinced, from her appearance, that no imposition whatever has been practised.

London Chronicle (1809)

Sir John, on his arrival home, at once sent for his solicitors, Messrs. Hutchinson & Harper, and ordering his will to be produced, demanded there and then that the pen of persuasion be dipped into the ink of revenge and spread thickly along the paragraph of blood-related charity to blank the intolerable words that referred to the woman he was now convinced, beyond doubt, had braved the bridge of bigamy.

Being beforehand acquaint with the numerous and costly tombstones erected individually, regardless of price, the wearied and sickly woman of former healthy tread was not long in observing the latest tablet, of towering height, at the northeast end of the sacred plot.

The misty dust blinded his sight . . . landing him on the slippery rock of smutty touch.

AMANDA M'KITTRICK ROS, *Irene Iddesleigh*

Lady Kent articled with Sir Edward Herbert, that he should come to her when she sent for him, and stay with her as long as she would have him, to which he set his hand; then he articled with her, that he should go away when he pleased, and stay away as long as he pleased, to which she set her hand. This is the epitome of all the contracts in the world.

The tone in preaching does much in working upon the people's affections. If a man should make love in an ordinary tone, his mistress would not regard him; and therefore he must whine. If a man should cry Fire, or Murder, in an ordinary voice, nobody would come out to help him.

JOHN SELDEN, *Table Talk*

SALE OF A WIFE.—On Tuesday afternoon, at 2 o'clock, a number of persons assembled in the neighbourhood of Portman-market to witness an exhibition of the above description. At the appointed time the husband, accompanied by his wife, entered the crowded arena, the latter having been led to the spot in the usual manner, with a halter round her neck. The business then commenced amid the hissings and hootings of the populace, who showered stones and other missiles on the parties. The first bidding was 4s., and the next 4s. 6d., after which an interval elapsed, amidst the call of "Going, going," from the auctioneer. At last a dustman stepped forward and exclaimed "I wool give five bob" (5s.). The woman was "knocked down" for the sum, and the dustman carried her off, nothing loth, amidst the hisses of the crowd.

The Times, London (1833)

A number of vulgar persons, admirers of the writings of Thomas Paine, met on Wednesday, in the Brewer-street Assembly-rooms, to celebrate that individual's birth-day. . . . We were content to take, for once, the hazard of a head-ache to see what manner of trash the self-constituted philosophers would take. . . .

At five o'clock, nearly 300 persons being assembled, Citizen Clio Rickman was called to the chair. Dinner was soon after put upon the tables. It was a hasty, ill-dressed, ill-served, coarse, clumsy, repast . . . scarcely fit to eat at any charge.

The Times, London (1823)

> Since in a bed a man, a maid
> May bundle and be chaste,
> It doth no good to burn up wood,
> It is a needless waste.

ANON.

Foote used to say of [Garrick] that he walked out with an intention to do a generous action; but turning the corner of a street, he met with the ghost of a halfpenny, which frightened him.

Mr. Langton . . . repeated the anecdote of Addison having distinguished between his powers in conversation and in writing, by saying "I have only ninepence in my pocket, but I can draw for a thousand pounds." *Johnson:* "He had not that retort ready, Sir; he had prepared it beforehand." *Langton* (turning to me): "A fine surmise. Set a thief to catch a thief."

B O S W E L L, *Life of Johnson*

When he [Edmund Gunter] was a student at Christ Church, it fell to his lot to preach the Passion sermon, which some old divines that I knew did hear, but 'twas said of him then in the University that our Saviour never suffered so much since his Passion as in that sermon, it was such a lamentable one . . .

[Sir Hierome Sanchy] challenged Sir William [Petty] to fight with him. Sir William is extremely shortsighted, and being the challengee it belonged to him to nominate place and weapon. He nominates, for the place, a dark cellar, and the weapon to be a great carpenter's ax. This turned the knight's challenge into ridicule, and so it came to naught.

Aubrey's Brief Lives

Lord B[yron]'s establishment consists, besides servants, of ten horses, eight enormous dogs, three monkeys, five cats, an eagle, a crow, and a falcon; and all these, except the horses, walk about the house . . . as if they were the masters of it. . . . After I have sealed my letter, I find that my enumeration . . . was defective . . . I have just met on the grand staircase five peacocks, two guinea hens, and an Egyptian crane.

S H E L L E Y, Letter to Thomas Love Peacock

There be many witches at this day in Lapland, who sell winds to mariners for money.

T H O M A S   F U L L E R (1642)

The flute is not an instrument with a good moral effect. It is too exciting.

Aristotle, *Politics*

> She leaped upon a pile, and lifted high
> Her mad looks to the lightning, and cried: "Eat!"

Shelley, *The Revolt of Islam*

[Dr. Johnson, complaining to his hostess, Mrs. Thrale:] *"Toujours* strawberries and cream."

The city of London, though handsomer than Paris, is not so handsome as Philadelphia.

Thomas Jefferson, Letter to John Page

Any Pole who can read and write is a nobleman.

Anon.

The perfect hostess will see to it that the works of male and female authors be properly separated on her book shelves. Their proximity, unless they happen to be married, should not be tolerated.

Lady Gough, *Etiquette* (1863)

The chimpanzee yearns for a tail.

West African proverb

This gallows is for us and our children.

Notice on an English gallows (circa 1700)

An Irishman is never at peace except when he's fighting.

Irish proverb

In Afrikaans, remarks Paul Jennings, "Hamlet, I am thy father's ghost" sounds like "Omlet, ek is de papap spook."

From *A Poetess*

A poetess I should like to be
And miscellaneously see
Much that will enlighten me
And in darkness never to be
For inspiration to flee,
Or Muse that leads to sonnetry,
For competent compositions to be.

From *Profoundlyness*

Profoundlyness we all should perceive
And dispositionally receive;
As Nature gives to one and all,
The foundation of all in all
And from it we should never fall,
For literature to drawl.

From *Hotels*

In fashionable hotels many dwell
To tell yarns of their ostrich farms
And sparkishly appear.

IDELLA CLARENCE HOOBLER,
Souvenir: Poems of the New England Coast and Others

After her lord's death . . . she [Eleanor Radcliffe, Countess of Sussex] sends for one (formerly her footman) and makes him groom of the chamber. He had the pox and she knew it . . . He was not very handsome, but his body of an exquisite shape . . . His nostrils were stuffed and borne out with corks in which were quills to breath through. About 1666 this countess died of the pox.

Aubrey's Brief Lives

> With heaving breast the Dean undressed
> The Bishop's wife to lie on.
> She thought it crude done in the nude,
> So he kept his old school tie on.

ANON.

Murger told us the funeral oration pronounced over Planche [the once-famous French critic] by Buloz [editor of the *Revue des Deux Mondes*]: "I had as lief have lost 20,000 francs."

[Gautier on George Sand:] You've heard that she goes back to work at midnight and works until four in the morning. Let me tell you what happened to her. Something fantastic. One day she finished a novel at one o'clock in the morning . . . and immediately started another.

The Goncourt Journals

(trans. Lewis Galantière)

Taking soup gracefully, under the difficulties opposed to it by a dinner dress at that time fashionable, was reared into an art about forty-five years ago by a Frenchman who lectured upon it to ladies in London; and the most brilliant duchess of that day, viz. the Duchess of Devonshire, was amongst his best pupils. Spitting, if the reader will pardon the mention of so gross a fact, was shown to be a very difficult art, and publicly prelected upon, about the same time in the same great capital. The professors in this faculty were the hackney-coachmen; the pupils were gentlemen, who paid a guinea each for three lessons; the chief problem in this system of hydraulics being to throw the salivating column in a parabolic curve from the centre of Parliament Street, when driving four-in-hand, to the foot pavements, right and left, so as to alarm the consciences of guilty peripatetics on either side. The ultimate problem, which closed the *curriculum* of study, was held to lie in spitting round a corner; when *that* was mastered, the pupil was entitled to his doctor's degree.

THOMAS DE QUINCEY, "Conversation"

[A description of Bertrand Russell in a suit to cancel his appointment as lecturer at City College, New York, 1940:] Lecherous, salacious, libidinous, lustful, venerous, erotomaniac, aphrodisiac, atheistic, irreverent, narrow-minded, untruthful and bereft of moral fibre.

When a great many people are unable to find work, unemployment results.

CALVIN COOLIDGE

A real way to relieve unemployment would be to give employment.

ARTHUR BRISBANE

Dancing

Dancing can reveal all the mystery that music conceals.

BAUDELAIRE, *Fanfarlo des paradis artificiels*

A correct execution of an *adagio* is the *ne plus ultra* of our art; and I look on it as the touchstone of the dancer.

CARLO BLASIS, *Code of Terpsichore*

[Nijinsky] had a perfectly proportioned body. . . . His legs were so muscular that the hard cords stood out on his thighs like bows. With his unusually powerful arms . . . he could pick up and lift his partners with such ease that it seemed as if he only held a doll of straw. He did not, like other male dancers, support the girl with both hands on her hip, but with one single arm he raised her straight from his side.

ROMOLA NIJINSKY, *Nijinsky*

One night a dancer's mother, sobbing, entered her daughter's dressing room just as she had completed her make-up.

"Oh, my child, your poor father is dead!"

The daughter dabbed her eyes with a handkerchief, then, stifling a sob, she said:

"Oh, mother, why did you tell me this now? How can I cry? It would ruin my make-up."

ANON., *Ces Demoiselles de l'Opéra*

On seeing the Tsar seated in his box, chatting instead of watching her dancing, [Rosita Mauri] grumbled:

"Well, I shall certainly not eat any more caviar!"

ANON.

[Marie Camargo] has lived in a peaceful and honourable retirement, with half a dozen dogs, and the one friend who remains to her out of all her thousand and one lovers. . . .

[Camargo's friend] gave her a magnificent burial, and everyone admired the white hangings, symbol of virginity, which unmarried persons have the right to use in their funeral ceremonies.

BARON VON GRIMM, *Correspondance littéraire*

Death

Causes of Death

Bursten and Rupture	15
Colick and Gripes	15
Convulsions	3,463
Croop	81
Evil	2
Flux	9
French Pox	29
Grief	5
Jaw Locked	4
Livergrown	21
Mortification	167
Overjoy	1
Palsy	123
Spasm	24
St Anthony's Fire	2
Stoppage in the Stomach	20
Strangury	1
Thrush	39
Water in the Head	252
Worms	5

The [English] Annual Register, 1809

Denunciation

A Glass of Beer

The lanky hank of a she in the inn over there
Nearly killed me for asking the loan of a glass of beer;

May the devil grip the whey-faced slut by the hair,
And beat bad manners out of her skin for a year.

That parboiled ape, with the toughest jaw you will see
On virtue's path, and a voice that would rasp the dead,
Came roaring and raging the minute she looked at me,
And threw me out of the house on the back of my head!

If I asked her master he'd give me a cask a day;
But she, with the beer at hand, not a gill would arrange!
May she marry a ghost and bear him a kitten, and may
The High King of Glory permit her to get the mange.

JAMES STEPHENS

From *Epistle to a Lady: Of the Characters of Women*

But what are these to great Atossa's mind?
Scarce once herself, by turns all womankind!
Who, with herself, or others, from her birth
Finds all her life one warfare upon earth:
Shines in exposing knaves, and painting fools,
Yet is, whate'er she hates and ridicules. . . .
From loveless youth to unrespected age,
No passion gratified except her rage.
So much the fury still outran the wit,
The pleasure missed her, and the scandal hit. . . .
Offend her, and she knows not to forgive;
Oblige her, and she'll hate you while you live.

.   .   .   .   .   .

With every pleasing, every prudent part,
Say, what can Cloe want?—She wants a heart.
She speaks, behaves, and acts just as she ought;
But never, never reached one generous thought.
Virtue she finds too painful an endeavour,

Content to dwell in decencies forever. . . .
She, while her lover pants upon her breast,
Can mark the figures on an Indian chest;
And when she sees her friend in deep despair,
Observes how much a chintz exceeds mohair. . . .
Of all her dears she never slandered one,
But cares not if a thousand are undone.
Would Cloe know if you're alive or dead?
She bids her footman put it in her head.

ALEXANDER POPE

Eccentrics

✠ Here is a "short" extract from one of the longest single works in all literature, the *Memoirs* of the Duc de Saint-Simon (1675–1755). It is also one of the most extraordinary works and, in portraying the world of Louis XIV, one of the most panoramic depictions of worldliness. In it Saint-Simon pictured not just the most lustrous court life of modern history, but what may in places be the most ambitious, the most licentious, the most hideous, the most rigid and most rotten. In this gilded world of dinners and balls, musicales and masquerades, the gilt bit by bit peels off: at these dinners who may not be poisoned? at these masquerades what dark machinations may not be pierced? No king has exceeded Louis XIV in kingliness and all its graces and grandeurs; and few have exceeded, in power and authority, the man who said, "L'état, c'est moi." Saint-Simon, if a great snob whose lifelong obsession was to topple the King's bastards from sitting higher than the dukes, was also an incomparable observer who portrayed the comedy, the drama, the melodrama of envious, treacherous, conspiratorial worldlings intriguing for position and thirsty for favor and power. There was a scattering of good men, a multitude—including the King's—of mistresses. Louis XIV's Versailles was a palace, a promenade, a prison, a brothel; and something close to a madhouse which displayed people whom it was never excessive, and often euphemistic, to describe as eccentrics. You will not, I think, find the Prince de Condé mislabeled. But what is greatest in Saint-Simon is the vast narrative of court life itself, with characters entering and exiting, re-entering and re-exiting over thousands of pages, and with such masterpieces of writing as the death of Monseigneur, Louis XIV's Dauphin son. No novelist, not even Proust, has dealt so superbly with Saint-Simon's subject matter; Proust, moreover, pored continually over the *Memoirs* and in them doubtless found the name Charlus.

M. le Prince [the Prince de Condé], who for more than two years had not appeared at the Court, died at Paris a little after midnight on the night between Easter Sunday and Monday, the last of March and the first of April, and in his seventy-sixth year. No man had ever more ability of all kinds,—extending even to the arts and mechanics,—more valor, and, when it pleased him, more discernment, grace, politeness, and nobility. But then no man had ever before so many useless talents, so much genius of no avail, or an imagination so calculated to be a bugbear to itself and a plague to others. Abjectly and vilely servile even to lackeys, he scrupled not to use the lowest and paltriest means to gain his ends. Unnatural son, cruel father, terrible husband, detestable master, pernicious neighbor; without friendship, without friends —incapable of having any—jealous, suspicious, even restless, full of slyness and artifices to discover and to scrutinize all (in which he was unceasingly occupied, aided by an extreme vivacity and a surprising penetration), choleric and headstrong to excess even for trifles, difficult of access, never in accord with himself, and keeping all around him in a tremble; to conclude, impetuosity and avarice were his masters, which monopolized him always. With all this he was a man difficult to be proof against when he put in play the pleasing qualities he possessed.

Madame la Princesse, his wife, was his continual victim. She was disgustingly ugly, virtuous, and foolish, a little humpbacked, and stunk like a skunk, even from a distance. All these things did not hinder M. le Prince from being jealous of her even to fury up to the very last. The piety, the indefatigable attention of Madame la Princesse, her sweetness, her novice-like submission, could not guarantee her from frequent injuries, or from kicks, and blows with the fist, which were not rare. She was not mistress even of the most trifling things; she did not dare to propose or ask anything. He made her set out from one place to another the moment the fancy took him. Often when seated in their coach he made her descend, or return from the end of the street, then recommence the journey after dinner, or the next day. This seesawing lasted once fifteen days running, before a trip to Fontainebleau. At other times he sent for her from church, made her quit high mass, and sometimes sent for her the moment she was going to receive the Sacrament; she was obliged to return at once and put off her communion to another occasion. It was not that he wanted her, but it was merely to gratify his whim that he thus troubled her.

He was always of uncertain habits, and had four dinners ready for him every day; one at Paris, one at Ecouen, one at Chantilly, and one where the Court was. But the expense of this arrangement was not great; he dined on soup, and the half of a fowl roasted upon a crust of bread; the other half serving for the next day. He rarely invited anybody to dinner, but when he did, no man could be more polite or attentive to his guests.

Formerly he had been in love with several ladies of the Court; then, nothing cost too much. He was grace, magnificence, gallantry in person—a Jupiter transformed into a shower of gold. Now he disguised himself as a lackey, another time as a female broker in articles for the toilet; and now in another fashion. He was the most ingenious man in the world. He once gave a grand *fête* solely for the purpose of retarding the journey into Italy of a lady with whom he was enamored, with whom he was on good terms, and whose husband he amused by making verses. He hired all the houses on one side of a street near St. Sulpice, furnished them, and pierced the connecting walls, in order to be able thus to reach the place of rendezvous without being suspected. . . .

During the last fifteen or twenty years of his life, he was accused of something more than fierceness and ferocity. Wanderings were noticed in his conduct, which were not exhibited in his own house alone. Entering one morning into the apartment of the Maréchale de Noailles (she herself has related this to me) as her bed was being made, and there being only the counterpane to put on, he stopped short at the door, crying with transport, "Oh, the nice bed, the nice bed!" took a spring, leaped upon the bed, rolled himself upon it seven or eight times, then descended and made his excuses to the Maréchale, saying that her bed was so clean and so well made, that he could not hinder himself from jumping upon it; and this, although there had never been anything between them; and when the Maréchale, who all her life had been above suspicion, was at an age at which she could not give birth to any. Her servants remained stupefied, and she as much as they. She got out of the difficulty by laughing and treating it as a joke. It was whispered that there were times when M. le Prince believed himself a dog, or some other beast, whose manners he imitated; and I have known people very worthy of faith who have assured me they have seen him at the going to bed of the King suddenly throw his head into the air several times running, and open his mouth quite wide, like a dog when barking, yet without making a noise. It is certain, that for a long time nobody saw him except a single valet, who had control over him, and who did not annoy him.

In the latter part of his life he attended in a ridiculously minute manner to his diet and its results, and entered into discussions which drove his doctors to despair. Fever and gout at last attacked him, and he augmented them by the course he pursued. Finot, our physician and his, at times knew not what to do with him. What embarrassed Finot most, as he related to us more than once, was that M. le Prince would eat nothing, for the simple reason, as he alleged, that he was dead, and that dead men did not eat! It was necessary, however, that he should take something, or he would have really died. Finot and another doctor who attended him, determined to agree with him that he was dead, but to maintain that dead men sometimes eat. They offered to produce dead men of this kind; and in point of fact, led to M. le Prince some persons unknown to him, who pretended to be dead, but who ate nevertheless. This trick succeeded, but he would never eat except with these men and Finot. On that condition he ate well, and this jealousy lasted a long time, and drove Finot to despair by its duration; who, nevertheless, sometimes nearly died of laughter in relating to us what passed at these repasts, and the conversation from the other world heard there.

M. le Prince's malady augmenting, Madame la Princesse grew bold enough to ask him if he did not wish to think of his conscience, and to see a confessor? He amused himself tolerably long in refusing to do so. Some months before he had seen in secret Père de la Tour. He had sent to the reverend father asking him to come by night and disguised. Père de la Tour, surprised to the last degree at so wild a proposition, replied that the respect he owed to the cloth would prevent him visiting M. le Prince in disguise; but that he would come in his ordinary attire. M. le Prince agreed to this last imposed condition. He made the Père de la Tour enter at night by a little back door, at which an attendant was waiting to receive him. He was led by this attendant, who had a lantern in one hand and a key in the other, through many long and obscure passages, and through many doors, which were opened and closed upon him as he passed. Having arrived at last at the sick chamber, he confessed M. le Prince, and was conducted out of the house in the same manner and by the same way as before. These visits were repeated during several months.

The Prince's malady rapidly increased, and became extreme. The doctors found him so ill on the night of Easter Sunday that they proposed to him the Sacrament for the next day. He disputed with them, and said that if he was so very bad it would be better to take the Sacraments at once, and have done with them. They in their turn opposed this, saying there was no need of so much hurry. At last, for fear of incensing him, they consented, and he received all-hurriedly the last Sacraments. A little while after he called M. le Duc to him, and spoke of the honors he wished at his funeral, mentioning those which had been omitted at the funeral of his father, but which he did not wish to be omitted from his. He talked of nothing but this and of the sums he had spent at Chantilly, until his reason began to wander.

Not a soul regretted him; neither servants nor friends, neither child nor wife. Indeed the Princess was so ashamed of her tears that she made excuses for them.

SAINT-SIMON, *Memoirs*

English Public-School Lingo

(EARLY TWENTIETH CENTURY)

Afternoon tea—Detention after three o'clock (Edinburgh Royal High School).

Ancient mariner—A rowing Don.

Behind—A back at football. At Eton, *short behind* and *long behind*. At Winchester, *second behind* and *last behind*.

Biddy—A bath in college (from French *bidet*) (Winchester).

Bond Street—A walk along one side of the playground (Stonyhurst).

Bum curtain—A short, scant academic gown (Cambridge).

Bunny grub—Green vegetables (Cheltenham).

Cathedral—A silk hat (Winchester).

Clean straw—Clean sheets. Worth recording because the shift to proper bedding was put into effect by someone named Dean Fleshmonger (Winchester).

Dolphin—A leading swimmer and diver (Harrow).

Gold hatband—A nobleman undergraduate (the Universities).

Mud student—A student at an agricultural college.

On and off—Lemonade. Two possible derivations: a melee of lemonade-seeking boys tramping down and kicking one another; or, because of the tap from which the lemonade flows (Tonbridge).

Playing fields—Though every one knows the phrase, perhaps not well known is the fact that there are seven of them: Upper Club, Lower Club, Upper Sixpenny, Sixpenny, Jordan, Mesopotamia, and (circa 1900) "the new ground in Agars Plough" (Eton).

Sodom—Wadham College (Oxford).

Vaseline—Butter (Royal Military Academy).

Fables

The Lion called the Sheep to ask if his breath smelt. She said, Ay, and he bit off her head for a fool. He called the Wolf; he said No, and was torn to pieces for a flatterer. He called the Fox, who said he had a cold, and could not smell.

A man who had been traveling kept bragging and boasting, after he returned home, of various great feats he had accomplished. Thus, in Rhodes he had taken so great a leap that no one could come near him; and there were witnesses there to prove it. "Possibly," said one of his hearers; "but if it's so, pretend that this is Rhodes and try the leap again."

A young Mole said to her Mother, "I can see." To try her out, the Mother put a lump of frankincense in front of her and asked her what it was. "A stone," said the young Mole. "My dear child," said the Mother, "not only do you not see; you cannot even smell."

There was great commotion among all the beasts, as to which boasted the largest family. They came to the Lioness, asking "How many do you have at a birth?" "Just one," she said, "but that one is a Lion."

A Hound chased a Hare for some distance, but the Hare got away. A Goatherd coming by jeered at the Hound for being out-run. "You forget," the Hound answered, "that it is one thing to be running for your dinner, and another for your life."

AESOP

Two benevolent Fairies were present at the birth of a Prince, who later became one of the great Monarchs in his country's history.

"I bestow on my protégé," said the one, "the piercing eye of the Eagle, from whose sight not the tiniest Fly can escape in his vast kingdom."

"A noble gift!" broke in the second Fairy. "The Prince will become a discerning Monarch. But the Eagle is not blest with such keen sight merely to discover the tiniest Flies; he also possesses a supreme contempt for chasing them. And this gift do I bestow on the Prince."

An old church in whose chinks the Sparrows had built countless nests, was repaired. Returning to it in its fine new lustre, the Sparrows sought out their old homes, to find them all bricked up. "Of what earthly use," they cried, "can so large a building be now? We can only leave such a worthless heap of stones to its fate."

A Wolf lay dying and cast back at the events of his life. "No doubt," he said, "I am a sinner, but not, I would hope, a very great one. I have done harm, but also much good. I remember once a bleating Lamb, that had wandered from the flock, came so near me that I could easily have destroyed it; yet I did nothing. That same time I listened to the sneers and jibes of a Sheep without the slightest irritation, though there were no watch-dogs to fear."

"I can account for all that," said his friend the Fox, who was assisting in the Wolf's preparations for death. "I remember perfectly the attendant circumstances. It was when you almost choked to death from a bone, which a kindhearted Crane afterwards pulled out of your mouth."

"Oh," groaned a miser to his neighbor, "what a miserable wretch I am! Last night some devil of a thief stole the treasure which I had buried in the garden, leaving a stone in its place."

"You'd have made no use of your gold," said the neighbor, "so just imagine that the stone is your treasure; you'll be no poorer."

"Even if I *weren't* any poorer," moaned the miser, "isn't someone else that much the richer? O I shall go mad!"

G. E. Lessing

A Mouse lived under a granary. In the granary floor there was a little hole through which grain slipped down. The Mouse led a happy life, but was filled with desire to display her good fortune, gnawed a larger hole, and invited other Mice in. "Let's have a feast," she said, "there will be ample food for us all."

But, on bringing the Mice to the feast, she found there was no hole at all. The farmer had noticed the big hole in the floor and sealed it up.

A man who had been blind from birth asked a man who could see: "What color is milk?"

The man who could see answered: "The color of milk is like white paper."

The blind man asked: "Then the color rustles in your hands like paper?"

Said the man who could see: "No, it's white, like white flour."

Asked the blind man: "Oh, then it's soft and dry like flour?"

Said the man who could see: "No, no—it's simply white, like a rabbit."

Asked the blind man: "Oh, then it's downy and soft like a rabbit?"

Said the the man who could see: "No. White is a *color,* exactly like snow."

Asked the blind man: "Oh, it's cold like snow, is it?"

And despite all the comparisons made by the man who could see, the blind man was completely unable to grasp what the color of milk really was.

T O L S T O I

A Writer of Fables was passing through a lonely forest, when he met a Fortune. Greatly alarmed, he tried to climb a tree, but the Fortune pulled him down and bestowed itself upon him with cruel persistence.

"Why did you try to run away?" said the Fortune, when his struggles had ceased and his screams were stilled. "Why did you glare at me so inhospitably?"

"I don't know what you are," replied the Writer of Fables, deeply disturbed.

"I am wealth; I am respectability," the Fortune explained; "I am elegant houses, a yacht and a clean shirt every day. I am leisure, I am travel, wine, a shiny hat and an unshiny coat. I am enough to eat."

"All right," said the Writer of Fables, in a whisper; "but for goodness' sake speak lower!"

"Why so?" the Fortune asked, in surprise.

"So as not to wake me," replied the Writer of Fables, a holy calm brooding upon his beautiful face.

A M B R O S E B I E R C E

"Look around you," said the Citizen. "This is the largest market in the world."

"Oh, surely not," said the Traveler.

"Well, perhaps not the largest," said the Citizen, "but much the best."

"You are certainly wrong there," said the Traveler. "I can tell you . . ."

They buried the Stranger in the dusk.

ROBERT LOUIS STEVENSON

Famous Passages

Warren Hastings

The place [Westminster Hall] was worthy of such a trial. It was the great hall of William Rufus, the hall which had resounded with acclamations at the inauguration of thirty kings, the hall which had witnessed the just sentence of Bacon and the just absolution of Somers, the hall where the eloquence of Strafford had for a moment awed and melted a victorious party inflamed with just resentment, the hall where Charles had confronted the High Court of Justice with the placid courage which has half redeemed his fame. Neither military nor civil pomp was wanting. The avenues were lined with grenadiers. The streets were kept clear by cavalry. The peers, robed in gold and ermine, were mashalled by the heralds under Garter King-at-Arms. The judges in their vestments of state attended to give advice on points of law. Near a hundred and seventy lords, three-fourths of the Upper House as the Upper House then was, walked in solemn order from their usual place of assembling to the tribunal. The junior Baron present led the way . . . The long procession was closed by the Duke of Norfolk, Earl Marshal of the realm, by the great dignitaries, and by the brothers and sons of the King. Last of all came the Prince of Wales, conspicuous by his fine person and noble bearing. The grey old walls were hung with scarlet. The long galleries were crowded by an audience such as has rarely excited the fears or the emulation of an orator. There were gathered together, from all parts of a great, free, enlightened, and prosperous empire, grace and female loveliness, wit and learning, the represent-

atives of every science and of every art. There were seated round
the Queen the fair-haired young daughters of the house of Brunswick. There the Ambassadors of great Kings and Commonwealths
gazed with admiration on a spectacle which no other country in
the world could present. There Siddons, in the prime of her majestic beauty, looked with emotion on a scene surpassing all the
imitations of the stage. There the historian of the Roman Empire
thought of the days when Cicero pleaded the cause of Sicily
against Verres, and when, before a senate which still retained
some show of freedom, Tacitus thundered against the oppressor
of Africa. There were seen, side by side, the greatest painter and
the greatest scholar of the age. The spectacle had allured Reynolds from that easel which has preserved to us the thoughtful
foreheads of so many writers and statesmen, and the sweet smiles
of so many noble matrons: It had induced Parr to suspend his
labours in that dark and profound mine from which he had ex-
tracted a vast treasure of erudition . . . There appeared the voluptuous charms of her to whom the heir of the throne had in
secret plighted his faith. There too was she, the beautiful mother
of a beautiful race, the Saint Cecilia, whose delicate features,
lighted up by love and music, art has rescued from the common
decay. There were the members of that brilliant society which
quoted, criticised, and exchanged repartees, under the rich peacock hangings of Mrs. Montague. And there the ladies whose lips,
more persuasive than those of Fox himself, had carried the Westminster election against palace and treasury, shone round Geor-
giana, Duchess of Devonshire.

The Serjeants made proclamation. Hastings advanced to the
bar, and bent his knee. The culprit was indeed not unworthy of
that great presence. He had ruled an extensive and populous
country, had made laws and treaties, had sent forth armies, had
set up and pulled down princes. And in his high place he had so
borne himself, that all had feared him, that most had loved him,
and that hatred itself could deny him no title of glory, except
virtue. He looked like a great man, and not like a bad man. A
person small and emaciated, yet deriving dignity from a carriage

which, while it indicated deference to the Court, indicated also habitual self-possession and self-respect, a high and intellectual forehead, a brow pensive, but not gloomy, a mouth of inflexible decision, a face pale and worn, but serene, on which was written, as legibly as under the picture in the council-chamber at Calcutta, *Mens æqua in arduis;* such was the aspect with which the great proconsul presented himself to his judges.

M A C A U L A Y, *Warren Hastings*

Marie Antoinette

It is now sixteen or seventeen years since I saw the Queen of France, then the dauphiness, at Versailles; and surely never lighted on this orb, which she hardly seemed to touch, a more delightful vision. I saw her just above the horizon, decorating and cheering the elevated sphere she just began to move in—glittering like the morning star, full of life, and splendour, and joy. Oh! what a revolution! and what a heart must I have, to contemplate without emotion that elevation and that fall! Little did I dream when she added titles of veneration to those of enthusiastic, distant, respectful love, that she should ever be obliged to carry the sharp antidote against disgrace concealed in that bosom; little did I dream that I should have lived to see such disasters fallen upon her in a nation of gallant men, in a nation of men of honour, and of cavaliers. I thought ten thousand swords must have leaped from their scabbards to avenge even a look that threatened her with insult. But the age of chivalry is gone. That of sophisters, economists and calculators has succeeded; and the glory of Europe is extinguished forever. Never, never more shall we behold that generous loyalty to rank and sex, that proud submission, that dignified obedience, that subordination of the heart, which kept alive, even in servitude itself, the spirit of an exalted freedom. The unbought grace of life, the cheap defence of nations, the nurse of manly sentiment and heroic enterprise is gone! It is gone, that sensibility of principle, that chastity of honour, which felt a stain like a wound, which inspired courage whilst it mitigated ferocity, which ennobled whatever it touched, and under which vice itself lost half its evil, by losing all its grossness.

EDMUND BURKE, *Reflections on the Revolution in France*

But the iniquity of oblivion blindly scattereth her poppy, and deals with the memory of men without distinction to merit of perpetuity. Who can but pity the founder of the pyramids? Herostratus lives that burned the temple of Diana, he is almost lost that built it. Time hath spared the epitaph of Adrian's horse, confounded that of himself. In vain we compute our felicities by the advantage of our good names, since bad have equal durations; and Thersites is like to live as long as Agamemnon. Who knows whether the best of men be known? or whether there be not more remarkable persons forgot, than any that stand remembered in the known account of time? Without the favour of the everlasting register, the first man had been as unknown as the last, and Methuselah's long life had been his only chronicle.

SIR THOMAS BROWNE, *Hydriotaphia*

The presence that rose thus so strangely beside the waters, is expressive of what in the ways of a thousand years men had come to desire. Hers is the head upon which all "the ends of the world are come," and the eyelids are a little weary. It is a beauty wrought out from within upon the flesh, the deposit, little cell by cell, of strange thoughts and fantastic reveries and exquisite passions. Set it for a moment beside one of those white Greek goddesses or beautiful women of antiquity, and how would they be troubled by this beauty, into which the soul with all its maladies has passed! All the thoughts and experience of the world have etched and moulded there, in that which they have of power to refine and make expressive the outward form, the animalism of Greece, the lust of Rome, the mysticism of the middle age with its spiritual ambition and imaginative loves, the return of the Pagan world, the sins of the Borgias. She is older than the rocks among which she sits; like the vampire, she has been dead many times, and learned the secrets of the grave; and has been a diver in deep seas, and keeps their fallen day about her; and trafficked for strange webs with Eastern merchants, and, as Leda, was the mother of Helen of Troy, and, as Saint Anne, the mother of Mary; and all this has been to her but as the sound of lyres and flutes, and lives only in the delicacy with which it has moulded the changing lineaments, and tinged the eyelids and the hands. The fancy of a perpetual life, sweeping together ten thousand experiences, is an old one; and modern philosophy has conceived the idea of humanity as wrought upon by, and summing up in itself, all modes of thought and life. Certainly Lady Lisa might stand as embodiment of the old fancy, the symbol of the modern idea.

WALTER PATER, *The Renaissance*

O eloquent, just, and mighty Death! whom none could advise, thou hast persuaded; what none have dared, thou hast done; and whom all the world hath flattered, thou only hast cast out of the world and despised. Thou hast drawn together all the far-stretched greatness, all the pride, cruelty, and ambition of man and covered it all over with these two narrow words, *Hic jacet.*

SIR WALTER RALEIGH, *The History of the World*

Food and Drink

✠ One touch of nature—in addition to Shakespeare's—makes the whole world kin: their desire to eat. To eat in caves, or in bumboats, or in the world's great capitals; but the last of these invites another famous line: "Civilized man cannot live without cooks." Cooked food is perhaps as old as the rubbing together of flints for a fire, and fancy food must go back well beyond Apicius: Lucullus, indeed, remains the symbol of magnif-

icent dining and wining—Lucullus, the former warrior who, if
he could not bring peace to Italy, was the first to introduce cherries there. And in our day, when cooks must be largely referred
to in the past tense, civilized men—and women—cannot live
without cookbooks. And uncivilized men also: one thinks of those
dreary, greedy, self-proclaimed gourmets who are certainly entitled to live to eat, but not to hold forth on what to eat, and what
to eat with what, and when to eat it—after the game course, or
only in April, and so on. But they are at any rate better than the
wine "experts" who have been satirized a thousand times without
profiting by the satire.

In spite of all the pretentious jabber and parvenu ritualism,
food and wine are often worth talking about, and have always,
it would seem, been written about: Plato on Homer and sauces,
I confess, surprises me, and is conceivably a gag; but I encountered it under reliable auspices and pass it along. Sir Epicure
Mammon, in Jonson's *The Alchemist*, is as much concerned with
the table setting as the menu, with emeralds and sapphires as an
"exquisite and poignant sauce," but he is a kind of poet of palatial
cookery and carnality. For the rest, food has played all kinds of
roles in all kinds of eating places, from being roasted on a musical
turnspit in Italy to being offered up, in the grave language of
French cuisine, to a war-shattered, starving Paris. Myself, I love
food, but chiefly (and increasingly as I get older) in simple,
even boyhood form. I am rather a byword for my enjoyment of
the drearier puddings (an uncle of mine said he wondered for
years who ordered such things on menus as sago pudding, cabinet
pudding, and tapioca pudding, and then took me to lunch and
found out); I seriously consider a liking for peanut butter a
sine qua non of nice people; I love all innards and bemoan the
terrific amount of cholesterol in calf's brains. At home, when
I was a boy, I always had to eat for lunch, on pain of no dessert,
a "nutritious" cereal bowl full of creamed carrots or creamed
celery or creamed spinach; and today I'm crazy about them all,
particularly creamed spinach.

I much prefer (this may result from going out at night, for

twenty-three years, to cover the theatre) dining at home to dining out. I like fine foods served up with fine sauces, but only one such to a meal; I have enjoyed bear steak and fried squirrel and raw fish, and I can tolerate a bit of dulse, if that can be called food, and have had both a mother and a wife whose cakes and tortes and soufflés are superb; but, beyond a compliment to the hostess or the cook, I don't want to talk food while eating it, and just so, I prefer a cheerful glutton to an articulate gourmet.

Drink I know little about, beyond the vocabulary. Wine, un-happily, doesn't agree with me: anything beyond a glass or so of white wine leaves me, next morning, feeling very seedy. I can tell a really good wine from a really bad one, and possibly a very great one from a good one; but I can't tell much else; the Moselle, the Nahe, and the Rhine all flow alike to me, and I can only spot a a burgundy from a claret by its making me, next day, feel worse than a claret does. I mostly drink bourbon, I detest rye, and I love hot milk, particularly at bedtime, this passion having origi-nated when I was young and when a dab of inserted butter made it look like an oyster stew; by now, an oyster stew looks to me like *it*.

A cook they hadde with hem for the nones
To boille the chiknes with the marybones,
And poudre-marchant tart, and galingale.
Wel coude he know a draughte of London ale.
He coude roste, and sethe, and broille, and frye,
Maken mortreux, and wel bake a pye. . . .
For blankmanger, that made he with the beste.

CHAUCER, Prologue to *The Canterbury Tales*

My meat shall all come in, in Indian shells,
Dishes of agate, set in gold, and studded
With emeralds, sapphires, hyacinths, and rubies.
The tongues of carps, dormice, and camels' heels,

Boiled i' the spirit of sol, and dissolved pearl,
Apicius' diet, 'gainst the epilepsy,—
And I will eat these broths with spoons of amber,
Headed with diamond and carbuncle.
My foot-boy shall eat pheasants, calvered salmons,
Knots, godwits, lampreys: I myself will have
The beards of barbels served, instead of salads;
Oiled mushrooms; and the swelling, unctuous paps
Of a fat, pregnant sow, newly cut off,
Dressed with an exquisite and poignant sauce,
For which I'll say unto my cook, "There's gold;
Go forth and be a knight!"

BEN JONSON, *The Alchemist*

Game owes a great part of its value to the nature of its native soil.
The taste of a Périgord partridge is not the same as that of a
partridge from Sologne; and though a hare, killed on the plains
around Paris, is just an insignificant dish, a leveret born on the
sun-scorched hills of Valromey or High Dauphiné is perhaps the
most deliciously scented of all four-legged things.

ANTHELME BRILLAT-SAVARIN, *The Physiology of Taste*

"Have you lunched?" asked the English steward of the Channel-
crossing Frenchman, to receive the pithy answer, *"Au contraire!"*

T. EARLE WELBY

Homer has not, if I remember correctly, ever said a word about
sauces.

PLATO

A woman should never be seen eating or drinking, unless it be
lobster salad and champagne, the only truly feminine viands.

BYRON

Neither is the art of cookery greater in Turkey than with us in Wales, for toasting of cheese in Wales, and seething of rice in Turkey, will enable a man freely to profess the art of cookery.

FYNES MORYSON

Breakfast for my lord and lady [non-flesh days]: First a loaf of bread in trenchers, two manchets, a quart of beer, a quart of wine, two pieces of salt fish, six bacon'd herring or a dish of sprouts.

Northumberland Book (1572)

Dined with the Prime Minister [Lord Palmerston] who was upwards of eighty years of age. He ate for dinner two plates of turtle soup; he was then served very amply to a plate of cod and oyster sauce; he then took a pâté; afterwards he was helped to two very greasy looking entrées; he then despatched a plate of roast mutton; there then appeared before him the largest, and to my mind the hardest, slice of ham that ever figured on the table of a nobleman, yet it disappeared, just in time to answer the inquiry of his butler, "Snipe, my Lord, or pheasant?" He instantly replied "Pheasant," thus completing his ninth dish of meat at that meal.

JOHN EVELYN DENISON, VISCOUNT OSSINGTON

Never did any one succeed in making [Napoleon] eat his dinner while it was hot, for once he settled down to work no one knew when he would leave off. Accordingly, when it was time for dinner, chickens were put on the spit for him at intervals of half an hour, and I have personally seen dozens of them roasted in such fashion before arriving at the one finally presented to him.

EMANUEL DE LAS CASES

✠ There is a similar story, which I cannot track down, concerning Tolstoi and omelets, which were constantly being prepared in the kitchen in case he should call for one.

[Paris during the Franco-Prussian War:] By the beginning of January 1871 some 650 horses a day were being killed to provide food for the starving population. In the Place de l'Hôtel de Ville there was a rat market, and a well known restaurant was said to transform these rodents into quite a succulent dish with the aid of champagne and spices. Recipes were exchanged for transforming prize poodle or common mongrel into a dainty dinner . . .

The Jardin d'Acclimatation—the Paris zoo—sold all its animals, for it had nothing to feed them on. Almost all the animals, yaks, zebra and buffaloes, were bought by a butcher of the Boulevard Haussmann named Deboos, who cut them up and sold them, morsel by morsel, at an enormous profit. He paid 27,000 francs for the two famous elephants, Castor and Pollux, which were shot and sold for meat.

COLIN CLAIR, *Kitchen and Table*

✠ A menu reported in *Les Nouvelles*, a Paris newspaper, December 4, 1870, for a grand dinner at which were present many well-known persons:

> consommé of horse with birdseed
> skewered dog liver, maître d'hôtel
> minced cat's back, mayonnaise sauce
> shoulder of dog, tomato sauce
> stewed cat with mushrooms
> dog cutlets with peas
> ragout of rats, Robert
> dog leg flanked with ratlets
> escarole salad
> elephant's ear au jus
> plum pudding with horse marrow
> dessert and wines

[Of a musical turnspit which played twenty-four tunes in the kitchens of an affluent Italian nobleman:] The spits of this machine turned 130 roasts at the same time; and the chef was informed, by the progress of the melodies, when the moment had arrived for removing each piece of meat.

J. C. JEAFFRESON, A Book about the Table

[On the origins of the canning industry:] An Englishman named Peter Durand had the idea of packing heat sterilized food in containers made of iron plate rendered rustproof by a thin coating of tin. . . . The early containers needed a hammer and chisel to open them . . .

COLIN CLAIR, Kitchen and Table

When we sat down to dinner, I asked Byron if he would take soup. No; he never took soup.—Would he take some fish? No; he never took fish.—Presently I asked him if he would eat some mutton. No; he never ate mutton.—I then asked if he would take a glass of wine. No; he never tasted wine.—It was now necessary to inquire what he *did* eat and drink; and the answer was, "Nothing but hard biscuits and soda water." Unfortunately, neither hard biscuits nor soda water were at hand; and he dined upon potatoes bruised down on his plate and drenched with vinegar. . . . Some days after, meeting Hobhouse, I said to him: "How long will Lord Byron persevere in his present diet?" He replied, "Just as long as you continue to notice it." I did not then know, what I now know to be a fact, that Byron, after leaving my house, had gone to a Club in St James's Street and eaten a hearty meat-supper.

SAMUEL ROGERS, Table Talk

✠ The great classical scholar Richard Porson (1759–1808) was an even greater drinker. Paying a visit to the painter John Hoppner, he could not long acquiesce in Hoppner's explaining that his wife had gone away, taking with her the key to the liquor closet. Porson suggested that surely she must have

at least a bottle of something in her bedroom; Hoppner denied
this, but a search at Porson's insistence did, to Hoppner's surprise, turn up a bottle, which Porson quickly drained, pronouncing it to be the best gin he had drunk in a long time. When
Mrs. Hoppner returned and her husband a little irritably told
her of the discovery of the bottle and of Porson's drinking every
drop of it, she said: "Every drop of it! Good God, that was spirits
of wine for the lamp."

> Bring us in no brown bread, for that is made of bran,
> Nor bring us in no white bread, for therein is no game.
> But bring us in good ale, and bring us in good ale;
> For our blessed Lady's sake, bring us in good ale!
>
> Bring us in no beef, for there is many bones,
> But bring us in good ale, for that goeth down at once;
> And bring us in good ale, etc.
>
> Bring us in no bacon, for that is passing fat,
> But bring us in good ale, and give us enough of that:
> And bring us in good ale, etc.
>
> Bring us in no mutton, for that is often lean,
> Nor bring us in no tripës, for they are seldom clean;
> But bring us in good ale, etc.
>
> Bring us in no eggës, for there are many shells,
> But bring us in good ale, and give us nothing else;
> And bring us in good ale, etc.
>
> Bring us in no butter, for therein are many hairs;
> Nor bring us in no piggës flesh, for that will make us
>   boars;
> But bring us in good ale, etc.
>
> Bring us in no puddings, for therein is all God's good;
> Nor bring us in no venison, for that is not for our blood;
> But bring us in good ale, etc.

Bring us in no capon's flesh, for that is often dear;
Nor bring us in no duck's flesh, for they slobber in the
    mere;
But bring us in good ale, and bring us in good ale,
For our blessed Lady's sake, bring us in good ale!

A N O N .

I was to dine at Northumberland House, and went a little after-hour: there I found the Countess, Lady Betty Mackenzie, Lady Strafford; my Lady Finlater, who was never out of Scotland before; a tall lad of fifteen, her son; Lord Drogheda, and Mr. Worseley. At five arrived Mr. Mitchell, who said the Lords had begun to read the Poor Bill, which would take at least two hours, and perhaps would debate it afterwards. We concluded dinner would be called for, it not being very precedented for ladies to wait for gentlemen: no such thing. Six o'clock came—seven o'clock came—our coaches came—well! we sent them away . . . We wore out the wind and the weather, the opera and the play, Mrs. Cornelys's and Almack's, and every topic that would do in a formal circle. We hinted, represented—in vain. The clock struck eight: my Lady at last said she would go and order dinner; but it was a good half-hour before it appeared. We then sat down to a table for fourteen covers, but instead of substantials, there was nothing but a profusion of plates striped red, green and yellow, gilt plate, blacks and uniforms! . . . The first course stayed as long as possible, in hopes of the Lords: so did the second. The dessert at last arrived, and the middle dish was actually set on when Lord Finlater and Mr. Mackay arrived!—would you believe it, the dessert was remanded, and the whole first course brought back again! Stay, I have not done: just as this second first course had done its duty, Lord Northumberland, Lord Strafford and Mackenzie came in, and the whole began a third time! Then the second course and the dessert! I thought we should have dropped from our chairs with fatigue and fumes! When the clock struck eleven, we were asked to return to the drawing-room and drink tea and coffee, but I said I was engaged to supper, and came home to bed. My dear lord, think of four hours and a half in a circle of mixed company, and three great dinners, one after another, without interruption.

HORACE WALPOLE, letter to the Earl of Hertford

Cleanliness does not presage civilization. It results from it. . . . Tablecloths, already in use at the time of Augustus, had disappeared, and their white surfaces were not seen on our tables until the close of the thirteenth century, and then only for kings and princes.

Napkins did not come into use until forty years later . . .

Our first ancestors, the Celts, wiped their hands on the bales of hay that served them for seats. The Spartans put a piece of soft bread beside each guest for the same purpose.

You may travel round the world, but you will find no professional cook, whether *cordon rouge* or *cordon bleu,* who can make an omelet like the French housewife preparing dinner for her children.

Bear meat is now eaten everywhere in Europe. From the most ancient times, the front paws have been regarded as the most delicate morsel.

Bishop—A beverage [made] of orange juice, sugar, and light wine. . . . If it is made with Bordeaux or Burgundy, it is a Bishop's drink. If it is made with an aged Rhine wine, it is a Cardinal's drink. But if you make it with Tokay, it is a Pope's drink.

German cherry soup—It is only for the record that we mention this execrable dish of crushed cherries and ground-up pits, ferociously spiced, drowned in wine, and served cold.

ALEXANDRE DUMAS PÈRE, *Dictionary of Cuisine*

(trans. Louis Colman)

It was amusing to look round the filthy little scullery and think that only a double door was between us and the dining-room. There sat the customers in all their splendour—spotless table-cloths, bowls of flowers, mirrors and gilt cornices and painted cherubim; and here, just a few feet away, we in our disgusting filth. For it really was disgusting filth. There was no time to sweep the floor till evening, and we slithered about in a compound of soapy water, lettuce-leaves, torn paper and trampled food. A dozen waiters with their coats off, showing their sweaty armpits, sat at the table mixing salads and sticking their thumbs into the cream pots. The room had a dirty mixed smell of food and sweat. Everywhere in the cupboards, behind the piles of crockery, were squalid stores of food that the waiters had stolen. There were only two sinks, and no washing basin, and it was nothing unusual for a waiter to wash his face in the water in which clean crockery was rinsing. But the customers saw nothing of this. There were a coco-nut mat and a mirror outside the dining-room door, and the waiters used to preen themselves up and go in looking the picture of cleanliness.

It is an instructive sight to see a waiter going into a hotel dining-room. As he passes the door a sudden change comes over him. The set of his shoulders alters; all the dirt and hurry and irritation have dropped off in an instant. He glides over the carpet, with a solemn priest-like air . . . and [sails] across it dish in hand, graceful as a swan. . . . And you could not help thinking, as you saw him bow and smile, with that benign smile of the trained waiter, that the customer was put to shame by having such an aristocrat to serve him. . . .

The customer pays, as he sees it, for good service; the employee is paid, as he sees it, for the *boulot*—meaning, as a rule, an imitation of good service. The result is that, though hotels are miracles of punctuality, they are worse than the worst private houses in the things that matter.

Take cleanliness, for example. The dirt in the Hôtel X., as soon as one penetrated into the service quarters, was revolting.

Our cafeteria had year-old filth in all the dark corners, and the bread-bin was infested with cockroaches. Once I suggested killing these beasts to Mario. "Why kill the poor animals?" he said reproachfully. . . .

In the kitchen the dirt was worse. It is not a figure of speech, it is a mere statement of fact to say that a French cook will spit in the soup—that is, if he is not going to drink it himself. He is an artist, but his art is not cleanliness. To a certain extent he is even dirty because he is an artist, for food, to look smart, needs dirty treatment. When a steak, for instance, is brought up for the head cook's inspection, he does not handle it with a fork. He picks it up in his fingers and slaps it down, runs his thumb round the dish and licks it to taste the gravy, runs it round and licks it again, then steps back and contemplates the piece of meat like an artist judging a picture, then presses it lovingly into place with his fat, pink fingers, every one of which he has licked a hundred times that morning. When he is satisfied, he takes a cloth and wipes his finger-prints from the dish, and hands it to the waiter. And the waiter, of course, dips *his* fingers into the gravy—his nasty, greasy fingers which he is for ever running through his brilliantined hair. Whenever one pays more than, say, ten francs for a dish of meat in Paris, one may be certain that it has been fingered in this manner. . . .

Dirtiness is inherent in hotels and restaurants, because sound food is sacrificed to punctuality and smartness. The hotel employee is too busy getting food ready to remember that it is meant to be eaten. A meal is simply *"une commande"* to him, just as a man dying of cancer is simply "a case" to the doctor. A customer orders, for example, a piece of toast. Somebody, pressed with work . . . has to prepare it. . . . All he knows is that it must look right and must be ready in three minutes. Some large drops of sweat fall from his forehead on to the toast. Why should he worry? Presently the toast falls among the filthy sawdust on the floor. Why trouble to make a new piece? It is much quicker to wipe the sawdust off. . . . The only food at the Hôtel X. which was ever prepared cleanly was the staff's, and the *patron's*. . . .

In spite of all this the Hôtel X. was one of the dozen most expensive hotels in Paris, and the customers paid startling prices. The ordinary charge for a night's lodging, not including breakfast, was two hundred francs. . . . If a customer had a title, or was reputed to be a millionaire, all his charges went up automatically. One morning on the fourth floor an American who was on diet wanted only salt and hot water for his breakfast. Valenti was furious. "Jesus Christ!" he said, "what about my ten per cent? Ten per cent of salt and water!" And he charged twenty-five francs for the breakfast. The customer paid without a murmur.

According to Boris, the same kind of thing went on in all Paris hotels, or at least in all the big, expensive ones. But I imagine that the customers at the Hôtel X. were especially easy to swindle, for they were mostly Americans . . . They would . . . eat marmalade at tea, and drink vermouth after dinner, and order a *poulet à la reine* at a hundred francs and then souse it in Worcester sauce. One customer, from Pittsburgh, dined every night in his bedroom on grape-nuts, scrambled eggs and cocoa.

G E O R G E   O R W E L L, *Down and Out in Paris and London*

We always remember the excitement at the Hostellerie de la Poste at Avallon, one of the greatest restaurants of France, when one day a client ordered the most expensive bottle of wine on the list, a Romanée Conti 1894 that cost $140. . . . Restaurateurs scarcely desire to sell [their collectors' items] because the very old wines have often passed their prime and it would be impossible to charge $140 for a bottle of pink water.

Thus, when the Romanée Conti 1894 was ordered, the sommelier went to M. Hure, the proprietor, who had to verify that the customer was not joking. The bottle was fetched, so swathed in cobwebs that it had lost its shape. The top management of the restaurant followed in procession as M. Hure carried out the Romanée Conti like a reliquary. It was uncorked with the greatest care, and by candlelight it was gently poured into a crystal jug.

The color was beautiful—pale but distinct, as transparent as a garnet. M. Hure sniffed the bouquet, then hesitantly nodded his approval. The restaurant was as silent as a tomb while the wine settled. Twenty minutes later, M. Hure returned, poured himself a taste of the Romanée Conti 1894, and drank it, trembling. The customer himself was on the edge of his chair. M. Hure let the wine vaporize in his mouth, drawing a light, whistling breath through pursed lips. The venerable lady, thus coaxed, revealed her most delicate secrets. M. Hure blushed, then looked the customer straight in the eye. "Monsieur," he said, "it is thirty years since I have sold a bottle of 1894. By ordering it you have permitted me to have one of the greatest emotions of my life. I am not talking about the cost of the bottle, although had it been necessary I would willingly have opened each of my five remaining bottles until I found a good one. But the miracle has been accomplished with the first. It is admirable. And of course, *cher monsieur*, I offer it to you with my compliments."

HENRI GAULT and CHRISTIAN MILLAU,
"France's Two Greatest Wines"

[Dr. Johnson:] Claret is the liquor for boys; port for men; but he who aspires to be a hero . . . must drink brandy.

BOSWELL, *Life of Johnson*

Nor have we one or two kinds of drunkards only, but eight kinds. The first is ape drunk, and he leaps, and sings, and hollows, and danceth for the heavens; the second is lion drunk, and he flings the pots about the house, calls his hostess whore, breaks the glass windows with his dagger, and is apt to quarrel with any man that speaks to him; the third is swine drunk, heavy, lumpish, and sleepy, and cries for a little more drink, and a few more clothes; the fourth is sheep drunk, wise in his own conceit, when he cannot bring forth a right word; the fifth is maudlin drunk, when a fellow will weep for kindness in the midst of his ale, and kiss you, saying: By God, Captain, I love thee, go thy ways, thou dost not think so often of me as I do of thee; I would (if it pleased God) I could not love thee so well as I do, and then he puts his fingers in his eye, and cries; the sixth is martin drunk, when a man is drunk and drinks himself sober ere he stir; the seventh is goat drunk, when in his drunkenness he hath no mind but on lechery; the eighth is fox drunk, when he is crafty drunk, as many of the Dutch men be, that will never bargain but when they are drunk.

THOMAS NASHE, Pierce Penniless (1592)

If you wish to grow thinner, diminish your dinner,
    And take to light claret instead of pale ale;
Look down with an utter contempt upon butter,
    And never touch bread till it's toasted—or stale.

H. S. LEIGH

The family that dines the latest
Is in our street esteemed the greatest.

HENRY FIELDING

Then each tuck'd his napkin up under his chin,
That his holiday-band might be kept very clean;
And pinned up his sleeves to his elbows, because
They should not hang down and be greased in the sauce.
Then all went to work, with such rending and tearing,
Like a kennel of hounds on a quarter of carrion.
When done with the flesh, they clawed off the fish,
With one hand at mouth and th'other in the dish.
When their stomachs were cloyed, what their bellies de-
    nied
Each clapped in his pocket to give to his bride,
With a cheese-cake and custard for my little Johnny,
And a handful of sweetmeats for poor daughter Nanny.

EDWARD WARD, "O Raree-Show" (1698)

It was Mr. Western's custom every afternoon, as soon as he was drunk, to hear his daughter play on the harpsichord.

HENRY FIELDING, *Tom Jones*

The Frontier

Australia

There is a very foolish custom prevalent in both these colonies of giving servants Tea & Sugar morning and evening; so that a man who has been transported for a Robbery, or even Murder, gets daily 1½ to 2 lb Bread, 1½ lb Meat (generally fine fresh mutton) every day, with 3 ounces of Tea and a pound Sugar every week. If he is a Mechanic, or in short any kind of tradesman, he can make his 3 pounds a week with ease by working over hours. Those Prisoners who are not assigned to Settlers work for Government till 2 o'clock, and the remainder of the day they have to themselves. You have a very erroneous idea in **England** of the situation of Convicts transported to this place. There is not one of them (if he is steady and industrious) but might become independent in a few years. Several emancipated Convicts possess great wealth; for instance, there is a man of the name of F—— residing here who has about 3000 head of horned cattle and from 3000 to 4000 sheep, and this man was a Prisoner not many years ago. We are not in that dread of the Convicts as you imagine. They will, to be sure, rob you if they can; but murder is very rarely committed, and I would as soon ride 20 miles at night here as I would from Chester to Bromborow. . . .

You can form no opinion of the depravity of some of the Prisoners. They all drink to excess, generally raw spirits, very seldom less than a half pint of Rum at one time. It is no uncommon thing for one of them to expend in drink from £20 to £40 of a Night . . .

Do not make my Letters public, which I know is the Custom in Cheshire.

WILLIAM BARNES, letters from Launceston, Van Diemen's Land
(May 5 and September 9, 1824)

Canada

Mar. 14 [1802]. In a drinking match at the Hills yesterday, Gros Bras in a fit of jealousy stabbed Aupusoi to death with a hand-dague; the first stroke opened his left side, the second his belly, and the third his breast; he never stirred, although he had a knife in his belt, and died instantly. Soon after this Aupusoi's brother, a boy about ten years of age, took the deceased's gun, loaded it with two balls, and approached Gros Bras' tent. Putting the muzzle of the gun through the door the boy fired the two balls into his breast and killed him dead, just as he was reproaching his wife for her affection for Aupusoi, and boasting of the revenge he had taken. The little fellow ran into the woods and hid. Little Shell found the old woman, Aupusoi's mother, in her tent; he instantly stabbed her. Ondainoiache then came in, took the knife, and gave her a second stab. Little Shell, in his turn taking the knife, gave a third blow. In this manner did these two rascals continue to murder the old woman, as long as there was any life in her. The boy escaped into Langlois' house, and was kept hid until they were all sober. Next morning a hole was dug in the ground, and all three were buried together. This affair kept the Indians from hunting, as Gros Bras was related to the principal hunters.

Nov. 26th [1802]. One of my men, who was much in debt, offered me his services as long as he could perform any duty, on condition I would clothe him and allow him to take a woman he had fallen in love with; for himself he asked nothing but dressed leather to make a shirt, capot and trousers, all the year round, and a little tobacco. He is an able-bodied young man. This proposal did not surprise me, having seen several people as foolish as he is, who would not hesitate to sign an agreement of perpetual bondage on condition of being permitted to have a woman who struck their fancy.

ALEXANDER HENRY, *Journals*

Gambling

✠ No nation has gambled oftener, more oddly, or more compulsively than the English, and they never so unrestrainedly as in the eighteenth century. The betting books of the great London clubs suggest fantasy and jesting rather than facts; members made high wagers that one woman would have a child before another ("N.B. Miscarriages go for nothing"); that a duke would die before 5:30 P.M., June 27, 1773; that Beau Nash would die before Colley Cibber, both bettors having committed suicide before either was in a position to collect. Members even bet (and lost) that they wouldn't gamble in the future. Children away at school were taught whist and casino, and the London *Times* (November 1797) wrote: "It is calculated that a clever child, by its Cards, and its novels, may pay for its own education." A few weeks later the *Times* reported that "at a private Ball, last week, a gentleman asking a young lady from Bath to dance the next two dances, she very ingenuously replied: 'Yes, if you will play two rubbers at Casino.' "

The betting book at Brooks's records in 1772: "Mr. Thynne, having won only 12,000 guineas during the last two months, retired in disgust." The *Morning Post* remarks in 1805: "The sum lately lost at play by a lady of high rank is variously stated. Some say it does not amount to more than £200,000, while others assert that it is little short of £700,000." (£700,000 in our money today would come to something like $20,000,000.)

Perhaps the most famous and most unfortunate of eighteenth-century gamblers was Charles James Fox, who by turns took to leading the Whigs and losing at whist; the following account in

Andrew Steinmetz's *The Gaming Table* covers a few days in Fox's life:

Fox's best friends are said to have been half ruined in annuities given by them as securities for him to the Jews. . . . [Horace] Walpole wondered what Fox would do when he had sold the estates of his friends. Walpole further notes that in the debate on the Thirty-nine Articles . . . Fox did not shine; nor could it be wondered at. He had sat up playing at Hazard, at Almack's, from Tuesday evening [February] 4th, till five in the afternoon of Wednesday, the 5th. An hour before he had recovered £12,000 that he had lost; and by dinner, which was at five o'clock, he had ended losing £11,000! On the Thursday he spoke in the above debate, went to dinner at half past eleven at night; from thence to White's, where he drank till seven the next morning; thence to Almack's, where he won £6,000; and, between three and four in the afternoon he set out for Newmarket. His brother Stephen lost £11,000 two nights after, and Charles £10,000 more on the 13th; so that in three nights the two brothers—the eldest not *twenty-five* years of age—lost £32,000!

Ghost Words and Phrases

✠ Herewith some slang phrases, pleasantries, and unpleasantries from Victorian days:

Afters—Pies, puddings, any sweet last course; a word often used of them when they failed to appear.

All his buttons on—Keen, sharp, not to be taken in.

Bald-headed butter—Butter free from hairs.

Born a bit tired—Said of somebody who is chronically lazy.

Breath strong enough to carry coal—Drunk.

Champagne shoulders—Sloping ones; from the shape of a champagne bottle.

Clock stopped—A refusal of credit; from the much commoner "no tick," which is actually "no ticket."

Eat vinegar with a fork—Extremely acid and cutting conversation.

Fried carpets—Extremely short ballet skirts, as seen on the stage.

Gin and fog—Hoarseness derived from hitting the bottle.

Hospital game—Football, from its frequent injuries.

Irish draperies—Cobwebs.

Looking as if he hadn't got his right change—Having a mad or wild appearance.

Parrot and monkey time—A quarrelsome period.

Pint o' mahogany—Coffee.

Please, mother, open the door—Said to an attractive girl encountered in passing, in hopes of a pickup.

Robbing the barber—Wearing long hair.

Throw mud at the clock—Shorten one's life from despair; have thoughts of suicide. More figurative than literal.

Two inches beyond upright—A lying hypocrite.

Yard of satin—Glass of gin.

Guidebooks

DIÁLOGO 18	DIALOGUE 18
Pâra montár â cavállo	For to ride a horse

Eis úm cavállo quê mê parêce máo. Dême ôutro; não quéro êste. Êlle não poderá andár. Ê asmático; está aguádo. Vm. não sê envergônha dê mê dár úm rossím semelhânte? Êlle está desferrádo ê encravádo. É necessário mandál-o âo ferradôr. Elle manqueêja; está estropeádo, ê é cégo. Ésta sélla mê ferirá. Ôs estríbos são múito comprídos, múito cúrtos. Estênda ôs estríbos, encôlha-os. Âs cílhas estão pôdres. Quê péssimo frêio! Dê-me ô mê chicóte. Áte â mála ê ó mêu capôte.

Here is a horse who have a bad looks. Give me another; I will not that. He not sall know to march, he is pursy, he is foundered. Don't you are ashamed to give me a jade as like? he is undshoed, he is with nails up, it want to lead to the farrier. He go limp, he is disable, he is blind. That saddle shall hurt me. The stirrups are too long, very shorts. Stretch out the stirrups, shorten the stirrups. The saddles girths are roted, what bat bridle? Give me my whip. Fasten the cloak-bag and my cloak.

Âs súas pistólas estão carregádas?

Não. Esquecêu-me vomprár pólvora ê bála. Piquêmos, vâmos máis depréssa. Núnca vi peior bêsta. Não quér andár, nêm pâra diânte, nêm pâra tráz.

Alárgue-lhe â rédea. Encúrtelhe âs rédeas. Esporêie-o rijamênte; fáça-o andár.

Your pistols are its loads?

No; I forgot to buy gunpowder and balls. Let us prick. Go us more fast never I was seen a so much bad beast; she will not nor to bring forward neither put back.

Strek him the bridle, hold him the reins sharters. Pique strongly, make to marsh him.

Pôr máis quê ô píco, não ô
pósso fazêr caminhár.
Desapêie-se; êu ô farêi avan-
çar.
Tôme seutído não lhê atíre
algúm côuce.
Êlle dá côuces pêlo quê
vêjo. Ólhe cômo êu ô súbe
domár.

I have pricked him enough.
But I can't to make march him.
Go down, I shall make march.
Take care that he not give
you a foot kick's.

Then he kicks for that I
look? Sook here if I knew to
tame hix.

DIÁLOGO 24
Dâ comédia

Â quê theátro irêmos ésta
nôite?
Sê lhê agráda, irêmos â——.

Vío Vm. já â nóva tragédia?
Elogíãoa múito.

Applaudírâo-a nâ representa-
ção.

DIÁLOGO 24
For the comedy

At what theatre shall we go
the night.
We shall go if you will go,
to——.
Have you seen already the
new tragedy? They praise her
very much.
It was played with applauses.

Há enchênte.
Tomêmos logár.
Núnca ví ô theátro tão chêio.

Erguem ô pânno.
Â orchéstra é dirigída opti-
mamênte.
Êste actôr desempênha bêm
ô sêu papêl.
Êlle represênta côm múito
acêrto.
Ésta peça é interessantíssima.
Élla enlevôu ôs especadô-
res.

It is multitude already.
Take us our rank.
Never I had seen the parlour
so full.
Its rise the curtains.
The orchestra is conducted
perfectly.
This actor he make very well
her part.
He plays very well.

That piece is full of interest.
It have wondered the spectators.

Crêio quê permanecerá nô theátro.	*I think shall stay to the the-atre.*
Báixão ô pânno.	*The curtains let down.*
Vâmos-nos.	*Go out us.*

PEDRO CAROLINO, *The New Guide of the Conversation
in Portuguese and English* (reprinted 1883)

High Comedy

Scene V. [*Mrs.*] *Millamant*, [*Edward*] *Mirabell*

. . . . . .

MILLA: . . . There is not so impudent a thing in nature, as the sawcy look of an assured man, confident of success. The pedantick arrogance of a very husband has not so pragmatical an air. Ah! I'll never marry, unless I am first made sure of my will and pleasure.

MIRA: Would you have 'em both before marriage? Or will you be contented with the first now, and stay for the other 'till after grace?

MILLA: Ah, don't be so impertinent—My dear liberty, shall I leave thee? My faithful solitude, my darling contemplation, must I bid you then adieu? Ay-h, adieu—my morning thoughts, agreeable wakings, indolent slumbers, all ye *douceurs,* ye *sommeils du matin,* adieu—I can't do't, 'tis more than impossible—Positively, Mirabell, I'll lye abed in a morning as long as I please.

MIRA: Then I'll get up in a morning as early as I please.

MILLA: Ah! Idle creature, get up when you will—And d'ye hear, I won't be called names after I'm married; positively I won't be called names.

MIRA: Names!

MILLA: Ay, as wife, spouse, my dear, joy, jewel, love, sweetheart, and the rest of that nauseous cant, in which men and their wives are so fulsomly familiar—I shall never bear that—Good Mirabell, don't let us be familiar or fond, nor kiss before folks, like my Lady Fadler and Sir Francis: nor go to Hide Park together the first Sunday in a new chariot, to provoke eyes and whispers; and then never be seen there together again; as if we were proud of one another the first week, and ashamed of one another ever after. Let us never visit together, nor go to a play together, but let us be very strange and well bred: let us be as strange as if we had been married a great while; and as well bred as if we were not married at all.

MIRA: Have you any more conditions to offer? Hitherto your demands are pretty reasonable.

MILLA: Trifles,—as liberty to pay and receive visits to and from whom I please; to write and receive letters, without interrogatories or wry faces on your part; to wear what I please; and chuse conversation with regard only to my own taste; to have no obligation upon me to converse with wits that I don't like, because they are your acquaintance; or to be intimate with fools because they may be your relations. Come to dinner when I please, dine in my dressing-room when I'm out of humour, without giving a reason. To have my closet inviolate; to be sole empress of my tea-table, which you must never presume to approach without first asking leave. And lastly, wherever I am, you shall always knock at the door before you come in. These articles subscribed, if I continue to endure you a little longer, I may by degrees dwindle into a wife.

MIRA: Your bill of fare is something advanced in this latter account. Well, have I liberty to offer conditions—that when you are dwindled into a wife, I may not be beyond measure enlarged into a husband?

MILLA: You have free leave, propose your utmost, speak and spare not.

MIRA: I thank you. *Imprimis* then, I covenant that your acquaintance be general; that you admit no sworn confident, or intimate of your own sex; no she friend to skreen her affairs under your countenance, and tempt you to make trial of a mu-

tual secresie. No decoy-duck to wheadle you a *fop—scrambling* to
the play in a mask—then bring you home in a pretended fright,
when you think you shall be found out—and rail at me for missing the play, and disappointing the frolick which you had to pick
me up and prove my constancy.

MILLA: Detestable *imprimis!* I go to the play in a mask!

MIRA: *Item,* I article, that you continue to like your own face as
long as I shall: and while it passes currant with me, that you
endeavour not to new coin it. To which end, together with all
vizards for the day, I prohibit all masks for the night, made of
oiled-skins and I know not what—hog's bones, hare's gall, pig
water, and the marrow of a roasted cat. In short, I forbid all commerce with the gentlewoman in *what-d'ye-call-it* Court. *Item,* I
shut my doors against all bauds with baskets, and pennyworths of
muslin, china, fans, atlasses, etc.—*Item,* when you shall be breeding—

MILLA: Ah! name it not.

MIRA: Which may be presumed, with a blessing on our endeavours—

MILLA: Odious endeavours!

MIRA: I denounce against all strait lacing, squeezing for a shape,
'till you mould my boy's head like a sugar-loaf; and instead of a
man-child, make me father to a crooked-billet. Lastly, to the dominion of the *tea-table* I submit.—But with *proviso,* that you ex-
ceed not in your province; but restrain yourself to native and
simple *tea-table* drinks, as *tea, chocolate,* and *coffee.* As likewise
to genuine and authorised *tea-table* talk—such as mending of
fashions, spoiling reputations, railing at absent friends, and so
forth—but that on no account you encroach upon the men's
prerogative, and presume to drink healths, or toast fellows; for
prevention of which, I banish all *foreign forces,* all auxiliaries to
the *tea-table,* as *orange-brandy,* all *anniseed, cinamon, citron* and
Barbado's-waters, together with *ratafia* and the most noble spirit
of *clary.*—But for *couslip-wine, poppy-water,* and all *dormitives,*
those I allow.—These *provisos* admitted, in other things I may
prove a tractable and complying husband.

MILLA: O horrid *provisos*! filthy strong waters! I toast fellows, odious men! I hate your odious *provisos*.

MIRA: Then we're agreed. Shall I kiss your hand upon the contract? and here comes one to be a witness to the sealing of the deed.

Scene VI. [To *them*] *Mrs. Fainall*

MILLA: Fainall, what shall I do? Shall I have him? I think I must have him.

MRS. FAIN: Ay, ay, take him, take him, what should you do?

MILLA: Well then—I'll take my death I'm in a horrid fright— Fainall, I shall never say it—Well—I think—I'll endure you.

MRS. FAIN: Fy, fy, have him, have him, and tell him so in plain terms: for I am sure you have a mind to him.

MILLA: Are you? I think I have—and the horrid man looks as if he thought so too—Well, you ridiculous thing you, I'll have you —I won't be kissed, nor I won't be thanked—Here, kiss my hand though—so, hold your tongue now, don't say a word.

WILLIAM CONGREVE, *The Way of the World,* Act IV

Hors d'Oeuvres Variés

[The Thomas Carlyles' maidservant:] Escorted to the National Gallery and confronted by a picture of the Madonna and Child, probably by an Italian primitive very free with gold leaf and bright colours, her only comment was "Ah, how expensive!"

D. M. STUART, *The English Abigail*

[A London dinner party:] The entertainment offered a few evenings before Easter was a discharge of obligations not insistently incurred, and had thereby, possibly, all the more, the note of this almost Arcadian optimism: a large, dull, murmurous, mild-eyed, middle-aged dinner, involving for the most part very bland, though very exalted, immensely announceable and hierarchically placeable couples, and followed, without the oppression of a later contingent, by a brief instrumental concert.

HENRY JAMES, *The Golden Bowl*

She had indeed no sense of humour and, with her pretty way of holding her head on one side, was one of those persons whom you want, as the phrase is, to shake, but who have learnt Hungarian by themselves. She conversed perhaps in Hungarian with Corvick; she had remarkably little English for his friend. . . . I remember his saying of her that she felt in italics and thought in capitals.

HENRY JAMES, "The Figure in the Carpet"

[The publisher John Murray's reader, on Carlyle:] The Author of *Teufelsdröckh* . . . has no great tact; his wit is frequently heavy; and reminds one of the German baron who took to leaping on tables, and answered that he was learning to be lively.

If he write a book which he intends *not* to be understood, we shall be very happy indeed not to understand it; but if he write a book which he means to be understood . . . we can only say that he is an ass—and this, to be brief, is our private opinion of Mr. Carlyle . . .

EDGAR ALLAN POE

Talleyrand [in his *Memoirs*] gives himself all the advantage to be got by depreciating others. . . . Friends enjoy no immunity from his satiric temper; and he is severe toward his tutor, Langfois, his secretary, Des Renaudes, and his intimate associate, Narbonne. He says that the choice of Necker was the worst the King could have made; Lafayette is beneath the level of mediocrity; Breteuil is fit for the second place anywhere; Sieyès would not be a rogue if he was not a coward; the hands of Carnot are dripping with blood; Fesch is a corsair disguised as a cardinal; Joseph and Jerome are inglorious libertines; the most prosperous of the marshals, Suchet, is *quelque peu bel esprit;* his own successor, Champagny, begins every day trying to repair his blunders of the day before; Humboldt is a bore; Metternich is tortuous and second-rate; Wellington has no head for principles; Castlereagh strains the Englishman's prerogative of ignorance.

LORD ACTON, *Historical Essays and Studies*

Those who, like the first Queen of Prussia, demand to know *le pourquoi du pourquoi.*

LORD ACTON

In Paradise what have I to win? . . . Thither go these same old priests, and halt old men and maimed, who all day and night cower continually before the altars, and in the crypts; and such folk as wear old amices and old clouted frocks, and naked folk and shoeless, and covered with sores, perishing of hunger and thirst, and of cold, and of little ease. . . . But into Hell would I fain go; for into Hell fare the goodly clerks, and goodly knights that fall in tourneys and great wars, and stout men at arms, and all men noble. . . . And thither pass the sweet ladies and courteous that have two lovers, or three, and their lords also thereto. Thither goes the gold, and the silver, and cloth of vair, and cloth of gris, and harpers, and makers, and the princes of this world. With these I would gladly go, let me but have with me Nicolette, my sweetest lady.

ANON., *Aucassin et Nicolette*

(trans. Andrew Lang)

Why dost thou lament my death, or call me miserable that am much more happy than thyself? what misfortune is befallen me? Is it because I am not so bald, crooked, old, rotten, as thou art? What have I lost—some of your good cheer, gay clothes, music, singing, dancing, kissing, merry-meetings, *thalami lubentias,* etc.:

is that it? Is it not much better not to hunger at all than to eat;
not to thirst than to drink to satisfy thirst; not to be cold than to
put on clothes to drive away cold?

ROBERT BURTON

[Proclamation, 1796:] Soldiers, you are naked and ill fed; the
Government owes you much and can give you nothing. Your patience and the courage you show here among these rocks are admirable; but they bring you no glory and no renown reflects on
you. I want to lead you to the world's most fertile plains. Rich
provinces will be in your power, and big cities; you will find
honor there, and glory, and wealth. Soldiers of Italy, will you fall
short of courage or of constancy?

NAPOLEON

This is no longer a time for jesting: witty things do not go well
with massacres . . . Busirises in wigs destroy, in the midst of horrible tortures, children of sixteen! And that in face of the verdict
of ten upright and humane judges! . . . Here Calas broken on
the wheel, there Sirven condemned to be hung, further off a gag
thrust into the mouth of a lieutenant-general, a fortnight after
that five youths condemned to the flames for extravagances that
deserve nothing worse than Saint-Lazare. . . . Is this the country
of philosophy and pleasure? It is the country rather of the Saint
Bartholomew massacre. Why, the Inquisition would not have
ventured to do what these Jansenist judges have done.

VOLTAIRE, letter to D'Alembert

(trans. John Morley)

✠ [Richard Porson] was in his customary state one
night. Wishing to blow out his candle, and seeing, as is said to
be the way of the inebriated, two flames side by side where there
was actually only one, he three times advanced with swaying
steps toward the wrong image, and three times blew on it with

no effect. After the third try he drew back, balanced himself, and passed sweeping judgment: "Damn the nature of things!"

I went to the woods because I wished to live deliberately, to front only the essential facts of life, and see if I could not learn what it had to teach, and not, when I came to die, discover that I had not lived. I did not wish to live what was not life, living is so dear; nor did I wish to practice resignation, unless it was quite necessary. I wanted to live deep and suck out all the marrow of life, to live so sturdily and Spartan-like as to put to rout all that was not life, to cut a broad swath and shave close, to drive life into a corner, and reduce it to its lowest terms, and, if it proved to be mean, why then to get the whole and genuine meanness of it, and publish its meanness to the world . . .

THOREAU, *Walden*

The most important ceremony in which I was officially concerned was the Coronation of King Edward [VII]. . . . Before the Coronation I had a remarkable dream. The State coach had to pass through the Arch at the Horse Guards on the way to Westminster Abbey. I dreamed that it stuck in the Arch, and that some of the Life Guards on duty were compelled to hew off the Crown upon the coach before it could be freed. When I told the Crown Equerry, Colonel Ewart, he laughed and said, "What do dreams matter?" "At all events, I replied, "let us have the coach and Arch measured." So this was done and, to my astonishment, we found that the Arch was nearly two feet too low to allow the coach to pass through. I returned to Colonel Ewart in triumph and said, "What do you think of dreams now?" "I think it's damned fortunate you had one," he replied. It appears that the State coach had not been driven through the Arch for some time, and that the level of the road had since been raised during repairs. So I am not sorry that my dinner disagreed with me that night; and I only wish all nightmares were as useful.

THE DUKE OF PORTLAND, *Men, Women and Things*

I will not claim to have been a perfect guest. Nor indeed was
I. . . . I was rather *too* quiet, and I did sometimes contradict.
And, though I always liked to be invited anywhere, I very often
preferred to stay at home. If anyone hereafter shall form a collection of the notes written by me in reply to invitations, I am afraid
he will gradually suppose me to have been more in request than
ever I really was, and to have been also a great invalid, and a
great traveller.

MAX BEERBOHM, *And Even Now*

Future tyrants were encouraged to believe that the blood which
they might shed in a long reign would instantly be washed away
in the waters of regeneration.

GIBBON, *The Decline and Fall of the Roman Empire*

The taste of arsenic was so really in my mouth when I described
how Emma Bovary was poisoned, that it cost me two indigestions
one upon the other—quite real ones, for I vomited my dinner.

FLAUBERT, letter to Hippolyte Taine

Life is a hospital where every patient is dominated by a wish to
change his bed. One would prefer to suffer near the fire, and another feels sure he would get well if he were by the window.

BAUDELAIRE, *Petits Poèmes en prose*

To do exactly the opposite is also a form of imitation.

G.C.LICHTENBERG

Milton, in the person of Satan, has started speculations hardier
than any which the feeble armory of the atheist ever furnished;
and the precise, straitlaced Richardson has strengthened Vice,
from the mouth of Lovelace, with entangling sophistries and ab-
struse pleas against her adversary Virtue, which Sedley, Villiers,

and Rochester wanted depth of libertinism enough to have invented.

C H A R L E S   L A M B

Mr. Young ought never to condescend to play comedy, nor aspire to play tragedy.

W I L L I A M   H A Z L I T T

[Ingres, to his students, in coming upon some paintings of Delacroix:] *"Saluez, mais ne regardez pas."*

People who found literary reviews feel an extraordinary kind of self-congratulation. They feel they're much more important than the people who write books.

A L D O U S   H U X L E Y, an interview

The same battle in the clouds will be known to the deaf only as lightning and to the blind only as thunder.

To feel beauty is a better thing than to understand how we come to feel it.

. . . the glorious monotony of the stars.

G E O R G E   S A N T A Y A N A

[Lord Orford to the Norwich Bible Society:] I have long been addicted to the Gaming Table. I have lately taken to the Turf. I fear I frequently blaspheme. But I have never distributed religious tracts. All this was known to you and your Society. Notwithstanding which you think me a fit person to be your president. God forgive your hypocrisy.

Wordsworth does not like even to share his reputation with his *subject,* for he would have it *all* to proceed from his own power and originality of mind.

W I L L I A M   H A Z L I T T

When they told Louis XV that if he went on with his extravagance, he would bring about a Revolution and be sent over to England with a pension, he merely asked, "Do you think the pension would be a pretty good one?"

WILLIAM HAZLITT, *The Conversations of James Northcote*

Individualists

✠ John Jay Chapman (1862–1933) was, sometimes for better and a few times for worse, an extraordinary man, to be better remembered for individualism than for eccentricity. Two very extraordinary facts in his life are understandably very well known: that in his college days, having brutally thrashed a man he disapproved of, he went home filled with guilt and in expiation thrust his left hand into the fire until it was so badly burned that it had to be amputated; and that late in life, on the first anniversary of a hideous Negro lynching in Coatesville, Pennsylvania, Chapman went to Coatesville to do penance, as it were, for the whole country, by holding a prayer meeting to which—in a town hostile with guilt—just two people came. So passionate and protestant a man in his later years could be strongly misled, as in becoming very anti-Catholic and at length anti-Semitic. But in most of his life, and in many things, there was a tang, a pungency, a vividness of phrase, a shrug at the proprieties, that made him a good critic and writer, and a remarkably good letter writer. In his letters Chapman could be delightfully picturesque: "I hate the young . . . Give me some good old rain-soaked clubmen who *can't* be improved"; and impressively incisive: "You cannot criticize the New Testament. It criticizes you." In his letters and *Memoirs* one comes upon all sorts of quotable things—anecdotes, observations, aphorisms.

Mrs. Ritchie had given Miss Georgina Schuyler a letter to Tennyson. Miss Schuyler was a very distinguished, experienced, public-

spirited lady of New York. Throughout the visit Tennyson be-
haved toward her with his usual boorishness. In saying good-bye
he endeavored to force out a polite word of some sort. Miss Schuyler coldly assured him that "She was always glad to meet any
friend of Mrs. Ritchie's."

After all, what do literature and family life amount to compared
to a first-rate restaurant?

[Henry Lee Higginson, who founded the Boston Symphony Orchestra:] Mr. Higginson's rather simple philosophy of life was
once expressed in my hearing at a lunch-party at Mrs. Whitman's
at Beverly Shore, where the question was asked, whether he
would give orders to the members of his orchestra as to how they
should vote at election-time. He replied that he certainly *should*.

A thing is not truth till it is so strongly believed in that the be-
liever is convinced that its existence does not depend upon him.

Did you hear what [William Dean] Howells once said to a bor-
ing author who was trying to wring a compliment out of him? "I
don't know how it is," said the author, "I don't seem to *write* as
well as I used to do." "Oh, yes you do—indeed you do. You write
as well as you ever did;—But your *taste* is improving."

I should say at a guess that people who are fundamentally theo-
retical—and require to understand and pigeonhole the world—
would be apt to boggle over Shakespeare. They want him to
stand and deliver—and he is dead and they can't get at him and
corner him . . . After all, life and the world—hunger, thirst,
and the instant stream of experience in which we live are vivid,
rapid, mysterious, and unfathomable, and Shakespeare has the
same effect on us—you cannot size him up and pocket him . . .
The only safe way is to say O, O, O, like a child looking at fire-
works.

John Jay Chapman and His Letters

✠ These days, however, the professors are often kind
enough to tell us exactly what Shakespeare meant.

Journals

Samuel Butler

If virtue had everything her own way she would be as insufferable as dominant factions generally are. It is the function of vice to keep virtue within reasonable bounds.

Morality turns on whether the pleasure precedes the pain or follows it. . . . Thus, it is immoral to get drunk because the headache comes after the drinking, but if the headache came first, and the drunkenness afterwards, it would be moral to get drunk.

The world will only, in the end, follow those who have despised as well as served it.

Bodily offspring I do not leave, but mental offspring I do. Well, my books do not have to be sent to school and college and then insist on going into the Church or take to drinking or marry their mother's maid.

A man said one day, talking about his wife, who was ill: "If God were to take one or other of us, I should go and live in Paris."

I remember hearing [my uncle] say shortly after Dickens's death: "I must say, I think a good deal more of him now that I know he left so considerable a personality behind him."

Lilian Jones asked her mother once whether riding or driving was the more difficult. "Well, my dear," answered her mother, "if you don't take pains, everything is difficult." "Now you know," said Lil, "that is the kind of answer that makes one hate people."

I have been told lately that Fuseli was travelling by coach and a gentleman opposite him said: "I understand, Mr. Fuseli, that you are a painter; it may interest you to know that I have a daughter

who paints on velvet." Fuseli rose instantly and said in a strong
foreign accent, "Let me get out."

The Notebooks of Samuel Butler

Greville

✠ Charles Cavendish Fulke Greville (1794–1865) was
born into the great English Whig aristocracy and became, in
the way of politics and society, England's best-informed and
most important diarist of his time. Early in life he managed the
stables of the Duke of York who, had he not died, would have
succeeded George IV as King of England. For forty years of his
life he was Clerk of the Privy Council, hence privy to almost
everything of importance. He was far from awed by royalty; he
called George IV a pig, William IV a clown, and thought Queen
Victoria anything but perfect. Herewith some bonbons:

[1818] Oatlands [the Duke of York's country place] is the worst
managed establishment in England; there are a great many servants, and nobody waits on you; a vast number of horses, and none
to ride or drive.

[1828] M'Gregor told me the other day that not one of the physi-
cians and surgeons who attended the Duke of York through his
long and painful illness had ever received the smallest remunera-
tion, although their names and services had been laid before the
King. He told me in addition that during sixteen years that he
attended the Duke and his whole family he never received one
guinea by way of fee or any payment whatever.

[1829] [George IV] leads a most extraordinary life—never gets
up till six in the afternoon. . . . He breakfasts in bed, does
whatever business he can be brought to transact in bed too, he
reads every newspaper quite through, dozes three or four hours,
gets up in time for dinner, and goes to bed between ten and

eleven. He . . . rings his bell forty times in the night; if he wants to know the hour, though a watch hangs close to him, he will have his *valet de chambre* down rather than turn his head to look at it. The same thing if he wants a glass of water; he won't stretch out his hand to get it. His valets were nearly destroyed, and at last Lady Conyngham prevailed on him to agree to an arrangement by which they wait on him alternate days. . . . The days they are in waiting their labours are incessant, and they cannot take off their clothes at night, and hardly lie down.

[1838] I dined yesterday at the Palace . . . When we went into the drawing room . . . the Queen [Victoria] advanced to meet us, and spoke to everybody in succession, and if everybody's "palaver" was as deeply interesting as mine, it would have been worth while to have had Gurney to take it down in short-hand. . . . I shall now record my dialogue with accurate fidelity.

Q. Have you been riding today, Mr. Greville?
G. No, Madam, I have not.
Q. It was a fine day.
G. Yes, Ma'am, a very fine day.
Q. It was rather cold though.
G. (like Polonius) It *was* rather cold, Madam.
Q. Your sister, Lady Francis Egerton, rides, I think, does not she?
G. She does ride sometimes, Madam.
　(A pause, when I took the lead, though adhering to the same topic.)
G. Had your Majesty been riding today?
Q. (with animation) O, yes, a very long ride.
G. Has your Majesty got a nice horse?
Q. O, a very nice horse.

　—gracious smile and inclination of head on part of Queen, profound bow on mine, and then she turned again to Lord Grey.

[1843] Went to Frankfort yesterday; went to see the Jews' street, the most curious part of the town. It is very narrow, the houses all of great antiquity, and not one new or modern in the whole street. . . . Strange figures were loitering about the street, standing in the doorways or looking out of the windows. There was a man who might have presented himself on the stage in the character of Shylock, with the gaberdine and long beard; there were old crones of the most miserable and squalid, but strange aspect. We had the good luck to see the old mother of the Rothschilds, and a curious contrast she presented. The house she inhabits appears not a bit better than any of the others; it is the same dark and decayed mansion. In this narrow gloomy street, and before this wretched tenement, a smart *calèche* was standing, fitted up with blue silk, and a footman in blue livery was at the door. Presently the door was opened, and the old woman was seen descending down a dark, narrow staircase, supported by her granddaughter, the Baroness Charles Rothschild, whose carriage was also in waiting at the end of the street. Two footmen and some maids were in attendance to help the old lady into the carriage, and a number of the inhabitants collected opposite to see her get in. A more curious and striking contrast I never saw than the dress of the ladies, both the old and the young one, and their equipages and liveries, with the dilapidated locality in which the old woman persists in remaining. The family allow her £4,000 a year, and they say she never in her life has been out of Frankfort, and never inhabited any other house than this, in which she is resolved to die.

CHARLES CAVENDISH FULKE GREVILLE, *Memoirs*

Charles Baudelaire

Immense depths of thought in expression of common speech; holes dug by generations of ants.

We love women in so far as they are strangers to us.

Whenever you receive a letter from a creditor, write fifty lines upon some extra-terrestrial subject, and you will be saved.

If a poet demanded from the State the right to have a few bourgeois in his stable, people would be very much astonished, but if a bourgeois asked for some roast poet, people would think it quite natural.

What is exhilarating in bad taste is the aristocratic pleasure of giving offence.

Stoicism, a religion which has but one sacrament: suicide!

Anyone, provided that he can be amusing, has the right to talk of himself.

I have no [political] convictions, as men of my century understand the word, because I have no ambition.

Belief in Progress . . . is the individual relying upon his neighbors to do his work.

She [George Sand] has good reasons for wishing to abolish Hell.

What is annoying about Love is that it is a crime in which one cannot do without an accomplice.

For the merchant, even honesty is a financial speculation.

Stupidity always preserves beauty, it keeps away the wrinkles, it is the divine cosmetic . . .

BAUDELAIRE, *Intimate Journals*

(trans. Christopher Isherwood)

Augustus Hare

From my *Journal. Rome, Dec. 21, 1865.*—Cardinal Cecchi died last week and lay in state all yesterday in his palace, on a high bier, with his face painted and rouged, wearing his robes, and with his scarlet hat on his head. Cardinals always lie in state on a high catafalque, contrary to the general rule, which prescribes that the higher the rank the lower the person should lie. Princess Piombino lay in state upon the floor itself, so very high was her rank . . .

Today at 10 A.M. the Cardinal was buried in the church at the back of the Catinari. According to old custom, when he was put into the grave, his head-cook walked up to it and said, "At what time will your Eminence dine?" For a minute there was no response, and then the major-domo replied, "His Eminence will not want dinner any more" (*non vuol altro*). Then the head footman came in and asked, "At what time will your Eminence want the carriage?" and the major-domo replied, "His Eminence will not want the carriage any more." Upon which the footman went out to the door of the church, where the fat coachman sat on the box of the Cardinal's state carriage, who said, "At what time will his Eminence be ready for the carriage?" and when the footman replied, "*La sua Eminenza non vuol altro*," he broke his whip, . . . flung up his hands with a gesture of despair, and drove off.

In her early married life, Mrs. Rowley had lived much in Berkeley Square with her mother-in-law, old Lady Langford, who was the original of Lady Kew in *The Newcomes,* and many pitched battles they had . . . Lady Langford had been very beautiful, clever, and had had *une vie très orageuse*. She had much excuse, however. She had only once seen her cousin, Lord Langford, when he came to visit her grandmother, and the next day the old lady told her she was to marry him. "Very well, Grandmama, but when?"—"I never in my life heard such an impertinent question," said the grandmother; "what business is it of yours *when* you are to marry him? You will marry him when I tell you. However, whenever you hear me order six horses to the carriage, you may know that you are going to be married." And so it was.

AUGUSTUS HARE, The Story of My Life

Wilfrid Scawen Blunt

[1893] . . . I am constitutionally idle. Millais used to say of me, when we were young men, that I was so lazy that when I began to work, I was too lazy to stop.

[1893] "Bishops," [Sir William Harcourt] said, "are always the first to lay their hands on property when they can do it. I remember Bright telling me that he never knew a bishop express disapproval of a war but once, and that was a war to put down the slave trade."

[1894] I fancy in all history no team of four horses was ever driven before down [the steep descent of Coombe Bottom], not even by Tommy Onslow of happy memory . . .

> What can Tommy Onslow do?
> He can drive a coach and two,
> Can Tommy Onslow do no more?
> He can drive a coach and four.
> Where shall we his merits fix?
> He can drive a coach and six.

[1896] [William] Morris is dead. . . . It has come sooner than I expected, though I knew his case was hopeless. It is better as it is. He is the most wonderful man I have known, unique in this, that he had no thought for any thing or person, including himself, but only for the work he had in hand. He was not selfish in the sense of seeking his own advantage or pleasure or comfort, but he was too absorbed in his own thoughts to be either openly affectionate or actively kind. I suppose he had a real affection for Burne-Jones, they saw each other constantly and spent their Sunday mornings, always together, and I have seen him tender to his daughter Jenny and nice with her and with his wife, but I doubt if he thought of them much when he did not see them, and his life was not arranged in reference to them. To the rest of the world he seemed quite indifferent, and he never, I am sure, returned the affection I gave him. He liked to talk to me because I knew how to talk to him, and our fence of words furbished his wit, but I doubt if he would have crossed the street to speak to me. He was generous and open-handed in his dealings, and I fancy did many kindnesses in a money way for people in distress, but he fashed himself for no man and no woman. The truth is he would not give an hour of his *time* to anyone, he held it to be too valuable. Thus, while all the world admired and respected him, I doubt whether he had many friends; they got too little in return to continue their affection. I should say half-a-dozen were all the friends he had.

[1898] To luncheon at Malwood. Sir William [Harcourt] in excellent form, principally about the bishops, with whom he is now in violent conflict. He narrated to us a conversation he had had with the Duke of Devonshire as to the nomination to a bishopric. The Duke's account of it was this: "He had written two letters to Salisbury [then Prime Minister], recommending a fellow, he couldn't remember the fellow's name, and Salisbury hadn't even answered. He had written because Courtney and another fellow, he couldn't remember his name either, had wanted it." On inquiry it had turned out that the proposed nominee was Page Roberts, and Sir William had taken an opportunity of asking Lord Salisbury why he hadn't made Page Roberts a Bishop. "The fact is," said Salisbury, "I thought they were talking of Page Hopps, and we gave it to some one else." "That," said Sir William, "is the way they make bishops."

[1899] My final sitting to [George Frederick] Watts. . . . I told him of my visit to Herbert Spencer, and asked whether he had ever painted him? "How could you expect me," he said, "to paint a man with such an upper lip?"

[1900] Sibell writes . . . about the unselfishness of the [Boer] war, and the noble qualities of all concerned. One might think it was a crusade, instead of being the Stock Exchange swindle it is. The art of governing the world has become the art of deceiving, not only the people, but if possible one's own high-minded conscience.

[1900] [Betty Balfour told] of a voyage the Queen [Victoria] had made in her yacht. The Queen used to be a good sailor, but is disturbed now if it is at all rough and likes the doctor to sit with her in the cabin and look after her. It came on to blow and a wave struck the ship rather roughly, which alarmed and made her indignant. "Go up at once," she said, "Sir James, and give the

Admiral my compliments and tell him the thing must not occur again."

[1902] [Cecil] Rhodes is dead. I did the rogue an injustice when I thought he might be shamming as a pretext for getting away from the Cape and the prosecution of Princess Radziwill, in which he is implicated, but Rhodes was one of those of whom one always had to ask oneself, *"Quel intérêt peut-il avoir en mourant?"* ["What might he stand to gain by dying?"]

[1909] [Of Dingra, the Hindu patriot and executed assassin:] Dingra's last dying pronouncement is published in the *Daily News,* all other papers being silent about it. It is a noble declaration of his faith in the destinies of his motherland and in his own. "My wish," he says, "is that I should be born again of the same mother, and that I should die the same death for her again."

[1910] Today the King [Edward VII] was buried, and I hope the country will return to comparative sanity, for at present it is in delirium. The absurdities written in every newspaper about him pass belief. He might have been a Solon and a Francis of Assisi combined if the characters drawn of him were true. In no print has there been the smallest allusion to any of his pleasant little wickednesses, though his was not even in make-believe the life of a saint or in any strict sense a theologically virtuous man. Yet all the bishops and priests, Catholic, Protestant, and Nonconformist, join in giving him a glorious place in heaven, and there were eight miles of his loyal and adoring subjects marching on foot to see him lying in state at Westminster Hall. For myself I think he performed his public duties well. He had a passion for pageantry and ceremonial and dressing up, and he was never tired of putting on uniforms and taking them off, and receiving princes and ambassadors and opening museums and hospitals, and attending cattle shows and military shows and shows of every kind, while every night of his life he was to be seen at theatres and operas and music-halls. Thus he was always before the public and had come to have the popularity of an actor who plays his part in a variety of costumes, and always well. Abroad, too, there is no doubt he had a very great reputation. His little Bohemian tastes made him beloved at Paris, and he had enough of the *grand seigneur* to carry it off. He did not affect to be virtuous, and all sorts of publicans and sinners found their places at his table. The journalists loved him; he did not mind being snap-shotted, and was stand off to nobody. If not witty, he could understand a joke, and if not wise he was sensible. He quarrelled with nobody, and always forgave. He disliked family scandals, and spent much of his time patching up those of the Court and whitening its sepulchres. In this respect he has every right to the title of "Peacemaker" given to him.

WILFRID SCAWEN BLUNT, *My Diaries*

Eugène Delacroix

[1853] [On the question of the use of the model, and on imitation:] Jean-Jacques [Rousseau] says rightly that the best way to paint the charms of liberty is to be in prison, that the best way to describe a pleasant bit of country is to live in a wearisome city . . . With my nose to the landscape, surrounded by trees and charming spots, my landscape painting is heavy, too much worked out, more truthful in detail perhaps, but lacking harmony with the subject. When Courbet painted the background of his women bathing, he copied it scrupulously from a study I saw beside his easel. Nothing could be colder; it is a piece of inlaid woodwork. I didn't begin to do anything passable in my trip to Africa until the moment when I had sufficiently forgotten small details, and so remembered the striking and poetic side of things for my pictures; up to that point, I was pursued by the love of exactitude, which the majority of people mistake for truth.

[1853] In re-reading what I have said of Meyerbeer, under the head of *local color* it just occurs to me that he is too much taken up with it. . . . In *William Tell,* if he had composed it, he would have wanted to make us recognize the Swiss and the passions of the Swiss in his slightest duet. As for Racine, it is with broad strokes that he paints a few landscapes in which, if you like, one feels the air of the mountains, or rather that melancholy which seizes upon the soul in the presence of the great spectacles of nature, and against this background he has thrown men, passions, grace and elegance everywhere. . . . What matter if Achilles is a Frenchman! And who ever saw the Greek Achilles? Who would dare to make him speak as Homer has done, in any language but Greek? "What tongue are you going to use?" asks Pancrace of Sganarelle. "Good Lord! The one I have in my mouth!" One can speak only with one's tongue, but one can also speak with the spirit of one's time. . . . Produce the Greek Achilles! Why, bless you! did Homer himself do that? He produced an Achilles for the people of his time. The men who had seen the real Achilles were gone, long since. The old Achilles must have been more like a Huron than the hero in Homer. Those oxen and sheep that the poet describes him as putting on the spit with his own hands, were perhaps eaten raw by him after he had knocked them on the head. The luxury with which Homer adorns him comes from the poet's imagination; the tripods, the tents and the vessels are no other than those that Homer had before him in the world where he lived. They are a joke, those vessels with which the Greeks went to the siege of Troy! The entire host of the Greeks would have surrendered to the flotilla that goes forth from Fécamp or from Dieppe for the herring fishing. That has been the weakness of our time, in its poets and its artists—that idea that they had made a great conquest with the invention of local color.

[1854] At noon they were to launch a big ship that they call a *clipper*. Here is another American invention that will let people go faster: always faster. When they have got travelers comfortably lodged in a cannon, so that that cannon shall make them travel as fast as bullets in any direction they may care to take, civilization will doubtless have taken a long step: we are marching toward that happy time; it will have suppressed space but will not have suppressed boredom . . .

[1854] The claim that Chenavard makes for his blessed Michelangelo is that he has painted man above all, and I say that all he has painted is muscles and poses . . . He did not know a single one of the feelings of man, not one of his passions. When he was making an arm or a leg, it seems as if he were thinking only of that arm or leg and was not giving the slightest consideration to the way it relates with the action of the figure to which it belongs, much less to the action of the picture as a whole.

You are forced to admit that certain passages treated in this way, things that resulted from the artist's exclusive absorption in them, are of a character in which the only passion is their own. Therein lies his great merit: he brings a sense of the grand and the terrible into even an isolated limb.

[1854] Mme Berryer, the daughter-in-law, wants to abstain from meat, in spite of the dispensation from the Bishop of Orléans for the whole diocese. She is like the peasant who, during a sermon which drew tears from everyone else, remained indifferent. To the people who reproached him for his coldness he said that he did not belong to the parish.

Journal of Eugène Delacroix

(trans. Walter Pach)

A Second Round of Poetry

Lully, lulley; lully, lulley!
The falcon hath borne my mate away!
He bare him up, he bare him down,
He bare him into an orchard brown;
In that orchard there was a hall
That was hangèd with purple and pall;
And in that hall there was a bed,
It was hangèd with gold so red;

And in that bed there lieth a knight,
His wounds bleeding day and night;
By that bedside kneeleth a may,
And she weepeth both night and day;
And by that bedside there standeth a stone,
Corpus Christi written thereon.
Lully, lulley; lully, lulley!

ANON.

Once did I love, and yet I live,
Through love and truth be now forgotten;
Then did I joy, now do I grieve
That holy vows must now be broken.

Hers be the blame that caused it so,
Mine be the grief though it be mickle;
She shall have shame, I cause to know
What 'tis to love a dame so fickle.

Love her that list! I am content
For that chameleon-like she changeth,
Yielding such mists as may prevent
My sight to view her when she rangeth.

Let not him vaunt that gains my loss!
For when that he and time hath proved her,
She may him bring to Weeping Cross.—
I say no more, because I loved her.

ANON.

Principal Points of Religion

To pray to God continually,
To learn to know him rightfully.
To honor God in Trinity,

The Trinity in Unity.
The Father in his majesty,
The Son in his humanity,
The Holy Ghost's benignity,
Three persons one in Deity.
To serve him alway holily,
To ask him all thing needfully,
To praise him in all company,
To love him alway heartily,
To dread him alway christianly,
To ask him mercy penitently,
To trust him alway faithfully,
To obey him alway willingly,
To abide him alway patiently,
To thank him alway thankfully,
To live here alway virtuously,
To use thy neighbour honestly,
To look for death still presently,
To help the poor in misery,
To hope for Heaven's felicity,
To have faith, hope, and charity,
To count this life but vanity—
Be points of Christianity.

THOMAS TUSSER, *Five Hundred Points of Good Husbandry* (1573)

Pointing at graves, and in the rear,
Trembling and talking loud, went Fear.

CHARLES CHURCHILL

A Simile

Dear Thomas, didst thou never pop
Thy head into a tin-man's shop?
There, Thomas, didst thou never see
('Tis but by way of simile)

A squirrel spend his little rage
In jumping round a rolling cage?
The cage, as either side turned up,
Striking a ring of bells a-top?—

Moved in the orb, pleased with the chimes,
The foolish creature thinks he climbs:
But here or there, turn wood or wire,
He never gets two inches higher.

So fares it with those merry blades
That frisk it under Pindus' shades.
In noble songs, and lofty odes,
They tread on stars and talk with gods;
Still dancing in an airy round,
Still pleased with their own verses' sound;
Brought back, how fast soe'er they go,
Always aspiring, always low.

MATTHEW PRIOR

Lines Written in an Ovid

Ovid is the surest guide
    You can name to show the way
To any woman, maid or bride,
    Who resolves to go astray.

MATTHEW PRIOR

From *To a Child of Quality*

FIVE YEARS OLD, THE AUTHOR FORTY

Lords, knights and squires, the numerous band
    That wear the fair Miss Mary's fetters,

Were summoned by her high command
    To show their passions by their letters.

.   .   .   .   .   .

Nor quality, nor reputation,
    Forbid me yet my flame to tell,
Dear five years old befriends my passion,
    And I may write till she can spell.

.   .   .   .   .   .

She may receive and own my flame,
    For, though the strictest prudes should know it,
She'll pass for a most virtuous dame,
    And I for an unhappy poet.

.   .   .   .   .   .

For as our different ages move
    'Tis so ordained (would Fate but mend it)
That I shall be past making love
    When she begins to comprehend it.

                              MATTHEW PRIOR

Épitaphe de Tristan-Joachim-Édouard Corbière, philosophe, épave, mort-né

Mélange adultère de tout:
De *la fortune et pas* le sou,
De l'énergie et pas de force,
La liberté, mais une entorse.
Du coeur, du coeur! de l'âme, *non—*
Des amis, pas un compagnon,
De l'idée et pas une idée,
De l'amour, *et pas une aimée,*
La paresse et pas le repos.

Vertus chez lui furent défauts,
Âme blasée inassouvie.
Mort, mais pas guéri de la vie,
Gâcheur de vie hors de propos,
Le corps à sec et la tête ivre,
Espérant, niant l'avenir,
Il mourut en s'attendant vivre
Et vécut s'attendant mourir.

TRISTAN CORBIÈRE

✠ My translation of this:

Of many-sided mongrel birth,
Born to wealth, yet nothing worth;
Lacking strength, though strong in aim,
Free to move, yet sadly lame;
Of bursting heart, of spirit bare;
Companionless with friends to spare;
Bare of ideas, ideas to burn,
Loving, but never loved in turn;
Never at rest though always idle.
Virtues that scarcely bear recital;
Sated, he was yet unsatisfied;
Not yet fed up with life he died;
Unshaped, his life was spent in vain:
A dried-up body, a drunken brain,
His hopes all vaporous castles in Spain
He died holding on to every breath,
Yet lived a celebrant of death.

From *Mark Antony*

Whenas the nightingale chaunted her vespers,
And the wild forester couched on the ground,
Venus invited me in the evening whispers
Unto a fragrant field with roses crowned

Where she before had sent
My wishes' compliment;
Unto my heart's content
Played with me on the green.
   Never Mark Antony
   Dallied more wantonly
   With the fair Egyptian Queen.

First on her cherry cheeks I mine eyes feasted,
Thence fear of surfeiting made me retire;
Next on her warmer lips, which when I tasted,
My duller spirits made active as fire.
   Then we began to dart
   Each at another's heart,
   Arrows that knew no smart,
   Sweet lips and smiles between.
   Never Mark Antony
   Dallied more wantonly
   With the fair Egyptian Queen.

JOHN CLEVELAND

Madrigal

My love in her attire doth show her wit,
   It doth so well become her:
For every season she hath dressings fit,
   For winter, spring and summer.
   No beauty she doth miss
   When all her robes are on:
   But Beauty's self she is
   When all her robes are gone.

ANON.

From *Ulysses and the Siren*

Come worthy Greek, Ulysses come
Possess these shores with me:
The winds and seas are troublesome,
And here we may be free.
Here may we sit and view their toil
That travail on the deep,
And joy the day in mirth the while,
And spend the night in sleep.

SAMUEL DANIEL

From *The Tragedy of Philotas*

And therefore since I have outlived the date
Of former grace, acceptance and delight,
I would my lines late-born beyond the fate
Of her spent line, had never come to light.
So had I not been taxed for wishing well,
Nor now mistaken by the censuring Stage,
Nor, in my fame and reputation fell,
Which I esteem more than what all the age
Of the earth can give. But years hath done this wrong,
To make me write too much, and live too long.

SAMUEL DANIEL

Because I Could Not Stop for Death

Because I could not stop for Death,
He kindly stopped for me;
The carriage held but just ourselves
And Immortality.

We slowly drove, he knew no haste,
And I had put away

My labor, and my leisure too,
For his civility.

We passed the school where children played
At wrestling in a ring;
We passed the fields of gazing grain,
We passed the setting sun.

We paused before a house that seemed
A swelling of the ground;
The roof was scarcely visible,
The cornice but a mound.

Since then 'tis centuries, but each
Feels shorter than the day
I first surmised the horses' heads
Were toward eternity.

EMILY DICKINSON

He that lies at the stock
Shall have the gold rock;
He that lies at the wall
Shall have the gold ball;
He that lies in the middle
Shall have the gold fiddle.

NURSERY RHYME

Midnight's bell goes ting, ting, ting, ting, ting;
Then dogs do howl, and not a bird does sing
But the nightingale, and she cries twit, twit, twit:
Owls then on every bough do sit.
Ravens croak on chimneys' tops;
The cricket in the chamber hops
    And the cats cry mew, mew, mew.
The nibbling mouse is not asleep,

But he goes peep, peep, peep, peep, peep,
    And the cats cry mew, mew, mew,
And still the cats cry mew, mew, mew.

THOMAS MIDDLETON

An idle poet, here and there,
    Looks round him; but, for all the rest,
The world, unfathomably fair,
    Is duller than a witling's jest.

Love wakes men, once a lifetime each;
    They lift their heavy lids and look;
And lo, what one sweet page can teach
    They read with joy, then shut the book.

And some give thanks, and some blaspheme,
    And most forget; but, either way,
That and the child's unheeded dream
    Is all the light of all their day.

COVENTRY PATMORE

BOSOLA.   Methinks
The manner of your death should much afflict you.
This cord should terrify you.
DUCHESS.   Not a whit:
What would it pleasure me to have my throat cut
With diamonds? or to be smotherèd
With cassia? or to be shot to death with pearls?
I know death hath ten thousand several doors
For men to take their exits . . .
                        Tell my brothers
That I perceive death, now I am well awake,
Best gift is they can give or I can take.

I would fain put off my last woman's fault,
I'd not be tedious to you.

> JOHN WEBSTER, *The Duchess of Malfi*

> . . . smooth pillows, sweetest bed;
> A chamber deaf to noise and blind to light . . .

> SIR PHILIP SIDNEY, *Astrophel and Stella*

To Mistress Margery Wentworth

With margerain gentle,
   The flower of goodlihead,
Embroidered the mantle
   Is of your maidenhead.
Plainly, I cannot glose;
   Ye be, as I divine,
The pretty primrose,
   The goodly columbine.

Benign, courteous and meek,
   With wordes well devisèd;
In you, who list to seek,
   Be virtues well comprisèd.
With margerain gentle,
   The flower of goodlihead,
Embroidered the mantle
   Is of your maidenhead.

> JOHN SKELTON

From *Philip Sparrow*

Sometimes he would gasp
When he saw a wasp;
A fly or a gnat,

He would fly at that;
And prettily he would pant
When he saw an ant;
Lord, how he would pry
After the butterfly!
Lord, how he would hop
After the gressop!
And when I said, "Phip! Phip!"
Then he would leap and skip
And take me by the lip.

J OHN S KELTON

✠ I had a job with E. E. Cummings' publisher when, as part of a new book, "Olaf" came in in manuscript; inside a few days most of the office knew the poem by heart and went round chanting it to people not yet aware of its existence: and this was in peacetime. Some of it I can still recite from memory, and all of it is still, I think, tremendous.

i sing of Olaf

i sing of Olaf glad and big
whose warmest heart recoiled at war:
a conscientious object-or

his wellbelovéd colonel(trig
westpointer most succinctly bred)
took erring Olaf soon in hand;
but—though an host of overjoyed
noncoms(first knocking on the head
him)do through icy waters roll
that helplessness which others stroke
with brushes recently employed
anent this muddy toiletbowl,
while kindred intellects evoke
allegiance per blunt instruments—

Olaf(being to all intents
a corpse and wanting any rag
upon what God unto him gave)
responds, without getting annoyed
"I will not kiss your f.ing flag"

straightway the silver bird looked grave
(departing hurriedly to shave)

but—though all kinds of officers
(a yearning nation's blueeyed pride)
their passive prey did kick and curse
until for wear their clarion
voices and boots were much the worse,
and egged the firstclassprivates on
his rectum wickedly to tease
by means of skilfully applied
bayonets roasted hot with heat—
Olaf(upon what were once knees)
does almost ceaselessly repeat
"there is some s. I will not eat"

our president,being of which
assertions duly notified
threw the yellowsonofabitch
into a dungeon,where he died

Christ(of His mercy infinite)
i pray to see;and Olaf, too

preponderatingly because
unless statistics lie he was
more brave than me:more blond than you.

                    E. E. CUMMINGS

A Kindle of Cats

✠ Of the numerous odd and centuries-old terms—doubtless originating among sportsmen—used of groups of animals, birds, and fishes, at least two are known to most of us: *a pride of lions* and *a gaggle of geese.* Here are the designations for a great many others:

Animals

A shrewdness of apes
A sloth of bears
A leash of bucks
A flock of camels
A clowder of cats
A kindle of (young) cats
A rag of colts
A cowardice of curs
A business of ferrets
A skulk of foxes
A trip of goats
A trip of hares
A harras of (stud) horses

A sute of bloodhounds
A leap of leopards
A pride of lions
A richness of martens
A labor of moles
A barren of mules
A couple of spaniels
A dray of squirrels
A drift of (tame) swine
A sounder of (wild) swine
A route of wolves
A crash of rhinoceros

Birds

A dissimulation of (small) birds
A siege of bitterns
A peep of chickens
A clattering of choughs
A murder of crows
A dule of turtledoves
A paddling of ducks (on the water)

A team of ducks (in flight)
A charm of finches
A tidings of magpies
A watch of nightingales
A muster of peacocks
A congregation of plovers
An unkindness of ravens
A building of rooks

A murmuration of starlings
A spring of teal
A mutation of thrush
A company of widgeon
A gaggle of geese
A skein of geese (on the wing)
A cast of hawks

A deceit of lapwings
An exaltation of larks ("flight" is now considered more correct)
A trip of wildfowl
A descent of woodpeckers

Fishes

A swarm of eels
A shoal of fishes
A cran of herrings
A school of porpoises
A pod of seals

A quantity of smelts
A gam of whales
A troop of dogfish
A smuck of jellyfishes
A hover of trout

✠ Recent competitions in the United States to invent suitable terms for persons, occupations, organizations, and the like, were actually late runners, the game being a rather old one in England. Herewith a number of them:

Birds, Animals, Fishes, and Insects

A bask of crocodiles
A helluvalot of flies
A tower of giraffes
A pandemonium of parrots

A strop of razorbills
A college of red cardinals
A slither of sea serpents
A perruque of earwigs

Persons

A condescension of actors
A debauchery of bachelors
An argument of bridge fiends
A boodle of company promoters
A pitch of gypsies

An altitude of highbrows
A slink of mannequins
A heckle of socialists
A lack of cooks
An exaggeration of fishermen

Learning

✠ Richard Porson (1759–1808) was perhaps second only to Richard Bentley (1662–1742) as an English scholar. In different ways they were extraordinarily vivid personalities. Master, for forty-two years, of Trinity College, Cambridge, Bentley ruled with an iron fist, breaking Trinity rules as he did it; was again and again hailed into court as defendant, but much oftener strode there as plaintiff. Nothing could put him out of countenance, and nothing, out of office. When finally expelled, Bentley stayed in office for many years by refusing to let the official bearer of his expulsion deliver it. Porson, whose memory perhaps equaled Macaulay's, and whose love of drink is possibly unequaled, was an eccentric who, while advancing Greek scholarship, enlarged the field of anecdote. All else failing, he was said to drink ink; and he was known to drink up what other men left in their wineglasses. In a kind of duel, however, when his opponent chose quarts of brandy as the weapons, Porson sank to the floor after consuming two quarts, while the victor drank Porson's health. It was Porson who, after a visit to Germany, wrote the well-known verses:

> I went to Frankfort and got drunk
> With that most learned Professor Brunck;
> I went to Würtz and got more drunken
> With that more learned Professor Runcken.

It was also Porson who, when at dinner someone venturing to argue with him said, "Dr. Porson, my opinion of you is most contemptible," answered, "Sir, I never knew an opinion of yours that was not contemptible." Herewith an account of Porson while traveling in a hackney coach, when a "young gentleman, fresh from Oxford . . . dared to make a quotation from the Greek, in the hope of impressing the ladies":

The Professor, a stranger to him, had appeared to be asleep, but
was roused immediately by this daring on the part of the young
gentleman, and, leaning forward, he said: "I think, young gentleman, you favoured us just now with a quotation from Sophocles;
I do not happen to recollect it there." "Oh, sir," replied the un-
wary young gentleman, "the quotation is word for word as I have
repeated it, and in Sophocles too; but I suspect, sir, it is some
time since you were at college." The Professor, after fumbling for
some time in his greatcoat, produced a small pocket edition of
Sophocles, and commanded the young gentleman to produce the
quotation. After some moments' unhappy turning of the pages, he
was obliged to confess that he could not find it, recollecting upon
second thoughts, that "the passage is in Euripides." The Professor, with a frown gathering upon his brow, produced the works of
that author for the young gentleman's inspection, saying, "Then
perhaps, sir, you will be good enough to find it for me, in that
little book." The young gentleman was, by now, thoroughly terrified, but, unwilling to give way before the ladies, he ejaculated,
"Bless me, sir, how dull I am; I recollect now, yes, yes, I remember that the passage is in Aeschylus." The Professor produced a
book from his pocket. But the young gentleman . . . cried,
"Stop the coach. Let me out. Let me out, I say. There's a fellow
here has got the Bodleian Library in his pocket; let me out I say,
let me out, he must either be the devil, or Porson himself."

EDITH SITWELL, *English Eccentrics*

Letters

✠ All my grown-up life I have particularly enjoyed
reading letters (and for the most part hated writing them). I
have not enjoyed all published letters, of course; some are pain-
fully dull, or syntactically fatiguing, or concerned with matters
I know nothing or care nothing about, or bathed in flattery, or

aimed at posterity; but I find more *kinds* of letters interesting or enjoyable than I find, say, kinds of poetry or fiction. For one thing, they introduce you to more kinds of people, and for the most part (even with poets and novelists) *as* people. Again, letters tend to satisfy our curiosity, to satisfy our base instincts and our better ones, about those who write them and often those they write about; about the world they live in and the life they lead; about their merits and virtues; but even more about their indiscretions, their idiosyncrasies, their ability to gossip, their need to confide. By the life they lead and the gossip they trade in, we mean something rather better than middle-class suburban life and that Clara spilled hot coffee all over Priscilla's new dress. Yet even things like that can create a picture or suggest a "scene"; indeed, I have now and then picked up in the street an abandoned letter, and found it thin in substance and illiterate in style, yet still been curious about *why* Gertrude got a divorce or *why* the Slaters sold their car ten days after buying it.

At this level, however, we have no wish to read many of anyone's letters; where, at higher levels, that is precisely what we wish most. There are, of course, great single letters: I think that two I have included—William James's letter to his dying father, and Dr. Johnson's to Macpherson—say what needs to be said superbly, and in saying it tell us much about the writers. And there are notable sequences of letters, such as Henry Adams's from Japan, or Lady Mary Wortley Montagu's from Constantinople, or Horace Walpole's on the Grand Tour, which imbue a particular subject matter with great personality. But for me, with a good letter writer the greatest pleasure lies in reading, so to speak, the letters of a lifetime. For besides its intrinsic interest, a man's correspondence has a valuably cumulative one, which is why it can sometimes be undistinguished as writing yet fascinating as revelation. Among other things, every man's personal traits—his prejudices, contradictions, dissimulations—have a piquancy of their own. Thus, for one small example, it is amusing, in the famous Holmes-Pollock letters, to find Justice

Holmes asking Pollock, late in life, who in the world is Dorothy Osborne; and then, some years later, blandly remarking to Pollock that Dorothy Osborne has always been one of his favorite writers.

But a long career of letters reveals, of course, far greater things: it reveals a person in both character and personality; in what he professes and in what he proves to be; in what he speaks out about and what he conceals. On this account his life need not be dramatic nor his career formidable; many of the greatest letter writers—Thomas Gray and William Cowper outstandingly— led quiet, not to say retired, lives. Again, a man whose single letters cannot compare with those of Horace Walpole, Byron, Henry Adams, and others, and whose body of letters is not their equal either—I mean Matthew Arnold—is yet the letter writer whom I turn to oftenest and always read with pleasure. He was not at all a man who made of his correspondence a confessional, or streaked it with drama, or shaped it for generations to come; the same man asked, indeed, that no biography be written of him. But he was a man who brought you closer to him by his reticences than others do by their revelations; who made the prosaic aspects of his life somehow as vital as other men's dazzling or dramatic ones; and who found that marvelous resting place in self-regard that breathes neither coyness on the one hand nor conceit on the other.

The domain of superior letters is very large and dates from very long ago, from Cicero's and Pliny's. The great central phalanx of classic English letter writers begins with Holmes's Dorothy Osborne and includes, along with those already mentioned, Keats, Jane Carlyle, and Edward Fitzgerald; among great foreign ones are Madame de Sévigné, Flaubert, and Chekhov. There are also great bad letter writers, notably Queen Victoria; and great correspondences, particularly Flaubert's with George Sand. It would be pleasant to expatiate on the merits of all these and more, and to distinguish between their merits, which might lead to summarizing or psychologizing their lives. But that would be too formal a work—in a commonplace book, too out of place —and it would certainly run on too long. Furthermore, they are all in their way very good; one can choose blindfolded among them, and yet come up with a prize.

I must go back to my charming occupation of hearing students give lessons. Here is my programme for this afternoon: Avalanches—The Steam Engine—The Thames—India Rubber— Bricks—The Battle of Poictiers—Subtraction—The Reindeer— The Gunpowder Plot—The Jordan. Alluring, is it not? Twenty minutes each, and the days of one's life are only threescore years and ten.

M A T T H E W   A R N O L D, to Lady de Rothschild

Yes, that man has missed something who has never awakened in an anonymous bed beside a face he will never see again, and who has never left a brothel at sunrise feeling like throwing himself into the river out of pure disgust for life. And just their shameless way of dressing—the temptation of the chimera—the aura of the unknown, of the *maudit*—the old poetry of corruption and venality! During my first years in Paris, I used to sit in front of Tortoni's on hot summer evenings and watch the streetwalkers stroll by in the last rays of the sun. At such moments I overflowed with biblical poetry. I thought of Isaiah, of "fornication in high places," and I walked back along the rue de la Harpe saying to myself: "And her mouth is smoother than oil." I swear that I was never more chaste. My only complaint about prostitution is that it no longer exists. The kept woman has invaded the field of debauchery, just as the journalist has invaded poetry; everything is becoming mongrelized. There are no more courtesans, just as there are no more saints; there are only varieties of semi-prostitutes, each more sordid than the last.

F L A U B E R T, to Louise Colet
(trans. Francis Steegmuller)

Of domestic doings, there has been nothing since Lady D * *
Not a divorce stirring—but a good many in embryo, in the shape
of marriages.

BYRON, to Thomas Moore

I hate all intolerance, but most the intolerance of Apostacy . . .
It is no disgrace to Mr. Southey to have written *Wat Tyler,* and
afterwards to have written his birthday or Victory odes (I speak
only of their *politics*), but it is something, for which I have no
words, for this man to have endeavoured to bring to the stake
(for such would he do) men who think as he thought, and for no
reason but because they think so still, when he has found it con-
venient to think otherwise. Opinions are made to be changed, or
how is truth to be got at?

BYRON, to John Murray

In short, [the Italians] transfer marriage to adultery, and strike
the *not* out of that commandment. The reason is, that they marry
for their parents, and love for themselves. They exact fidelity from
a lover as a debt of honour, while they pay the husband as a
tradesman, that is, not at all. You hear a person's character, male
or female, canvassed, not as depending on their conduct to their
husbands or wives, but to their mistress or lover. And—and—
that's all. If I wrote a quarto, I don't know that I could do more
than amplify what I have here noted. It is to be observed that
while they do all this, the greatest outward respect is to be paid to
the husbands, not only by the ladies, but by their *Serventi*—particularly if the husband serves no one himself (which is not often
the case, however): so that you would often suppose them relations—the *Servente* making the figure of one adopted into the
family. Sometimes the ladies run a little restive and elope, or divide, or make a scene; but this is at starting, generally, when they
know no better, or when they fall in love with a foreigner, or

some such anomaly—and is always reckoned unnecessary and extravagant.

B Y R O N, to John Murray

You must not trust Italian witnesses: nobody believes them in their own courts: why should you? For 50 or 100 Sequins you may have any testimony you please, and the Judge into the bargain.

B Y R O N, to Thomas Moore

At the last warm debate in the House of Lords, it was unanimously resolved there should be no crowd of unnecessary auditors; consequently the fair sex were excluded, and the gallery destined to the sole use of the House of Commons. Notwithstanding which determination, a tribe of dames resolved to show on this occasion that neither men nor laws could resist them. These heroines were Lady Huntingdon, the Duchess of Queensberry, the Duchess of Ancaster, Lady Westmoreland, Lady Cobham, Lady Charlotte Edwin, Lady Archibald Hamilton and her daughter, Mrs. Scott, and Mrs. Pendarves and Lady Frances Saunderson. . . . They presented themselves at the door at nine o'clock in the morning, where Sir William Saunderson respectfully informed them that the Chancellor had made an order against their admittance. The Duchess of Queensberry, as head of the squadron, pished at the ill-breeding of a mere lawyer, and desired him to let them upstairs privately. After some modest refusals, he swore by G— he would not let them in. Her grace, with a noble warmth, answered by G— they would come in in spite of the Chancellor and the whole House. This being reported, the Peers resolved to starve them out; an order was made that the doors should not be opened till they had raised their siege. These Amazons now showed themselves qualified for the duty even of foot soldiers; they stood there till five in the afternoon, without either sustenance or evacuation, every now and then playing volleys of thumps, kicks, and raps against the door, with so much violence that the speakers in the House were scarce heard. When the Lords were not to be conquered by this, the two duchesses (very well apprised of the use of stratagems in war) commanded a dead silence of half an hour; and the Chancellor, who thought this a certain proof of their absence (the Commons also being very impatient to enter), gave order for the opening of the door; upon which they all rushed in, pushed aside their competitors, and placed themselves in the front rows of the gallery. They stayed there till after eleven, when the House rose; and during the debate gave applause, and showed marks of dislike, not only by smiles and winks (which have always been allowed in these cases), but by noisy laughs . . .

LADY MARY WORTLEY MONTAGU,
to the Countess of Pomfret

I had a visit in the beginning of these holidays of thirty horse of ladies and gentlemen, with their servants . . . They came with the kind intent of staying with me at least a fortnight, though I had never seen any of them before; but they were all neighbours within ten mile round. I could not avoid entertaining them at supper, and by good luck had a large quantity of game in the house, which with the help of my poultry furnished out a plentiful table. I sent for the fiddles; and they were so obliging as to dance all night, and even dine with me next day, though none of them had been in bed, and were much disappointed I did not press them to stay, it being the fashion to go in troops to one anothers' houses, hunting and dancing together, a month in each castle.

LADY MARY WORTLEY MONTAGU,
to her daughter, the Countess of Bute

I am going to tell you a thing the most astonishing, the most surprising, the most marvelous, the most miraculous, the most magnificent, the most confounding, the most unheard of, the most singular, the most extraordinary, the most incredible, the most unforeseen, the greatest, the least, the rarest, the most com-

mon, the most public, the most private till today, the most brilliant, the most enviable; in short, a thing of which there is but
one example in past ages, and that not an exact one neither; a
thing that we cannot believe at Paris; how then will it gain credit
at Lyons? a thing which makes everybody cry "Lord, have mercy
upon us!" a thing which causes the greatest joy to Madame de
Rohan and Madame de Hauterive; a thing, in fine, which is to
happen on Sunday next, when those who are present will doubt
the evidence of their senses; a thing which, though it is to be
done on Sunday, yet perhaps will not be finished on Monday. I
cannot bring myself to tell it you: guess what it is. I give you
three times to do it in. What, not a word to throw at a dog? Well
then, I find I must tell you. Monsieur de Lauzun is to be married
next Sunday at the Louvre, to—pray guess to whom! I give you
four times to do it in, I give you six, I give you a hundred. Says
Madame de Coulanges, "It is really very hard to guess: perhaps it
is Madame de la Vallière." Indeed, Madame, it is not. "It is
Mademoiselle de Retz, then." No, nor she neither; you are extremely provincial. "Lord, bless me," say you, "what stupid
wretches we are! it is Mademoiselle Colbert all the while." Nay,
now you are still farther from the mark. "Why then it must certainly be Mademoiselle de Créqui." You have it not yet. Well, I
find I must tell you at last. He is to be married next Sunday, at
the Louvre, with the King's leave, to mademoiselle, mademoiselle
de—mademoiselle—guess, pray guess her name: he is to be married to Mademoiselle, the great Mademoiselle, Mademoiselle,
daughter to the late Monsieur; Mademoiselle, granddaughter of
Henry the Fourth; Mademoiselle d'Eu, Mademoiselle de Dombes,
Mademoiselle de Montpensier, Mademoiselle d'Orléans, Mademoiselle, the King's cousin-german, Mademoiselle, destined to the
Throne, Mademoiselle, the only match in France that was worthy
of Monsieur. What glorious matter for talk! If you should burst
forth like a bedlamite, say we have told you a lie, that it is false,
that we are making a jest of you, and that a pretty jest it is without wit or invention, in short, if you abuse us, we shall think you
quite in the right; for we have done just the same things our-

selves. Farewell, you will find by the letters you receive this post, whether we tell you truth or not.

MADAME DE SÉVIGNÉ, to M. de Coulanges

Kirkaldy, Fifeshire, Nov. 9, 1776.

Dear Sir:

It is with a real, though a very melancholy pleasure, that I sit down to give you some account of the behavior of our late excellent friend, Mr. Hume, during his last illness.

Though in his own judgment his disease was mortal and incurable, yet he allowed himself to be prevailed upon, by the entreaty of his friends, to try what might be the effects of a long journey . . . Upon his return to Edinburgh, though he found himself much weaker, yet his cheerfulness never abated, and he continued to divert himself, as usual, with correcting his own works for a new edition, with reading books of amusement, with the conversation of his friends; and sometimes in the evening with a party at his favourite game of whist. His cheerfulness was so great, and his conversation and amusements ran so much in their usual strain, that notwithstanding all bad symptoms, many people could not believe he was dying. "I shall tell your friend Colonel Edmonstoune," said Dr. Dundas to him one day, "that I left you much better, and in a fair way of recovery." "Doctor," said he, "as I believe you would not choose to tell anything but the truth, you had better tell him I am dying as fast as my enemies, if I have any, could wish, and as easily and cheerfully as my best friends could desire." Colonel Edmonstoune soon afterwards came to see him, and take leave of him; and on his way home he could not forbear writing him a letter, bidding him once more an eternal adieu. Mr. Hume's magnanimity and firmness were such, that his most affectionate friends knew that they hazarded nothing in talking and writing to him as to a dying man; and that so far from being hurt by this frankness, he was rather pleased and flattered by it. I happened to come into his room while he was

reading [Colonel Edmonstoune's] letter, which he had just received, and which he immediately showed me. I told him that
though I was sensible how very much he was weakened, and that
appearances were in many respects very bad, yet his cheerfulness
was still so great, the spirit of life seemed still to be so very strong
in him, that I could not help entertaining some faint hopes. He
answered, "Your hopes are groundless. An habitual diarrhea of
more than a year's standing would be a very bad disease at any
age; at my age it is a mortal one. When I lie down in the evening
I feel myself weaker than when I rose in the morning; and when I
rise in the morning weaker than when I lay down in the evening.
I am sensible, besides, that some of my vital parts are affected, so
that I must soon die." "Well," said I, "if it must be so, you have
at least the satisfaction of leaving all your friends, your brother's
family in particular, in great prosperity." He said that he felt that
satisfaction so sensibly that when he was reading, a few days before, Lucian's *Dialogues of the Dead,* among all the excuses which
are alleged to Charon for not entering readily into his boat, he
could not find one that fitted him: he had no house to finish, he
had no daughter to provide for, he had no enemies upon whom
he wished to revenge himself. "I could not well imagine," said he,
"what excuse I could make to Charon, in order to obtain a little
delay . . ." He then diverted himself with inventing several
jocular excuses, which he supposed he might make to Charon,
and with imagining the very surly answers which it might suit the
character of Charon to return to them. "Upon further consideration," said he, "I thought I might say to him, 'Good Charon, I
have been correcting my works for a new edition. Allow me a
little time that I may see how the public received the alterations.'
But Charon would answer, 'When you have seen the effect of
these, you will be making other alterations. There will be no end
of such excuses.' . . . But I might still urge, 'Have a little patience, good Charon, I have been endeavouring to open the eyes
of the public. If I live a few years longer, I may have the satisfaction of seeing the downfall of some of the prevailing systems of
superstition.' But Charon would then lose all temper and de-

cency. 'You loitering rogue, that will not happen these many hundred years . . . Get into the boat this instant.' "

But though Mr. Hume always talked of his approaching disso- lution with great cheerfulness . . . he never mentioned the sub- ject but when the conversation naturally led to it, and never dwelt longer upon it than the course of the conversation hap- pened to require . . .

Thus died our most excellent, and never-to-be-forgotten friend . . . Upon the whole, I have always considered him, both in his lifetime, and since his death, as approaching as nearly to the idea of a perfectly wise and virtuous man as perhaps the nature of human frailty will admit.

ADAM SMITH, to William Strahan

Darling old Father,

. . . We have been so long accustomed to the hypothesis of your being taken away from us, especially during the past ten months, that the thought that this may be your last illness conveys no very sudden shock. You are old enough, you've given your message to the world in many ways and will not be forgotten . . . I should like to see you once again before we part. . . . Meanwhile . . . I scribble this line . . . just to tell you how full of the tenderest memories and feelings about you my heart has for the last few days been filled. In that mysterious gulf of the past into which the present soon will fall and go back and back, yours is still for me the central figure. All my intellectual life I derive from you; and though we have often seemed at odds in the expression thereof, I'm sure there's a harmony somewhere, and that our strivings will combine. What my debt to you is goes beyond all my power of estimating—so early, so penetrating and so constant has been the influence. . . . As for us, we shall live on each in his way—feel- ing somewhat unprotected, old as we are, for the absence of the parental bosoms as a refuge, but holding fast together in that common sacred memory. We will stand by each other and by Alice, try to transmit the torch in our offspring as you did in us, and when the time comes for being gathered in, I pray we may, if not all, some at least, be as ripe as you. As for myself, I know what trouble I've given you at various times through my peculiarities; and as my own boys grow up, I shall learn more and more of the kind of trial you had to overcome in superintending the development of a creature different from yourself, for whom you felt responsible. . . . And it comes strangely over me in bidding you good-bye how a life is but a day and expresses mainly but a single note. It is so much like the act of bidding an ordinary good-night. Good-night, my sacred old Father! If I don't see you again—Farewell!

W I L L I A M   J A M E S, to his father

I am sorry for H. Fielding's death, not only as I shall read no more of his writings, but I believe he lost more than others, as no man enjoyed life more than he did, though few had less reason to do so, the highest of his preferment being raking in the lowest sinks of vice and misery. I should think it a nobler and less nauseous employment to be one of the staff-officers that conduct the nocturnal weddings. His happy constitution (even when he had, with great pains, half demolished it) made him forget everything when he was before a venison pasty, or over a flask of champagne; and I am persuaded he has known more happy moments than any prince upon earth. His natural spirits gave him rapture with his cook-maid, and cheerfulness when he was fluxing in a garret. There was a great similitude between his character and that of Sir Richard Steele. He had the advantage both in learning and, in my opinion, genius: they both agreed in wanting money in spite of all their friends, and would have wanted it, if their hereditary lands had been as extensive as their imagination; yet each of them [was] so formed for happiness, it is a pity he was not immortal. . . .

This Richardson is a strange fellow. I heartily despise him, and eagerly read him, nay, sob over his works in a most scandalous manner. The two first tomes of *Clarissa* touched me, as being very resembling to my maiden days; and I find in the pictures of Sir Thomas Grandison and his lady, what I have heard of my mother, and seen of my father.

LADY MARY WORTLEY MONTAGU,
to the Countess of Bute

At ten o'clock I was at home and alone (Marianna was gone with her husband to a conversazione) when the door of my apartment opened, and in walked a well-looking and (for an Italian) *bionda* girl of about nineteen, who informed me that she was married to the brother of my *amorosa,* and wished to have some conversation with me. I made a decent reply, and we had some talk in Italian and Romaic (her mother being a Greek of Corfu) when lo! in a very few minutes, in marches, to my very great astonishment, Marianna Sergati, *in propria persona,* and after making a most polite curtsy to her sister-in-law and to me, without a single word seizes her said sister-in-law by the hair, and bestows upon her some sixteen slaps, which would have made your ear ache only to hear their echo. I need not describe the screaming which ensued. The luckless visitor took flight. I seized Marianna who, after several vain efforts to get away in pursuit of the enemy, fairly went into fits in my arms; and, in spite of reasoning, eau de Cologne, vinegar, half a pint of water, and God knows what other waters beside, continued so till past mdinight.

BYRON, to Thomas Moore

In spite of all my modesty, I cannot help thinking I have a little something of the prophet about me. At least we have not conquered America yet. I did not send you immediate word of our victory at Boston, because the success not only seemed very equivocal, but because the conquerors lost three to one more than the vanquished. The last do not pique themselves upon modern good breeding, but level only at the officers, of whom they have slain a vast number. We are a little disappointed, indeed, at their fighting at all, which was not in our calculation. We knew we could

conquer *America in Germany,* and I doubt had better have gone
thither now for that purpose, as it does not appear hitherto to be
quite so feasible in America itself. However, we are determined to
know the worst, and are sending away all the men and ammuni-
tion we can muster. The Congress, not asleep neither, have appointed a Generalissimo, Washington, allowed a very able officer,
who distinguished himself in the last war. Well! we had better
have gone on robbing the Indies; it was a more lucrative trade.

HORACE WALPOLE, to Sir Horace Mann (1775)

You will be diverted to hear that Mr. Gibbon has quarrelled with
me. He lent me his second volume in the middle of November. I
returned it with a most civil panegyric. He came for more in-
cense, I gave it, but alas! with too much sincerity; I added, "Mr.
Gibbon, I am sorry *you* should have pitched on so disgusting a
subject as the Constantinopolitan History. There is so much of
the Arians and Eunomians, and semi-Pelagians; and there is such
a strange contrast between Roman and Gothic manners, and so
little harmony between a Consul Sabinus and a Ricimer, Duke of
the palace, that though you have written the story as well as it
could be written, I fear few will have patience to read it." He
coloured; all his round features squeezed themselves into sharp
angles; he screwed up his button-mouth, and rapping his snuff-
box, said, "It had never been put together before"—*so well,* he
meant to add—but gulped it. He meant *so well* certainly, for
Tillemont, whom he quotes in every page, has done the very
thing. Well, from that hour to this I have never seen him, though
he used to call once or twice a week; nor has sent me the third
volume, as he promised. I well knew his vanity, even about his
ridiculous face and person, but thought he had too much sense to
avow it so palpably.

HORACE WALPOLE, to the Reverend William Mason

After [Dr. Johnson's] death, Burke, Sir Joshua Reynolds, and
Boswell sent an ambling circular-letter to me, begging subscrip-

tions for a monument for him—the last two, I think, imperti-
nently, as they could not but know my opinion, and could not
suppose I would contribute to a monument for one who had endeavoured, poor soul! to degrade my friend [Gray's] superlative
poetry. I would not deign to write an answer; but sent down
word by my footman, as I would have done to parish officers with
a brief, that I would not subscribe. In the two new volumes Johnson says . . . that Gray's poetry is *dull,* and that he was a *dull*
man! The same oracle dislikes Prior, Swift and Fielding. If an
elephant could write a book, perhaps one that had read a great
deal would say that an Arabian horse is a very clumsy ungraceful
animal.

HORACE WALPOLE, to Miss Mary Berry

Well, now, you have got home again—which I daresay is as agreeable as a "draught of cool small beer to the scorched palate of a
waking sot"—now you have got home again, I say, probably I
shall hear from you. Since I wrote last I have been transferred to
my father-in-law's, with my lady and my lady's maid, etc., etc.,
etc., and the treacle-moon is over, and I am awake, and find myself married. . . . Swift says "no *wise* man ever married"; but,
for a fool, I think it the most ambrosial of all possible future
states. I still think one ought to marry upon *lease,* but am very
sure I should renew mine at the expiration . . . Pray tell me
what is going on in the way of intriguery, and how the whores
and rogues of the upper Beggar's Opera go on . . . in or after
marriage; or who are going to break any particular commandment. Upon this dreary coast [Stockton-on-Tees, in northeast
England] we have nothing but county meetings and shipwrecks;
and I have this day dined upon fish, which probably dined upon
the crews of several colliers lost in the last gales. But I saw the sea
once more in all the glories of surf and foam—almost equal to the
Bay of Biscay . . .

My [father-in-law] Sir Ralpho, hath recently made a speech at
a Durham tax-meeting; and not only at Durham, but here, sev-

eral times since, after dinner. He is now, I believe, speaking it to himself (I left him in the middle) over various decanters, which can neither interrupt him nor fall asleep—as might possibly have been the case with some of this audience.

BYRON, to Thomas Moore

I suppose one does learn a little, even after forty; and whenever here I come across a man who says that he stands out . . . on the *principle* of the thing, I strike him off my list of useful allies. There's no need to talk about principles when you are really dying for your race or your religion; the talk chiefly comes in when you are dressing yourself, not to give anyone pleasure, but against rival beauties.

I wish I could get that Shakespeare begun. I fear I'm getting middle-aged and shan't capture the zest. Moreover I'm sick of my own syntax. It's stiff and monotonous, and I can't change it. . . .

Also I'm sick of what is called "the serious business of Scholarship—the baggage of the campaign." I've passed a wasted life; I ought to have written straight-on things. Now I can't acquire the art.

Doctorates are given daily to men who would never have got to be shop-walkers if they had been drapers' assistants. The academic business is, in the main, a small-minded affair. The Comedy of Pedantry seems to be two-thirds of life.

SIR WALTER RALEIGH (the Oxford professor),
to John Sampson

I received your foolish and impudent letter. Any violence offered me I shall do my best to repel; and what I cannot do for myself the law shall do for me. I hope I shall never be deterred from detecting what I think a cheat by the menaces of a ruffian.

What would you have me retract? I thought your book an imposture; I think it an imposture still. For this opinion I have given my reasons to the public, which I here dare you to refute. Your rage I defy. Your abilities since your Homer are not so for-

midable, and what I hear of your morals inclines me to pay regard not to what you shall say, but to what you shall prove. You
may print this if you will.

DR. JOHNSON, to James Macpherson

Do you know, and would you believe it, that the King [George
IV] will be obliged to hire the crown that will be placed on his
head at his Coronation, and that it has been the same with all the
coronations of the princes of Brunswick? It is paid for at so much
an hour.

PRINCESS LIEVEN, to Prince Metternich

I'm sick of portraits and wish very much to take my viol-da-gamba
and walk off to some sweet village when I can paint landskips and
enjoy the fag-end of life in quietness and ease. But these fine
ladies and their tea-drinkings, dancings, husband-huntings and
such will fob me out of the last ten years, and I fear miss getting
husbands too. But we can say nothing to these things, you know,
Jackson, we must jog on and be content with the jingling of the
bells, only, damn it, I hate a dust, the kicking up of a dust, and
being confined *in harness* to follow the track, whilst others ride in
the waggon, under cover, stretching their legs in the straw at ease,
and gazing at green trees and blue skies without half my taste,
that's damned hard. My comfort is, I have 5 viols-da-gamba, 3
Jayes and two Barak Normans. [Jaye made various musical instruments; Norman, cellos.]

THOMAS GAINSBOROUGH, to William Jackson

If I were to find funds, would you be ready on Wednesday morning to take a run into Wales, and make me a sketch of some rocks
in the bed of a stream, with trees above, mountain ashes, and so
on, scarlet in autumn tints? If you are later than Wednesday, you
will be too late; but if you can go on Wednesday, let me know by
return of post, or by bearer. I will send funds. I want you to go to

Pont-y-Monach, near Aberystwyth, and choose a subject there-
abouts. I shall be very much obliged to you if you will do this for
me.

You are a *very* odd creature, that's a fact. I said I would find
funds for you to go into Wales to draw something I wanted. I
never said I would for you to go to Paris, to disturb yourself and
other people, and I won't.

JOHN RUSKIN, to Dante Gabriel Rossetti

I should like Ruskin to know what he never knew—the want of
money for a year or two; then he might come to doubt his infalli-
bility and give an artist working on the right road the benefit of
any little doubt that might arise. The little despot imagines himself the Pope of Art and would wear 3 crowns as a right, only they
would make him look funny in London.

THOMAS WOOLNER, to Mrs. Tennyson

When one serves you coffee, do not think to find beer in it. When
I offer you a professor's ideas, trust me, and do not search in them
for Chekhov's ideas. Throughout the entire story there is only one
idea with which I agree—the one that comes to the mind of the
swindler, Knekker, the professor's son-in-law,—"The old man is
in his dotage."

CHEKHOV, to A. S. Souvorin

The literary brotherhood in Petersburg seems to talk of nothing
but the uncleanness of my motives. I have just received the good
news that I am to be married to the rich Madame Sibiryakov. I
get a lot of agreeable news, altogether.

CHEKHOV, to A. S. Souvorin

Oh, if you only knew what a plot for a novel I have in my mind!
What wonderful women! What funerals! What marriages!

CHEKHOV, to A. N. Pleshcheyev

Do you want my biography? Here it is. . . . In 1891 I made a
tour of Europe, where I drank excellent wine and ate oysters. In
1892 I took part in an orgy in the company of V. A. Tikhonov at
a name-day party. . . . I have been translated into all the languages with the exception of the foreign ones . . . The mysteries
of love I fathomed at the age of thirteen. . . . I am a bachelor. I
should like to receive a pension. I practise medicine . . . sometimes in the summer I perform post-mortems . . . Of authors my
favorite is Tolstoi, of doctors, Zakharin.

All that is nonsense though. Write what you like. If you
haven't facts, substitute lyricism.

CHEKHOV, to V. A. Tikhonov

"Chekhov belongs to the generation which has perceptibly begun
to turn away from the West . . ." . . . One would have to be a
bull to "turn away from the West" on arriving for the first time
in Venice or Florence. . . . I should like to know who is taking
the trouble to announce to the whole universe that I did not like
foreign parts. . . . I liked even Bologna. Whatever ought I to
have done? Howled with rapture? Broken the windows? Embraced Frenchmen?

CHEKHOV, to A. S. Souvorin

I am so poorly, I have been to a funeral, where I made a pun, to
the consternation of the rest of the mourners. . . . I can't describe to you the howl which the widow set up at proper intervals.

CHARLES LAMB, to P. G. Patmore

A terrible idea occurred to me as I wrote those words [about
oysters]. The oyster-cellars—what do they do when oysters are not
in season? Is pickled salmon vended there? Do they sell crabs,
shrimps, winkles, herrings? The oyster-openers—what do *they*
do? Do they commit suicide in despair, or wrench open tight
drawers and cupboards and hermetically-sealed bottles for prac-

tice? Perhaps they are dentists out of the oyster season. Who knows?

D I C K E N S, to C. C. Felton

A propos of dreams, is it not a strange thing if writers of fiction never dream of their own creations; recollecting, I suppose, even in their dreams, that they have no real existence? *I* never dream of any of my own characters, and I feel it so impossible that I would wager Scott never did of his, real as they are.

D I C K E N S, to C. C. Felton

Outside, an indeterminate horror on the increase; a little nearer, indifference and mockery, and then, suddenly, this old man [Cézanne] deep in his work, painting nudes only from old drawings done forty years ago in Paris, knowing that no model would be allowed him in Aix. "At my age," he says, "the most I could get is a hag of fifty, and I know that even such a creature is not to be found in Aix." So he paints from his old drawings. And lays his apples on counterpanes, which Madame Brémond is sure to find missing one day, and places his wine bottles in between. . . . And (like Van Gogh) makes his "saints" out of such things; forces them, *forces* them to be beautiful. . . . And sits in the garden like an old dog—the dog of this work which calls him again, and beats him, and lets him go hungry. And clings with all his strength to this incomprehensible master, who only allows him to turn back to God on Sunday, as to his first owner. . . . And outside, the people say "Cézanne," and gentlemen in Paris write his name with a flourish . . . proud of being so well informed.

R I L K E, to his wife

(trans. R. F. C. Hull)

Being abroad was something of a strain at first. You no longer know how to set about it; you . . . spent half the day reading

the names Houbigant, Roger & Gallet and Pinaud over the drug
stores . . . The confectioners did not impress me half so much,
so far I have bought no chocolate, but the soaps did for me, I was
entirely defenceless against the . . . displays in Zurich's Bahn-
hofstrasse. By these devious routes, however ridiculous they were,
I gradually got to the other things; to the French bookshops and
art salons, to the bustle of streets and business, and, with some
effort, even to Nature. It's a pity that she only seems to reveal
herself to me in Switzerland in exaggerations; how pompous these
lakes and mountains are, there is always too much of them, they
have been weaned from the simplicities. . . . Heavens alive! A
sort of parlor-Nature, all ups and downs, full of prodigies, dupli-
cates, underlined objects. A mountain? behold, dozens of them on
either hand, one behind the other; a lake? but of course, and a
very refined lake too, best quality, with reflections in the purest
water, a whole picture gallery of reflections and the Almighty explaining them one by one like a curator, if, that is to say, he is not
at the moment doing his film-director stunt and training the
searchlights of the blood-red evening on to the mountains, where
the snow clings day after day far into the summer.

RILKE, to Gertrud Duckama Knoop

(trans. R. F. C. Hull)

✠ Surely the last half of this passage might be assigned
to Jean Giraudoux.

[The Samoans,] the least imaginative people I ever met . . . are
pure Greek fauns. Their intellectual existence is made up of concrete facts. . . . They are not in the least voluptuous, they have
no longings and very brief passions; they live a matter-of-fact existence that would scare a New England spinster. Even their
dances—proper or improper—always represent facts. . . . Old
Samsoni, the American pilot here for many years . . . tells us
that the worst dance he ever saw here was a literal reproduction
of the marriage ceremony, and that the man went through the

entire form, which is long and highly peculiar, and ended with the consummation—openly before the whole village, delighted with the fun—but that never actors nor spectators showed a sign of emotion or passion, but went through it as though it had been a cricket match.

HENRY ADAMS, to John Hay

Your friend [Jean-Jacques] Rousseau (I doubt) grows tired of Mr. Davenport and Derbyshire. He has picked a quarrel with David Hume and writes him letter[s] of 14 pages folio upbraiding him with all his *noirceurs*. Take one only as a specimen, he says, that at Calais they chanced to sleep in the same room together, and that he overheard David talking in his sleep, and saying, *Ah! je le tiens, ce Jean-Jacques là.* In short (I fear) for want of persecution and admiration . . . he will go back to the continent.

THOMAS GRAY, to Thomas Wharton

I received the book [Walpole's *Historic Doubts on the Life and Reign of King Richard the Third*] you were so good to send me . . . You are universally read here [Pembroke College, Cambridge]; but what *we* think, is not so easy to come at. We stay as usual to see the success, to learn the judgment of the town, to be directed in our opinions by those of more competent judges. If they like you, we shall; if any one of name write against you, we give you up: for we are modest and diffident of ourselves, and not without reason. History in particular is not our *fort;* for (the truth is) we read only modern books and the pamphlets of the day. I have heard it objected, that you raise doubts and difficulties, and do not satisfy them by telling us what was *really* the case. I have heard you charged with disrespect to the King of Prussia; and above all to King William, and the revolution. These are seriously the most sensible things I have heard said, and all that I recollect. If you please to justify yourself, you may.

THOMAS GRAY, to Horace Walpole

Are dreams so very various and different, as you suppose? Or is there, taking into consideration our vast differences in point of mental and physical constitution, a remarkable sameness in them? Surely it is an extremely unusual circumstance to hear any narrative of a dream that does violence to our dreaming experience or enlarges it very much. And how many dreams are common to us all, from the Queen to the costermonger! We all fall off that Tower, we all skim above the ground at a great pace and can't keep on it, we all say "this must be a dream, because I was in this strange, low-roofed, beam-constructed place once before, and it turned out to be a dream," we all take unheard of trouble to go to a Theatre and never get in, or to go to a Feast which can't be eaten or drunk, or to read letters, placards or books, that no study will render legible, or to break some thraldom or other, from which we can't escape, we all confound the living with the dead, and all frequently have a knowledge or suspicion that we are doing it, we all astonish ourselves by telling ourselves, in a dialogue with ourselves, the most astonishing and terrific secrets, we all go to public places in our night dresses and are horribly disconcerted lest the company should observe it.

DICKENS, to Dr. Stone

You have been too near and dear a friend to me for many years . . . to admit of my any longer keeping silence to you on a sad domestic topic. I believe you are not quite unprepared for what I am going to say, and will, in the main, have anticipated it.

I believe my marriage has been for years and years as miserable a one as ever was made. I believe that no two people were ever created, with such an impossibility of interest, sympathy, confidence, sentiment, tender union of any kind between them, as there is between my wife and me. It is an immense misfortune to her—it is an immense misfortune to me—but Nature has put an insurmountable barrier between us, which never in this world can be thrown down.

You know me too well to suppose that I have the faintest

thought of influencing you on either side. I merely mention a fact which may induce you to pity us both, when I tell you that she is the only person I have ever known with whom I could not get on somehow or other, and in communicating with whom I could not find some way to come to some kind of interest. . . .

We have been virtually separated for a long time. We must put a wider space between us now, than can be found in one house. If the children loved her, or ever had loved her, this severance would have been a far easier thing than it is. But she has never attached one of them to herself, never played with them in their infancy, never attracted their confidence as they have grown older, never presented herself before them in the aspect of a mother. I have seen them fall off from her in a natural—not *un*natural—progress of estrangement, and at this moment I believe that Mary and Katey (whose dispositions are of the gentlest and most affectionate conceivable) harden into stone figures of girls when they can be got to go near her, and have their hearts shut up in her presence as if they were closed by some horrid spring. . . . It is her misery to live in some fatal atmosphere which slays every one to whom she should be dearest. It is my misery that no one can ever understand the truth in its full force, or know what a blighted and wasted life my married life has been.

DICKENS, to Angela Burdett-Coutts

It is impossible for me to continue any longer a correspondence that is becoming epileptic. Change it, I beg. What have I done to you that you should unfold before me, with all the pride of grief, the spectacle of a despair for which I know no remedy? If I had betrayed you, exposed you, sold your letters, etc., you could not write me things more atrocious or more distressing.

What have I done, good God? What have I done?

You know quite well that I cannot come to Paris. Are you trying to make me answer you brutally? I am too well brought up to do that, but it seems to me that I have said this often enough for you to remember it.

I had formed quite a different idea of love. I thought it was something independent of everything, even of the person who inspired it. Absence, insult, infamy—all that does not affect it. When two persons love, they can go ten years without seeing each other and without suffering any ill effects therefrom.

You claim that I treat you like "the lowest kind of woman." I don't know what "the lowest kind of woman" is, or the highest kind, or the next-highest. Women are relatively inferior or superior by reason of their beauty and the attraction they exert on us, that's all. You accuse me of being an aristocrat, but I have very democratic ideas about this. It is possible, as you say, that moderate affections are always lasting. But in saying that, you condemn your own, for it is anything but moderate. As for myself, I am weary of grand passions, exalted feelings, frenzied loves, and howling despairs. I love good sense above all, perhaps because I have none.

I don't understand why you constantly pick quarrels and sulk. You should not do this, for you are kind, good, and charming, and one cannot help holding it against you that you wantonly spoil all those qualities.

Calm yourself, work, and when we meet again welcome me with a good laugh and tell me you've been silly.

FLAUBERT, to Louise Colet
(trans. Francis Steegmuller)

Monsieur Gustave Flaubert presents his respects to Monsieur and Madame Charpentier. He will be proud and happy to appear next Friday in response to their honorable invitation.

He finds the fact that no bourgeois will be present a reassuring prospect. For he has now reached such a point of exasperation, when he finds himself in the company of persons of that species, that he is invariably tempted to strangle them, or rather to hurl them into the latrines (if such language is permitted)—an action

whose consequences would be embarrassing to the publishing
house of Charpentier . . .

F L A U B E R T , to the Georges Charpentiers
(trans. Francis Steegmuller)

I wot not how to answer your query about my father. He was a
New Hampshire man, 6 foot 2, a crack shot & a famous fly-
fisherman & a firstrate sailor (his sloop was named The Actress) &
a woodsman who could find his way through forests primeval
without a compass & a canoeist who'd still paddle you up to a deer
without ruffling the surface of a pond & an ornithologist & taxi-
dermist & (when he gave up hunting) an expert photographer (the
best I've even seen) & an actor who portrayed Julius Caesar in
Sanders Theatre & a painter (both in oils & watercolours) & a better carpenter than any professional & an architect who designed
his own houses before building them & (when he liked) a plumber
who just for the fun of it installed all his own waterworks & (while
at Harvard) a teacher with small use for professors—by whom
(Royce, Lanman, Taussig, etc.) we were literally surrounded
(but not defeated)—& later (at Doctor Hale's socalled South
Congregational really Unitarian church) a preacher who an-
nounced, during the last war, that the Gott Mit Uns boys were in
error since the only thing which mattered was for man to be on
God's side (& one beautiful Sunday in Spring remarked from the
pulpit that he couldn't understand why anyone had come to hear
him on such a day) & horribly shocked his pewholders by crying
"the Kingdom of Heaven is no spiritual roofgarden: it's inside
you" & my father had the first telephone in Cambridge & (long
before any Model T Ford) he piloted an Orient Buckboard with
Friction Drive produced by the Waltham watch company & my
father sent me to a certain public school because its principal was
a gentle immense coalblack negress & when he became a diplomat
(for World Peace) he gave me & my friends a tremendous party
up in a tree at Sceaux Robinson & my father was a servant of the
people who fought Boston's biggest & crookedest politician
fiercely all day & a few evenings later sat down with him cheer-

fully at the Rotary Club & my father's voice was so magnificent
that he was called on to impersonate God speaking from Beacon
Hill (he was heard all over the common) & my father gave me
Plato's metaphor of the cave with my mother's milk.

E. E. Cummings, to Paul Rosenfeld

It would be fun to send you some of my examination papers. My
rule in making them up is to ask questions which I can't myself
answer. It astounds me to see how some of my students answer
questions which would play the deuce with me.

Henry Adams, to Charles Milnes Gaskell

Ma très chère Soeur!
    . . . You must not gather from my not replying, that you and
your letters are a nuisance to me! . . . If the necessary business
of earning my living did not prevent me, God knows I would
answer your letters at once! And have I never sent you a reply?
Well, then—forgetfulness it cannot be—nor negligence, either;
therefore it is entirely due to positive hindrances—to genuine impossibility. . . . In Heaven's name, you [and my father] know
what Vienna is. In such a place has not a man (who has not a
kreuzer of assured income) enough to think about and to work at
day and night? Our father, when he has finished his duties in
church, and you, when you have done with your few pupils, can
both do what you like for the rest of the day and write letters
containing whole litanies. But it is not so with me. I described my
manner of life the other day to my father and I will repeat it to
you. My hair is always done by six o'clock in the morning and by
seven I am fully dressed. I then compose until nine. From nine to
one I give lessons. Then I lunch, unless I am invited to some
house where they lunch at two or even three o'clock, as, for example, today and tomorrow at Countess Zichy's and Countess
Thun's. I can never work before five or six o'clock in the evening,
and even then I am often prevented by a concert. If I am not
prevented, I compose until nine. I then go to my dear Constanze

[his future wife], though the joy of seeing one another is nearly always spoilt by her mother's bitter remarks. . . . At half past ten or eleven I come home—it depends on her mother's darts and on my capacity to endure them! . . . It is my custom (especially if I get home early) to compose a little before going to bed. I often go on writing until one—and am up again at six.

M O Z A R T , to his sister

Now I must tell you about Mozart's last days. Well, Mozart became fonder and fonder of our . . . mother [see previous letter] and she of him. . . . When Mozart fell ill, we both made him a night-jacket which he could put on frontways, since on account of his swollen condition he was unable to turn in bed. . . . I used to go into town every day to see him. Well, one Saturday when I was with him, Mozart said to me: "Dear Sophie, do tell Mamma that I am fairly well and that I shall be able to go and congratulate her on the octave of her name-day." Who could have been more delighted than I to bring such cheerful news to my mother . . . ? I hurried home therefore to comfort her, the more so as he himself really seemed to be bright and happy. The following day was a Sunday. . . . I said to our good mother: "Dear Mamma, I'm not going to see Mozart today. He was so well yesterday that surely he will be much better this morning, and one day more or less won't make much difference." Well, my mother said: ". . . Make me a bowl of coffee and then I'll tell you what you ought to do." . . . I went into the kitchen. . . . I had to light the lamp and make a fire. . . . I had made the coffee and the lamp was still burning. Then I noticed how wasteful I had been with my lamp . . . I stared into the flame and thought to myself, "How I should love to know how Mozart is." While I was . . . gazing at the flame, it went out, as completely as if the lamp had never been burning. . . . And yet there wasn't the slightest draught—that I can swear to. A horrible feeling came over me. I ran to our mother and told her all. She said: ". . . Go into town and bring me back news of him at once. . . ." Alas, how frightened I was when my sister [Mozart's wife], who was almost despairing and yet trying to keep calm, came out to me, saying: "Thank God that you have come, dear Sophie. Last night he was so ill that I thought he would not be alive this morning. . . . Go in to him for a little while and see how he is." I tried to control myself and went to his bedside. He immediately called me to him and said: "Ah, dear Sophie, how glad I am that you have come. You must stay here tonight and see me die." I tried hard to be brave and to persuade him to the contrary. But to all my attempts he only replied: "Why, I have already the taste of death on my tongue." And, "if you do not stay, who will support my dearest Constanze when I am gone?" "Yes, yes, dear Mozart," I assured him, "but I must first go back to our mother and tell her that you would like me to stay with you today. . . ." "Yes, do so," said Mozart, "but be sure and come back soon." . . . My poor sister followed me to the door and begged me . . . to go to the priests at St. Peter's and implore one of them to come to Mozart—a chance call, as it were. I did so, but for a long time they refused to come and I had a great deal of trouble to persuade one of those clerical brutes to go to him. Then I ran off to my mother . . . I then ran back as fast as I could to my distracted sister. Süssmayr was at Mozart's bedside. The well-known Requiem lay on the quilt and Mozart was explaining to him how, in his opinion, he ought to finish it, when he was gone. Further, he urged his wife to keep his death a secret until she should have informed Albrechtsberger [chief organist at St. Stephen's], who was in charge of all the services. A long search was made for Dr. Closset, who was found at the theatre, but who had to wait for the end of the play. He came and ordered cold poultices to be placed on Mozart's burning head, which, however, affected him to such an extent that he became unconscious and remained so until he died. His last movement was an attempt to express with his mouth the drum passages in the Requiem. That I can still hear. Müller from the Art Gallery came and took a cast of his pale, dead face. . . . His devoted wife . . . simply could not tear herself away from Mozart, however much I begged her to do so. . . . The day after that dreadful night . . . crowds of people walked past his corpse and wept and wailed for him. All my life I have never seen Mozart in a temper, still less, angry.

SOPHIE HAIBEL, to G. N. von Nissen

✠ Thirty-odd years after Mozart's death, his sister-in-law wrote this memoir to his widow's second husband, who was collecting material for a Mozart biography. The account you have just read of his strenuous working life and of his miserable, impoverished last days all the more sadly recalls the *tempo felice* of his child-prodigy triumphs and now and then of his grown-up ones, as here, in a letter from Prague, a few years before his death, to a friend and pupil:

At six o'clock I drove with Count Canal to the so-called Bretfeld ball, where the cream of the beauties of Prague is wont to gather. . . . I neither danced nor flirted with any of them . . . I looked on, however, with the greatest pleasure while all these people flew about in sheer delight to the music of my "Figaro," arranged for quadrilles and waltzes. For here they talk of nothing but "Figaro." Nothing is played, sung or whistled but "Figaro." No opera is drawing like "Figaro." Nothing, nothing but "Figaro."

MOZART, to Baron Gottfried von Jacquin

✠ I find it hard to write about Mozart, or about that other great musical genius who struggled and died young, Schubert. Magicians both, they differ for me in their magic, Mozart's producing music that might be called divine; Schubert's, music that might be called unearthly. Perhaps the most memorable tribute to Mozart is Rossini's, who, when asked to name the greatest composer, said: "Beethoven is the greatest composer"— and then added, "But Mozart is the only one."

Light Verse

✠ Favorite student though he was of Dr. Arnold of Rugby, Arthur Hugh Clough had a good deal of humor and wit, and wrote here, there, and elsewhere, some bright and light things in verse, of which "The Latest Decalogue," and the long series of stanzas beginning with the following one, are most famous:

> As I sat at the café I said to myself,
> They may talk as they please about what they call pelf,
> They may sneer as they like about eating and drinking,
> But help it I cannot, I cannot help thinking
>   How pleasant it is to have money, heigh-ho!
>   How pleasant it is to have money.

✠ But these stanzas on a different theme, though not so successful, are good of their kind and not at all well known:

> These juicy meats, this flashing wine,
>   May be an unreal mere appearance;
> Only—for my inside, in fine,
>   They have a singular coherence.
>
> This lovely creature's glowing charms
>   Are gross illusion, I don't doubt that;
> But when I pressed her in my arms
>   I somehow didn't think about that.
>
> This world is very odd, we see;
>   We do not comprehend it;
> But in one fact can all agree:
>   God won't, and we can't, mend it.

Being common sense, it can't be sin
　To take it as we find it;
The pleasure to take pleasure in:
　The pain, try not to mind it.

A R T H U R   H U G H   C L O U G H ,   "Dipsychus"

✠ Puzzling at first, this next poem is meant to be read
as an exposition of the use of the comma: "I saw a peacock, with
a fiery tail I saw a blazing comet, drop down hail I saw a cloud,"
etc.

I saw a peacock with a fiery tail
I saw a blazing comet drop down hail
I saw a cloud wrapped with ivy round
I saw an oak creep on along the ground
I saw a pismire swallow up a whale
I saw the sea brimful of ale
I saw a Venice glass full fathom deep
I saw a well full of men's tears that weep
I saw red eyes all of a flaming fire
I saw a house bigger than the moon and higher
I saw the sun at twelve o'clock at night
I saw the man that saw this wondrous sight.

A N O N .

Little Dickey Diller
Had a wife and siller;

He took a stick and broke her back
And sent her to the miller.

The miller, with his stone dish,
Sent her unto Uncle Fish.

Uncle Fish, the shoemaker,
Sent her unto John the baker.

John the baker, with his ten men,
Sent her unto Mistress Wren.

Mistress Wren, with grief and pain,
Sent her to the Queen of Spain.

The Queen of Spain, that woman of sin,
Opened the door and let her in.

ANON.

Your legs, so like the moon at crescent,
    A bathing-tub will scarce look neat in;
So here I send you, for a present,
    A drinking-horn to wash your feet in.

MARTIAL, *Epigrams*

(trans. W. T. Webb)

I care not for these ladies
That must be wooed and prayed:
Give me kind Amarillis
The wanton country maid.
Nature art disdaineth,
Her beauty is her own.
Her when he court and kiss,
She cries, Forsooth, let go!
But when we come where comfort is,
She never will say No!

If I love Amarillis
She gives me fruit and flowers:
But if we love these ladies
We must give golden showers.
Give them gold that sell love,
Give me the nut-brown lass
Who, when we court and kiss,

She cries, Forsooth, let go!
But when we come where comfort is,
She never will say No!

These ladies must have pillows,
And beds by strangers wrought:
Give me a bower of willows,
Of moss and leaves unbought,
And fresh Amarillis
With milk and honey fed,
Who, when we court and kiss,
She cries, Forsooth, let go!
But when we come where comfort is,
She never will say No!

THOMAS CAMPION

From *The Undertaking*

I have done one braver thing
   Than all the worthies did,
And yet a braver thence doth spring,
   Which is, to keep that hid.

JOHN DONNE

Literature

How hard it is to judge of Dickens's names I realized the other day when a friend exclaimed ecstatically, "Oliver Twist! What a perfect name." He was in fact praising Mr. Bumble's powers of invention, for it was he who named the foundlings as they arose. But there is surely no particular merit in the name. It is purely a matter of old affection. At any rate, I know where Dickens got it and it is my one literary discovery of which I am immensely proud. Wandering through the churchyard at Chalk, where Dickens spent his honeymoon, I came across three neighbouring tombstones bearing the names of Flight (not Flite), Guppy and Twist. The first two he kept in cold storage for years, till the time of *Bleak House,* but Twist he used almost immediately.

B E R N A R D D A R W I N, *Every Idle Dream*

✠ I myself had a possibly like experience: glancing at some of the mortuary inscriptions in Winchester Cathedral, where Jane Austen often went, and where she is buried, I noted that one of them commemorated someone or other, and "his wife, Lady Susan."

Every Poem must necessarily be a perfect Unity, but why Homer's is peculiarly so I cannot tell: he has told the story of Bellerophon, and omitted the Judgment of Paris, which is not only a part but a principal part of Homer's subject.

But when a work has Unity, it is as much in a part as in the whole: the Torso is as much a Unity as the Laocoön.

As Unity is the cloak of folly, so Goodness is the cloak of knavery. Those who will have Unity exclusively in Homer come out with a Moral like a sting in the tail. Aristotle says Characters are either Good or Bad; now Goodness or Badness has nothing to do with Character: an Apple tree, a Pear tree, a Horse, a Lion are Characters; but a Good Apple Tree or a Bad is an Apple tree still: a Horse is not more a Lion for being a Bad Horse; that is its Character; its Goodness or Badness is another consideration.

It is the same with the Moral of a whole poem as with the Moral Goodness of its parts. Unity and Morality are secondary considerations, and belong to Philosophy and not to Poetry, to Exception and not to Rule, to Accident and not to Substance. The ancients called it eating of the tree of good and evil.

The Classics! It is the Classics, and not Goths nor Monks, that desolate Europe with Wars.

B L A K E, "On Homer's Poetry"

I hate anything that occupies more space than it is worth. I hate to see a load of bandboxes go along the street, and I hate to see a parcel of big words without anything in them.

WILLIAM HAZLITT, "On Familiar Style"

> This common tale, alas! few can prevent:
> We first must sin, before we can repent.

ANON.

When [Samuel] Rogers produces a couplet, he goes to bed, and the knocker is tied up, and straw is laid down, and the caudle is made, and the answer to inquiries is, that Mr. Rogers is as well as can be expected.

SYDNEY SMITH

✠ Rogers is said to have spent days over his epigram on Ward:

> They say that Ward has no heart, but I deny it:
> He has a heart, and gets his speeches by it.

His daughters called in their father [Wordsworth], a plain, elderly, white-haired man, not prepossessing, and disfigured by green goggles. He sat down, and talked with great simplicity. . . .

I inquired if he had read Carlyle's critical articles and translations. He said he thought him sometimes insane. He proceeded to abuse Goethe's *Wilhelm Meister* heartily. It was full of all manner of fornication. It was like the crossing of flies in the air. He had never gone farther than the first part; so disgusted was he that he threw the book across the room. . . . He had just returned from a visit to Staffa, and within three days had made three sonnets on Fingal's Cave, and was composing a fourth when he was called in to see me. He said, "If you are interested in my verses perhaps you will like to hear these lines." I gladly assented, and he recollected himself for a few moments and then stood forth and repeated, one after the other, the three entire sonnets with great animation. . . . His opinions of [the] French, English, Irish and Scotch seemed rashly formulized from little anecdotes of what had befallen himself and members of his family, in a diligence or stagecoach.

EMERSON, *English Traits*

He [Wordsworth] seems impatient that even Shakespeare should be admired.

CARLYLE

I asked him [Wordsworth] abruptly what he thought of Shelley as a poet.

"Nothing," he replied, as abruptly.

Seeing my surprise, he added, "A poet who has not produced a good poem before he is twenty-five, we may conclude cannot, and never will do so."

"The *Cenci*," I said eagerly.

"Won't do," he replied, shaking his head, as he got into the carriage. . . .

E. J. TRELAWNY, *Recollections of the
Last Days of Shelley and Byron*

Michael Henchard's Will

That Elizabeth-Jane Farfrae be not told of my death, or made to grieve on account of me.

& that I be not bury'd in consecrated ground.

& that no sexton be asked to toll the bell.

& that nobody is wished to see my dead body.

& that no murners walk behind me at my funeral.

& that no flours be planted on my grave.

& that no man remember me.
To this I put my name.

Michael Henchard

T H O M A S   H A R D Y, *The Mayor of Casterbridge*

Richardson was, as it were, a saint among novelists,—and Fielding a sinner. Richardson laid himself out to support high-toned
feminine virtue. The praise of strict matrons and of severe elders
was the very breath of his nostrils. He placed himself on a pedes-
tal of morality, and dictated to Propriety at large what should and
what should not be considered becoming for young women. And
he lived up to his preaching, preferring good old ladies to
naughty young men, and a dish of tea to a glass of punch. Fielding was in every respect the reverse of his rival,—whom he loved
to flout.

A N T H O N Y   T R O L L O P E, *Four Lectures*

Even the best critics are mainly wise after the event. . . . It
would make a most illuminating anthology if someone—may it
soon be done!—would collect all the verdicts of famous critics
that time has turned to derision. It might even—but no, nothing
could do that—inspire a few momentary doubts in the minds of
some of their living successors. What name, for instance, more
eminent in criticism than Coleridge?—who yet found Gibbon's
prose detestable and Tennyson ignorant of what metre was; who
could discover nothing "sublime" in Greek literature and was so
grotesquely inappreciative of French, as to give public thanks to
God in a London lecture that he could not pronounce a line of
the language—much as if a man should claim to be publicly admired for going about with one eye shut. Think, again, of Hazlitt, unable "to make head or tail" of Shakespeare's *Sonnets;* dis-
missing Racine as one who cannot "lay bare the heart," and simply "reads lectures out of a commonplace book"; of De Quincey
denouncing Keats for having "trampled upon his mother-tongue
as with the hoofs of a buffalo," or talking glibly of "the prodi-

gious defects of the French in all the higher qualities of prose composition" and of the inferiority of Voltaire to Horace Walpole; of Swinburne, shocked by *Venus and Adonis* and by Walt Whitman, abusing Euripides as "a mutilated monkey" and Ibsen as "a Fracastoro" [author of a sixteenth-century poem called *Syphilis*] of the drama.

As a charming instance of the general appreciation of serious literature in France, I have always remembered the case of one Laurent, "dit Coco," accused of burglary in April 1909, who proved an alibi because "Juste à cette heure-là je me trouvais chez un marchand de vin de la rue de Tracy et je discutais avec un camarade au sujet de la mère de Britannicus dans la tragédie de Racine." This discussion was proved to have lasted three-quarters of an hour. No doubt burglars in England *might* discuss the character of Hamlet in a public-house; but no magistrate would believe it.

F. L. L u c a s, *Studies French and English*

In Endymion, I leaped headlong into the sea, and thereby have become better acquainted with the soundings, the quicksands, and the rocks, than if I had stayed upon the green shore, and piped a silly pipe, and took tea and comfortable advice.

K e a t s, letter to James Hessey

I have met with women whom I really think would like to be married to a poem, and to be given away by a novel.

K e a t s, letter to Fanny Brawne

"If I should die," said I to myself, "I have left no immortal work behind me—nothing to make my friends proud of my memory— but I have loved the principle of beauty in all things, and if I had had time I would have made myself remembered."

K e a t s, letter to Fanny Brawne

Love

You will not understand these English words, and *others* will not understand them—which is the reason I have not scrawled them in Italian. But you will recognize the handwriting of him who passionately loved you, and you will divine that, over a book which was yours, he could only think of love. In that word, beautiful in all languages, but most so in yours—*Amor mio*—is comprised my existence here and hereafter. I feel I exist here, and I fear that I shall exist hereafter—to *what* purpose you will decide; my destiny rests with you, and you are a woman, seventeen years of age, and two out of a convent. I wish that you had stayed there, with all my heart—or, at least, that I had never met you in your married state.

But all this is too late. I love you, and you love me—at least, you *say so,* and *act* as if you *did* so, which last is a great consolation in all events. But *I* more than love you, and cannot cease to love you.

Think of me, sometimes, when the Alps and the ocean divide us—but they never will, unless you *wish* it.

B Y R O N, letter to the Countess Guiccioli

And he [Lancelot] came to the window: and the Queen, who waited for him, slept not, but came thither. And the one threw to the other their arms, and they felt each other as much as they could reach. "Lady," said Lancelot, "if I could enter yonder, would it please you?" "Enter," said she, "fair sweet friend. How could this happen?" "Lady," said he, "if it pleasure you, it could happen lightly." "Certainly," said she, "I should it willingly above everything." "Then, in God's name," said he, "that shall well happen. For the iron will never hold." "Wait, then," said she, "till I have gone to bed." . . . Then he drew the irons from their sockets so softly that no noise was made and no bar broke.

. . . Great was the joy that they made each other that night, for long had each suffered for the other. And when the day came, they parted.

A N O N ., *Le Livre de Lancelot du Lac* (thirteenth century)

Noi leggevamo un giorno per diletto
    di Lancilotto, come amor lo strinse;
    soli eravamo e sanza alcun sospetto.
Per più fiate gli occhi ci sospinse
    quella lettura, e scolorocci il viso;
    ma solo un punto fu quel che ci vinse.
Quando leggemmo il disiato riso
    esser baciato da cotanto amante,
    questi, che mai da me no fia diviso
la bocca mi baciò tutto tremante:
    Galeotto fu il libro, e chi lo scrisse;
    quel giorno più non vi leggemmo avante.

D A N T E, *Inferno*

✠ The translation by Lord Byron is far short of the original.

We read one day for pastime, seated nigh,
    Of Lancilot, how love enchain'd him too.
    We were alone, quite unsuspiciously.
But oft our eyes met, and our cheeks in hue
    All o'er discolour'd by that reading were;
    But one point only wholly us o'erthrew;
When we read the long-sigh'd-for smile of her,
    To be thus kiss'd by such devoted lover,
    He who from me can be divided ne'er,
Kiss'd my mouth, trembling in the act all over.
    Accursèd was the book and he who wrote!
    That day no further leaf we did uncover.

✠ Perhaps no one has ever loved so passionately, so publicly, so hostilely as Catullus, whose feelings for his Lesbia were a fierce mingling of love and hate; indeed, one of his briefest and best known poems opens with *Odi et amo*—"I hate and love"—and continues, "Why, you may ask, is this so? I know not, but it pierces me and I am in torment." Here are two other poems in which Catullus's conflicting feelings for Lesbia are sounded:

None could ever say that she,
Lesbia! was so loved by me;
Never, all the world around,
Faith so true as mine was found.
If no longer it endures,
(Would it did!) the fault is yours.
I can never think again
Well of you: I try in vain.
But, be false, do what you will,
Lesbia! I must love you still.

(trans. Walter Savage Landor)

So loved has woman never been
    As thou hast been by me,
Nor lover yet was ever seen
    So true as I to thee.

But cruel, cruel Lesbia, thou
    Hast by thy falsehood wrought
Such havoc in my soul, and now
    So madly 'tis distraught,

'Twould prize thee not, though thou shouldst grow
    All pure and chaste as ice;
Nor could it cease to love thee, though
    Besmirched with every vice.

(trans. Theodore Martin)

This is the monstrosity in love, lady, that the will is infinite and the execution confined, that the desire is boundless and the act a slave to limit.

SHAKESPEARE, *Troilus and Cressida*

There's a blush for won't, and a blush for shan't,
And a blush for having done it;
There's a blush for thought and a blush for naught,
And a blush for just begun it.

.   .   .   .   .   .

There's a sigh for yes, and a sigh for no,
And a sigh for I can't bear it!
O what can be done, shall we stay or run,
Or cut the sweet apple and share it?

KEATS, "Sharing Eve's Apple"

Children of the future age
Reading this indignant page,
Know that in a former time,
Love, sweet Love, was thought a crime!

BLAKE, *Songs of Experience*

Your brother and my sister no sooner met, but they looked; no sooner looked, but they loved; no sooner loved, but they sighed; no sooner sighed, but they asked one another the reason; no sooner knew the reason, but they sought the remedy: and in these degrees have they made a pair of stairs to marriage, which they will climb incontinent, or else be incontinent before marriage. They are in the very wrath of love, and they will together. Clubs cannot part them.

SHAKESPEARE, *As You Like It*

From *Farewell to Love*

Ah cannot we
As well as cocks and lions jocund be
After such pleasures?

JOHN DONNE

It is not without reason that there is everywhere a temple of
Aphrodite as girl friend and nowhere in all Greece a single temple of Aphrodite as wife.

And suddenly, where injury of chance
Puts back leave-taking, jostles roughly by
All time of pause, rudely beguiles our lips
Of all rejoinder, forcibly prevents
Our locked embrasures, strangles our dear vows
Even in the birth of our own labouring breath:
We two, that with so many thousand sighs
Did buy each other, must poorly sell ourselves
With the rude brevity and discharge of one.
Injurious time now with a robber's haste
Crams his rich thievery up, he knows not how:
As many farewells as be stars in heaven,
With distinct breath and consigned kisses to them,
He fumbles up into a loose adieu
And scants us with a single famished kiss,
Distasted with the salt of broken tears.

SHAKESPEARE, *Troilus and Cressida*

On a time the amorous Silvy
Said to her shepherd, Sweet, how do you?
Kiss me this once, and then God be wee you,
    My sweetest dear.

Kiss me this once, and then God be wee you,
For now the morning draweth near.

With that, her fairest bosom showing,
Opening her lips, rich perfumes blowing,
She said, Now kiss me and be going,
            My sweetest dear.
Kiss me this once, and then be going,
For now the morning draweth near.

With that the shepherd waked from sleeping,
And spying where the day was peeping,
He said, Now take my soul in keeping,
            My sweetest dear.
Kiss me and take my soul in keeping,
Since I must go now, day is near.

ANON.

From *The Sun Rising*

        Busy old fool, unruly Sun,
        Why dost thou thus,
Through windows, and through curtains, call on us?
Must to thy motions lovers' seasons run?
        Saucy pedantic wretch, go chide
        Late schoolboys, and sour prentices,
    Go tell court-huntsmen that the King will ride,
    Call country ants to harvest offices;
Love, all alike, no season knows nor clime,
Nor hours, days, months, which are the rags of time.

JOHN DONNE

Go, restless ghost, tell that proud fair
    She was my cause of dying;

And if she still seem coy to hear,
   Importune her with crying.

If angry looks still threaten war
   Ah, then tell Beauty's jewel,
Though angels are less fair by far,
   Yet tigers are less cruel.

ANON.

The dainty young heiress of Lincoln's Inn Fields,
   Brisk, beautiful, wealthy and witty,
To the power of love so unwillingly yields,
   That 'tis feared she'll unpeople the city.
The sparks and the beaus all languish and die;
   Yet, after the conquest of many,
One little good marksman, that aims with one eye,
   May wound her heart deeper than any.

CHARLES SACKVILLE, EARL OF DORSET

The Good-Morrow

I wonder by my troth what thou and I
Did, till we loved? were we not weaned till then,
But sucked on country pleasures childishly?
Or snorted we in the seven sleepers' den?
'Twas so; but this all pleasures fancies be.
If ever any beauty I did see
Which I desired, and got, 'twas but a dream of thee.

And now good morrow to our waking souls
Which watch not one another out of fear;
For love, all love of other sights controls,
And makes one little room an everywhere.
Let sea-discoverers to new worlds have gone,

Let maps to others, worlds on worlds have shown,
Let us possess one world, each hath one and is one.

My face in thine eye, thine in mine appears,
And true plain hearts do in the faces rest,
Where can we find two better hemispheres
Without sharp North, without declining West?
Whatever dies was not mixed equally;
If our two loves be one, or thou and I
Love so alike, that none do slacken, none can die.

JOHN DONNE

Upon the Death of Sir Albert Morton's Wife

He first deceased; she for a little tried
To live without him, liked it not and died.

SIR HENRY WOTTON

Love consists in this, that two solitudes protect and touch and
greet each other.

RILKE, Letters to a Young Poet

(trans. M. D. Herter Norton)

My little pretty one,
My pretty honey one,
She is a jolly one
And gentle as can be.
With a beck she comes anon,
With a wink she will be gone.
No doubt she is alone
Of all that ever I see.

ANON.

[Katheryn Howard on the scaffold, 1542:] "Brothers, by the journey upon which I am bound, I have not wronged the King [Henry VIII]. But it is true that long before the King took me, I loved Culpeper, and I wish to God I had done as he wished me, for at the time the King wanted to take me, he urged me to say that I was pledged to him. If I had done as he advised me, I should not die this death, nor would he. I would rather have had him for a husband than be mistress of the world, but sin blinded me, and the greed of grandeur; and since mine is the fault, mine also is the suffering, and my great sorrow is that Culpeper should have had to die through me." She then turned to the headsman: "Pray, hasten with thy office." . . . "I die a Queen, but I would rather die the wife of Culpeper."

Wherever you are, whilst I have life, my soul shall follow you, my ever dear Lord Marl, and wherever I am I should only kill the time wishing for night that I may sleep . . .

S a r a h , D u c h e s s o f M a r l b o r o u g h , letter to the Duke

✠ A letter that appeared in an English newspaper; the writer of it died a few days after it was written:

Dear Alf,

I seen you last night in my dream. O my dear I cried at waking up. What a silly girl you been and got. The pain is bad this morning, but I laugh at the sollum cloks of the sisters and the sawbones. I can see they think I am booked but they don't know what has befalen between you and me. How could I die and leave my Dear. I spill my medecin this morning thinking of my Dear. Hopeing this finds you well no more now from yours truly Liz.

From *The Knight's Tale*

Allas the Wo! Allas, the peynès stronge
That I for yow have suffred, and so longe!
Allas, the deeth! allas, myn Emelye!

Allas, departynge of oure companye!
Allas, myn hertès quene; allas, my wyf!
Myn hertès lady, ender of my lyf!
What is this world? What asketh men to have?
Now with his love, now in his coldè grave
Allone, withouten any companye.
Far-wel, my swetè fo! myn Emelye!
And softè tak me in your armès tweye,
For love of God, and herkneth what I seye.

CHAUCER

A Lover's Anger

As Cloe came into the room t'other day,
I peevish began: Where so long could you stay?
In your lifetime you never regarded your hour:
You promised at two; and (pray look, child) 'tis four.
A lady's watch needs neither figures nor wheels:
'Tis enough that 'tis loaded with baubles and seals.
A temper so heedless no mortal can bear—
Thus far I went on with a resolute air.
Lord bless me! said she; let a body but speak:
Here's an ugly hard rosebud fallen into my neck:
It has hurt me and vexed me to such a degree—
See here: for you never believe me: pray see,
On the left side my breast what a mark it has made!
So saying, her bosom she careless displayed.
That seat of delight I with wonder surveyed;
And forgot every word I designed to have said.

MATTHEW PRIOR

A Mad World, My Masters

Gentlemen are requested, and servants are commanded, to keep off the grass.

Sign in London parks, early nineteenth century

You must think of me as not belonging to the present system of society, but as one looking with the greatest delight to its entire annihilation, so that ultimately not one stone of it shall be left upon another.

The Life of Robert Owen, by Himself

Our evening dress needs radical reform. How it happens that black cloth has come to be associated with occasions of public and private festivity in common with occasions of public and private mourning is a riddle which we must leave posterity to solve. But it is certain that in the existing state of society, Englishmen wear the same dress at an evening party and a funeral. Nor is this all, for many a host who entertains his friends at dinner has a butler behind his chair who is dressed precisely like himself. To add to this confusion, the clergyman who rises to say grace might, so far as his apparel goes, be mistaken for either.

CHARLES I. EASTLAKE,
Hints on Household Taste [1877]

I have long sought for some instances of invention or discovery by a woman. And the best I have been able to find is Thwaites's soda-water. A Miss Thwaites of Dublin . . . hit on an improvement in soda-water, which enabled her to drive all others out of the market.

RICHARD WHATELY, Archbishop of Dublin

Exposure of the face is one of the great tendencies of the time;
and though it is not exactly indelicate in itself, yet the bold con-
fronting of notice that is involved in going out with a totally unprotected countenance . . . cannot be modest in itself; nor does
a veil coming close over the nose materially alter the matter.

CHARLOTTE M. YONGE, *Womankind*

I was not six years old before my mother . . . began to follow
out a code of penance with regard to me. . . . The most delicious
puddings were talked of. . . . At length *"le grand moment"* arrived. They were put on the table before me, and then, just as I
was going to eat some of them, they were snatched away, and I
was told to get up and carry them off to some poor person in the
village.

AUGUSTUS HARE, *The Story of My Life*

The state of public affairs is not inviting, and I rejoice that we
take in no daily paper.

DR. ARNOLD of Rugby

Married a young parishioner of the name of Mahershallalashbaz
Tuck. He accounted for the possession of so extraordinary a name
thus: his father wished to call him by the shortest name in the
Bible, and for that purpose selected Uz. But, the clergyman making some demur, the father said in pique: "Well, if he cannot
have the shortest he shall have the longest."

THE REVEREND BENJAMIN J. ARMSTRONG,
A Norfolk Diary

I am now going to tell you the horrible and wretched plaege that
my multiplications gives me you can't conceive it. The most Dev-
ilish thing is 8 times 8 and 7 times 7 it is what nature itself cant
endure.

In my travels I met with a handsome lad named Charles Balfour, Esq., and from him I got ofers of marage—ofers of marage, did I say? Nay plenty heard me.

I am reading the Mysteries of Udolpho. I am much interested in the fate of poor, poor Emily.

The Diary of Marjorie Fleming, Aged 6 (1803–1811)

> Children she had five,
> Three are dead and two alive;
> Those that are dead choosing rather
> To die with their mother than live with their father.

An Epitaph in Cornwall

✠ An excerpt from one of the most prized of bad novels:

Looking fully into the face that seemed so lovely just now, with the dainty spots of blazing ire enlivening the pale cheeks of creeping sin, Sir John began—

"Irene, if I may use such familiarity, I have summoned you hither, it may be to undergo a stricter examination than your present condition probably permits; but knowing, as you should, my life must be miserable under this growing cloud of unfathomed dislike, I became resolved to end, if within my power, such contentious and unlady-like conduct as that practised by you towards me of late. It is now quite six months—yea, weary months —since I shielded you from open penury and insult, which were bound to follow you, as well as your much-loved protectors, who sheltered you from the pangs of penniless orphanage; and during these six months, which naturally should have been the pet period of nuptial harmony, it has proved the hideous period of howling dislike!

"I, as you see, am tinged with slightly snowy tufts, the result of stifled sorrow and care concerning you alone; and on the memorable day of our alliance, as you are well aware, the black and glossy locks of glistening glory crowned my brow. There dwelt

then, just six months this day, no trace of sorrow or smothered
woe—no variety of color where it is and shall be so long as I
exist—no furrows of grief could then be traced upon my visage.
But, alas! now I feel so changed. And why?

"Because I have dastardly and doggedly been made a tool of
treason in the hands of the traitoress and unworthy! I was enticed
to believe that an angel was always hovering around my footsteps, when moodily engaged in resolving to acquaint you of my
great love, and undying desire to place you upon the highest pinnacle possible of praise and purity within my power to bestow!

"I was led to believe that your unbounded joy and happiness
were never at such a par as when sharing them with me. Was I
falsely informed of your ways and worth? Was I duped to ascend
the ladder of liberty, the hill of harmony, the tree of triumph,
and the rock of regard, and when wildly manifesting my act of
ascension, was I to be informed of treading still in the valley of
defeat?

"Am I, who for nearly forty years was idolised by a mother of
untainted and great Christian bearing, to be treated now like a
slave? Why and for what am I thus dealt with? . . .

"Can it be that your attention has ever been, or is still, attracted by another, who, by some artifice or other, had the audac-
ity to steal your desire for me and hide it beneath his pillaged
pillow of poverty, there to conceal it until demanded with my
ransom?

"Speak! Irene! Wife! Woman! Do not sit in silence and allow
the blood that now boils in my veins to ooze through cavities of
unrestrained passion and trickle down to drench me with its
crimson hue! . . ."

[Irene] began now to stare her position fully in the face. On
this interview, she thought, largely depended her future welfare,
if viewed properly. Should she make her husband cognisant of her
inward feelings, matters were sure to end very unsatisfactorily.
These she kept barred against his entrance in the past, and she
was fully determined should remain so now, until forced from
their home of refuge by spirited action. . . .

"Sir and husband," she said, with great nervousness at first, "you have summoned me hither to lash your rebuke unmercifully upon me, provoked, it may be, by underhand intercourse. You accordingly, in the course of your remarks, fail not to tamper with a character which as yet defies your scathing criticism. Only this week have I been made the recipient of news concerning my deceased parents, of whom I never before obtained the slightest clue, and armed with equality, I am in a position fit to treat some of your stingy remarks with the scorn they merit.

"You may not already be aware of the fact that I, whom you insinuate you wrested from beggary, am the only child of the late Colonel Iddesleigh, who fell a victim to a gunshot wound inflicted by the hand of his wife, who had fallen into the pit of intemperance. Yes, Earl Peden's daughter was his wife and my mother, and only that this vice so actuated her movements, I might still have lent to Society the object it dare not now claim, and thereby would have shunned the iron rule of being bound down to exist for months at a time within such a small space of the world's great bed. . . .

"Relative to my affections, pray have those courted by me in the past aught to do with the present existing state of affairs? I am fully persuaded to answer 'Nothing whatever.'

"You speak of your snowy tufts appearing where once there dwelt locks of glossy jet. Well, I am convinced they never originated through me, and must surely have been threatening to appear before taking the step which links me with their origin.

"I now wish to retire, feeling greatly fatigued, and trusting our relations shall remain friendly and mutual, I bid thee goodnight."

A M A N D A   M ' K I T T R I C K   R O S , *Irene Iddesleigh*

At Bickley Hall, taken down a few years ago, used to be shown the room where the body of the Earl of Leicester was laid for a whole twelvemonth—1659 to 1660—he having been kept unburied all that time, owing to a dispute which of his heirs should pay his funeral expenses.

[An Englishman] used a queer expression in reference to the drowning of two college men; he said it was an "awkward" affair. I think this is equal to Longfellow's story of the Frenchman, who avowed himself very much "displeased" at the news of his father's death.

Mr. [Monckton] Milnes told me that he owns the land, in Yorkshire, whence some of the pilgrims of the Mayflower emigrated to Plymouth; and that Elder Brewster was the postmaster of the village. . . . He also said that, in the next voyage of the Mayflower, after she carried the pilgrims, she was employed in transporting a cargo of slaves from Africa. . . .

NATHANIEL HAWTHORNE, *The English Notebooks*

The Middle Ages

✠ I am not at all well read in the Middle Ages, but I have always dipped into them in one way or another. For me their great appeal rests on a certain eerie remoteness and kind of blur, on an unlikeness to what I am familiar with: they are the Dark Ages, possessing a romantic aura. But what I also particularly respond to is what appears of a sudden in a clear, distinct light—a scene or a sentence that is wholly familiar and domestic, realistic and recognizable. I can "connect," or think I connect, with classical Greece and Rome as true civilizations: I can walk their streets, I can spiritually speak their language, I can conceive of living their lives. But the Middle Ages are, for me, all mist or magnificence—vile hovels or Gothic cathedrals, wolf-infested forests or Crusader castles. And then I stumble on something that, though the language may be stilted or strange, brings me into the presence of people I can see and almost touch and understand; can watch them eat, hear them argue, come to know the games they play, the rules they go by, the things they laugh at, the ways they make love. It is, as I say, wonderfully realistic—not quite real—like something well mounted and well acted on the stage, with slightly heightened stage lighting. They really *did* do these things, I'm inclined to assure myself; but not, Why they're exactly like us!

This, though not very important, is what brings me into some kind of rapport with the Middle Ages, just as the Middle Ages themselves, with their mysticism and their miracles, their superstitions and "voices" and conflict of dialects, do not. This is true in part, I think, because most of us don't take the Dark Ages in stride, as part of our education, don't grow up with them as we do with Greece or Rome or, somewhat later, with the Renaissance and the Enlightenment. They are a chasm between the ancient world and the modern, and they are a chaos of ill-lighted scenes, dreamlike images, and haunting murmurations. We may know an eleventh-century church from a fourteenth-century one, but can we distinguish an eleventh-century man from a fourteenth-century man? I like the atmosphere of chasm and chaos, it is poetic and religious; I like being baffled by the "layout" of those centuries: it has a kind of magic, with its Queen Matildas and Queen Eleanors, its tourneys and pageants and feasts, its dark conspiracies and splendid chivalries, its gruesome murders and gorgeous coronations. But the Roger Bacons and the scholars at Oxford or Bologna seem isolated in their enlightenment, not at all like the Francis Bacons and sophisticated scholar-courtiers of the Renaissance. With their contrasting appeal, the Middle Ages have for me a true fascination: I am drawn to them by something mysterious and impenetrable, and I am delighted when they emerge into the light, into everyday practices and commonplace relationships.

Doctoring in the Twelfth Century

The [Arab] lord of al-Munaytirah wrote to my uncle asking him to dispatch a physician to treat certain sick persons among his people. My uncle sent him a Christian physician named Thabit.

Thabit was absent but ten days when he returned. So we said to him: "How quickly hast thou healed thy patients!"

He said: "They brought before me a knight in whose leg an abscess had grown; and a woman afflicted with imbecility. To the knight I applied a small poultice until the abscess opened and became well; and the woman I put on diet and made her humor wet. Then a Frankish physician came to them and said, 'This man knows nothing about treating them.' He then said to the knight, 'Which wouldst thou prefer, living with one leg or dying with two?' The latter replied, 'Living with one leg.' The physician said, 'Bring me a strong knight and a sharp ax.' A knight came with the ax. And I was standing by. Then the physician laid the leg of the patient on a block of wood and bade the knight strike his leg with the ax and chop it off at one blow. Accordingly he struck it—while I was looking on—one blow, but the leg was not severed. He dealt another blow, upon which the marrow of the leg flowed out and the patient died on the spot. He then examined the woman and said, 'This is a woman in whose head there is a devil which has possessed her. Shave off her hair.' Accordingly they shaved it off and the woman began once more to eat their ordinary diet—garlic and mustard. Her imbecility took a turn for the worse. The physician then said, 'The devil has penetrated through her head.' He therefore took a razor, made a deep cruciform incision on it, peeled off the skin at the middle of the incision until the bone of the skull was exposed, and rubbed it with salt. The woman also expired instantly. Thereupon I asked them whether my services were needed any longer, and when they replied in the negative I returned home, having learned of their medicine what I knew not before."

Memoirs of Usamah

(trans. Philip K. Hitti)

Chatting and Resting in the Twelfth Century

The Franks are void of all zeal and jealousy. One of them may be walking along with his wife. He meets another man who takes the wife by the hand and steps aside to converse with her while the husband is standing on one side waiting for his wife to conclude the conversation. If she lingers too long for him, he leaves her alone with the conversant and goes away. . . . One day [a] Frank went home and found a man with his wife in the same bed. He asked him, "What could have made thee enter into my wife's room?" The man replied, "I was tired, so I went in to rest." "But how," asked he, "didst thou get into my bed?" The other replied, "I found a bed that was spread, so I slept in it." "But," said he, "my wife was sleeping together with thee!" The other replied, "Well, the bed is hers. How could I therefore have prevented her from using her own bed?" "By the truth of my religion," said the husband, "if thou shouldst do it again, thou and I would have a quarrel." Such was for the Frank the entire expression of his disapproval and the limit of his jealousy.

Memoirs of Usamah

(trans. Philip K. Hitti)

Loving in the Twelfth Century

Love is a certain inborn suffering derived from the sight of and excessive meditation upon the beauty of the opposite sex, which causes each one to wish above all things the embraces of the other. . . .

[Some of the Rules:]

Marriage is no real excuse for not loving.
He who is not jealous cannot love.
It is well known that love is always increasing or decreasing.
When one lover dies, a widowhood of two years is required of the survivor.
No one should be deprived of love without the very best of reasons.
Love is always a stranger in the home of avarice.

It is not proper to love any woman whom one would be
ashamed to seek to marry.

When made public, love rarely endures.

Every lover regularly turns pale in the presence of his beloved.

A man in love is always apprehensive.

Real jealousy always increases the feeling of love.

Jealousy, and therefore love, are increased when one suspects
his beloved.

A lover can never have enough of the solaces of his beloved.

Nothing forbids one woman being loved by two men or one
man by two women.

ANDREAS CAPELLANUS, *The Art of Courtly Love*

(trans. John Jay Parry)

Valeting in the Fifteenth Century

In the morning, against your lord shall rise, take care that his
linen be clean, and warm it at a clear fire, not smoky, if [the
weather] be cold or freezing.

When he rises make ready the foot-sheet, and forget not to
place a chair or some other seat with a cushion on it before the
fire, with another cushion for the feet. Over the cushion and chair
spread this sheet so as to cover them; and see that you have a
kerchief and a comb to comb your lord's head before he is fully
dressed.

Then pray your lord in humble words to come to a good fire,
and array him thereby . . . First hold out to him his tunic, then
his doublet while he puts in his arms, and have his stomacher well
aired to keep off harm, also his vamps [short stockings] and socks,
and so shall he go warm all day. . . .

If your lord wishes to bathe and wash his body clean, hang
sheets round the roof, every one full of flowers and sweet green
herbs, and have five or six sponges to sit or lean upon, and see
that you have one big sponge to sit upon, and a sheet over so that
he may bathe there for a while, and have a sponge also for under
his feet, if there be any to spare, and always be careful that the

door is shut. Have a basin full of hot fresh herbs and wash his body with a soft sponge, rinse him with fair warm rose-water, and throw it over him; then let him go to bed; but see that the bed be sweet and nice; and first put on his socks and slippers that he may go near the fire and stand on his foot-sheet, wipe him dry with a clean cloth, and take him to bed to cure his troubles.

J O H N R U S S E L L, *Book of Nurture*

(trans. Edith Rickert)

Instructions to the Student

Learn how to entertain at table, to provide food and the sauces that go with the various dishes, and to serve seasonable wine in modest quantity. Once again I touch critically on manners in polite society so that my readers may become more genteel. According to good custom you should place the sauce on the right, the service plate on the left; you should have the servant take the first course to him who sits at the head of the table. Take hold of the base of a goblet so that unsightly finger marks may not show on the side. Polite diners pause over their cup but gluttons, who live like mules and weevils, empty it with one draught. Pour wine properly with both hands so as not to spill any. Always serve two pieces of bread. Have several well dressed servants in readiness to bring clean towels and to supply the wants of the guests. Lest I should seem to be in charge of the cooks like Nebuzaradan, I shall not go into the art of preparing fine dishes. Carve the meats which are not to be served in the broth, and skilfully take off the wings of fowl while they are hot. He who takes a walk or a brief nap after dinner preserves his health. If you wish to regain your strength as a convalescent, and keep your health when you are well, drink moderately. All Epicureans live impure lives; they lose their eyesight, they are rude, unclean, and are doomed to die a sudden death.

J O H N O F G A R L A N D, *Morale Scolarium* (thirteenth century)

(trans. L. J. Paetow)

✠ This has a certain piquancy from seeming, after seven centuries, rather modern in both its atmosphere and applicability; one wonders just what the Latin for "service plate" or even "broth" may be. The introduction of towels rather than napkins helps restore the balance, however—not to speak of the fate of Epicureans, which by no means confronts their current counterparts, the wine-and-food zealots.

In the month of March, about Mid-Lent, the king came to London with his son Henry and the Lord Uguccione, Legate of the Pope, who purposed to call together the clergy of England and hold a Council. When therefore the Papal Legate had taken his seat on a raised throne in the midst, and Richard Archbishop of Canterbury, by right of his primacy, had sat down on his right, then Roger Archbishop of York, puffed up with his own innate arrogance to reject the left-hand throne that was destined for him, strove irreverently to sit down between the Legate and his Grace of Canterbury, thrusting with the more uncomely quarters of his body so that he sat down upon the lap of his own Primate. Yet scarce had he struck my lord of Canterbury with that elbow of his wherewith he had been accustomed to fight, when he was ignominiously seized by certain bishops, clerics, and laymen, and torn from the Archbishop's lap, and cast upon the floor.

The Chronicle of Gervase

I have heard of one man who, wishing to do penance, even as he had likened himself to the beasts in sin, so he would make himself like to a beast in his food; wherefore he rose up at dawn and browsed on grass without touching it with his hands; and thus he would oftentimes eat daily. When therefore he had long lived thus, he began to ponder within himself, wondering of what Order of Angels he should be, seeing that he had done so great a penance; until at length it was answered to him through an angel: "By such a life thou hast not deserved to be of the Order of Angels, but rather of the Order of Asses."

I have heard how certain folk promise much to God, binding themselves by vows which they afterwards violate to the detriment of their souls, and seeking to mock Him with deceit. Such were a man and his wife who vowed to God that they would not drink wine save on solemn feast-days or when they had chanced to make a bargain. When therefore they had drunk water for a few days, then the man began to say to his wife: "We cannot abstain altogether today; let us make a bargain, that we may drink wine." So he sold his ass to the wife. Next day the wife said to her good man, "Buy back thine ass, and let us drink wine." Thus they bargained daily, that they might drink wine.

This fraud is committed by many. Such was the man who had vowed that he would eat no flesh save when he had guests; wherefore he invited guests for every day whereon men are wont to eat flesh. Such also are certain monks who, being forbidden to eat any flesh save hunted game, set hounds to chase their own home-bred swine through the monastery after the fashion of a hunting party . . .

JACQUES DE VITRY, *Exempla*

An Attempt to Enforce Clerical Celibacy

Geoffrey, the archbishop, having returned to Rouen from attending the council at Reims, held a synod in the third week of November, and stirred up by the late papal decrees, dealt sharply and rigorously with the priests of his diocese. Among other canons of the council which he promulgated was that which interdicted them from commerce with females of any description, and against such transgressors he launched the terrible sentence of excommunication. As the priests shrunk from submitting to this grievous burden, and in loud mutterings among themselves vented their complaints of the struggle between the flesh and the spirit to which they were subjected, the archbishop ordered one Albert, a man free of speech, who had used some offensive words, I know not what, to be arrested on the spot, and he was presently thrust into the common prison.

This prelate was a Breton and guilty of many indiscretions, warm and obstinate in temper, and severe in his aspect and manner, harsh in his censures, and, withal, indiscreet and a great talker. The other priests, witnessing this extraordinary proceeding, were utterly confounded; and when they saw that, without being charged with any crime or undergoing any legal examination, a priest was dragged, like a thief, from a church to a dungeon, they became so exceedingly terrified that they knew not how to act, doubting whether they had best defend themselves or take to flight. Meanwhile, the archbishop rose from his seat in a violent rage, and hastily leaving the synod, summoned his guards, whom he had already posted outside, with instructions what they were to do. The archbishop's retainers then rushed into the church with arms and staves, and began to lay about them, without respect of persons, on the assembled clergy, who were conversing together. Some of these ecclesiastics ran to their lodgings through the muddy streets of the city, though they were robed in their albs; others snatched up some rails and stones which they chanced to find, and stood on their defence; whereupon their cowardly assailants betook themselves to flight and sought refuge in the sacristy, followed closely by the indignant clergy. The archbishop's people, ashamed of having been discomfited by an unarmed, tonsured band, summoned to their aid, in the extremity of their fury, all the cooks, bakers, and scullions they could muster in the neighbourhood, and had the effrontery to renew the conflict within the sacred precincts. All whom they found in the church or cemetery, whether engaged in the broil or innocently looking on, they beat and cuffed, or inflicted on them some other bodily injury.

Then Hugh of Longueville and Ansquetil of Cropus, and some other ecclesiastics of advanced age and great piety, happened to be in the church, conversing together on confession and other profitable subjects, or reciting, as was their duty, the service of the hours to the praise of God. The archbishop's domestics were mad enough to fall on these priests, treated them shamefully, and so outrageously, that they hardly restrained themselves from taking their lives, though they asked for mercy on their bended knees. These old priests, being at length dismissed, made their escape from the city as soon as they could, together with their friends who had before fled, without stopping to receive the bishop's license and benediction. They carried the sorrowful tidings to their parishioners and concubines, and, to prove the truth of their reports, exhibited the wounds and livid bruises on their persons. The archdeacons, and canons, and all quiet citizens, were afflicted at this cruel onslaught, and compassionated with the servants of God who had suffered such unheard-of-insults. Thus the blood of her priests was shed in the very bosom of Holy Mother Church, and the holy synod was converted into a scene of riot and mockery.

The archbishop, overwhelmed with consternation, retired to his private apartments, where he concealed himself during the uproar, but shortly afterwards, when the ecclesiastics had betaken themselves to flight, as we have already related, his wrath subsided, and going to the church, he put on his stole, and sprinkling holy water, reconciled the church which he had polluted and his sorrowing canons.

ORDERIC VITALIS, *Ecclesiastical History*

A Picture of a Tyrant

Sigismondo, of the noble family of the Malatesta but illegitimate, was very vigorous in body and mind, eloquent, and gifted with great military ability. He had a thorough knowledge of history and no slight acquaintance with philosophy. Whatever he attempted he seemed born for, but the evil part of his character had the upper hand. He was such a slave to avarice that he was ready not only to plunder but to steal. His lust was so unbridled that he violated his daughters and his sons-in-law. When he was a lad he often played the bride and after taking the woman's part debauched men. No marriage was sacred to him. He ravished nuns and outraged Jewesses; boys and girls who would not submit to him he had murdered or savagely beaten. He committed adultery with many women to whose children he had been godfather and murdered their husbands. He outdid all barbarians in cruelty. His bloody hand inflicted terrible punishments on innocent and guilty alike. He oppressed the poor, plundered the rich, spared neither widows nor orphans. No one felt safe under his rule. Wealth or a beautiful wife or handsome children were enough to cause a man to be accused of crime. He hated priests and despised religion. He had no belief in another world and thought the soul died with the body. Nevertheless he built at Rimini a splendid church dedicated to St. Francis, though he filled it so full of pagan works of art that it seemed less a Christian sanctuary than a temple of heathen devil-worshippers. In it he erected for his mistress a tomb of magnificent marble and exquisite workmanship with an inscription in the pagan style as follows, "Sacred to the deified Isotta." The two wives he had married before he took Isotta for his mistress he killed one after the other with the sword or poison. The third, whom he married before these, he divorced before he had intercourse with her, but kept her dowry. Meeting not far from Verona a noble lady who was going from Germany to Rome in the jubilee year, he assaulted her (for she was very beautiful) and when she struggled left her wounded and covered with blood. Truth was seldom in his mouth. He was a past master of simulation and dissimulation. He showed himself a perjuror and traitor to Alfonso, king of Sicily, and his son Ferrante. He broke his word to Francesco, duke of Milan, to the Venetians, the Florentines and the Sienese. Repeatedly too he tricked the Church of Rome. Finally when there was no one left in Italy for him to betray, he went on to the French, who allied themselves with him out of hatred for Pope Pius but fared no better than the other princes. When his subjects once begged him to retire at last to a peaceful life and spare his country, which had so often been exposed to pillage on his account, he replied, "Go and be of good courage; never while I live shall you have peace."

Such was Sigismondo, intolerant of peace, a devotee of pleasure, able to endure any hardship, and greedy for war. Of all men who have ever lived or ever will live he was the worst scoundrel, the disgrace of Italy and the infamy of our times.

The Commentaries of Pius II

The Character and Customs of the Irish

I have considered it not superfluous to give a short account of the condition of this nation, both bodily and mentally; I mean their state of cultivation, both interior and exterior. This people are not tenderly nursed from their birth, as others are; for besides the rude fare they receive from their parents, which is only just sufficient for their sustenance, as to the rest, almost all is left to nature. They are not placed in cradles, or swathed, nor are their tender limbs either fomented by constant bathings, or adjusted with art. For the midwives make no use of warm water, nor raise their noses, nor depress the face, nor stretch the legs; but nature alone, with very slight aids from art, disposes and adjusts the limbs to which she has given birth, just as she pleases. As if to prove that what she is able to form she does not cease to shape also, she gives growth and proportions to these people, until they arrive at perfect vigour, tall and handsome in person, and with agreeable and ruddy countenances. But although they are richly endowed with the gifts of nature, their want of civilization, shown both in their dress and mental culture, makes them a barbarous people. For they wear but little woollen, and nearly all they use is black, that being the colour of the sheep in this country. Their clothes are also made after a barbarous fashion.

Their custom is to wear small, close-fitting hoods, hanging below the shoulders a cubit's length, and generally made of particoloured strips sewn together. Under these, they use woollen rugs instead of cloaks, with breeches and hose of one piece, or hose and breeches joined together, which are usually dyed of some colour. Likewise, in riding, they neither use saddles, nor boots, nor spurs, but only carry a rod in their hand, having a crook at the upper end, with which they both urge forward and guide their horses.

They use reins which serve the purpose both of a bridle and a bit, and do not prevent the horses from feeding, as they always live on grass. Moreover, they go to battle without armour, considering it a burthen and esteeming it brave and honourable to fight without it. . . .

The Irish are a rude people, subsisting on the produce of their cattle only, and living themselves like beasts—a people that has not yet departed from the primitive habits of pastoral life. In the common course of things, mankind progresses from the forest to the field, from the field to the town, and to the social condition of citizens; but this nation, holding agricultural labour in contempt, and little coveting the wealth of towns, as well as being exceedingly averse to civil institutions, lead the same life their fathers did in the woods and open pastures, neither willing to abandon their old habits nor learn anything new. They, therefore, only make patches of tillage; their pastures are short of herbage; cultivation is very rare, and there is scarcely any land sown. This want of tilled fields arises from the neglect of those who should cultivate them; for there are large tracts which are naturally fertile and productive. The whole habits of the people are contrary to agricultural pursuits, so that the rich glebe is barren for want of husbandmen, the fields demanding labour which is not forthcoming.

Very few sorts of fruit trees are found in this country, a defect arising not from the nature of the soil, but from want of industry in planting them; for the lazy husbandman does not take the trouble to plant the foreign sorts which would grow very well here. . . .

This people, then, is truly barbarous, being not only barbarous in their dress, but suffering their hair and beards (*barbis*) to grow enormously in an uncouth manner, just like the modern fashion recently introduced; indeed, all their habits are barbarisms. But habits are formed by mutual intercourse; and as this people inhabit a country so remote from the rest of the world, and lying at its farthest extremity, forming, as is were, another world, and are thus secluded from civilized nations, they learn nothing, and practise nothing but the barbarism in which they are born and bred, and which sticks to them like a second nature. Whatever natural gifts they possess are excellent, in whatever requires industry they are worthless. . . .

The faith having been planted in the island from the time of St. Patrick, so many ages ago, and propagated almost ever since, it is wonderful that this nation should remain to this day so very ignorant of the rudiments of Christianity. It is indeed a most filthy race, a race sunk in vice, a race more ignorant than all other nations of the first principles of the faith. Hitherto they neither pay tithes nor first fruits; they do not contract marriages, nor shun incestuous connections; they frequent not the church of God with proper reverence. Nay, what is most detestable, and not only contrary to the gospel, but to everything that is right, in many parts of Ireland brothers (I will not say marry) seduce and debauch the wives of their brothers deceased, and have incestuous intercourse with them; adhering in this to the letter, and not to the spirit, of the Old Testament; and following the example of men of old in their vices more willingly than in their virtues.

They are given to treachery more than any other nation, and never keep the faith they have pledged, neither shame nor fear withholding them from constantly violating the most solemn obligations, which, when entered into with themselves, they are above all things anxious to have observed. So that, when you have used the utmost precaution, when you have been most vigilant, for your own security and safety, by requiring oaths and hostages, by treaties of alliance firmly made, and by benefits of all kinds conferred, then begins your time to fear; for then especially their treachery is awake, when they suppose that, relying on the fulness of your security, you are off your guard. That is the moment for them to fly to their citadel of wickedness, turn against you their weapons of deceit, and endeavour to do you injury, by taking the opportunity of catching you unawares. . . .

It must be observed also, that the men who enjoy ecclesiastical immunity, and are called ecclesiastical men, although they be laics, and have wives, and wear long hair hanging down below

their shoulders, but only do not bear arms, wear for their protec-
tion, by authority of the pope, fillets on the crown of their heads,
as a mark of distinction. Moreover, these people, who have cus-
toms so very different from others, and so opposite to them, on
making signs either with the hands or the head, beckon when
they mean that you should go away, and nod backward as often
as they wish to be rid of you. Likewise, in this nation, the men pass
their water sitting, the woman standing. They are also prone to
the failing of jealousy beyond any other nation. The women, also,
as well as the men, ride astride, with their legs stuck out on each
side of the horse.

We come now to the clerical order. The clergy, then, of this
country are commendable enough for their piety; and among
many other virtues in which they excel, are especially eminent for
that of continence. They also perform with great regularity the
services of the psalms, hours, lessons, and prayers, and, confining
themselves to the precincts of the churches, employ their whole
time in the offices to which they are appointed. They also pay due
attention to the rules of abstinence and a spare diet, the greatest
part of them fasting almost every day till dusk, when by singing
complines they have finished the offices of the several hours for
the day. Would that after these long fasts, they were as sober as
they are serious, as true as they are severe, as pure as they are
enduring, such in reality as they are in appearance. But among so
many thousands you will scarcely find one who, after his devotion to long fastings and prayers, does not make up by night for
his privations during the day by the enormous quantities of wine
and other liquors in which he indulges more than is becoming.

Dividing the day of twenty-four hours into two equal parts, they
devote the hours of light to spiritual offices, and those of night to
the flesh; so that in the light they apply themselves to the works of
the light, and in the dark they turn to the works of darkness.
Hence it may be considered almost a miracle, that where wine has
the dominion lust does not reign also. This appears to have been
thought difficult by St. Jerome; still more so by the apostle; one of
whom forbids men to be drunken with wine, wherein there is

excess: the other teaches that the belly, when it is inflamed by drink, easily vents itself in lust.

There are, however, some among the clergy who are most excellent men, and have no leaven of impurity. Indeed this people are intemperate in all their actions, and most vehement in all their feelings. Thus the bad are bad indeed—there are nowhere worse; and than the good you cannot find better. But there is not much wheat among the oats and the tares. Many, you find, are called, but few chosen: there is very little grain, but much chaff.

GIRALDUS CAMBRENSIS, *Topography of Ireland*

The Vision of Viands

In a slumber visional,
Wonders apparitional
    Sudden shone on me:
Was it not a miracle?
Built of lard, a coracle
    Swam a sweet milk sea.

With high hearts heroical,
We stepped in it, stoical,
    Braving billow-bounds;
Then we rode so dashingly,
Smote the sea so splashingly,
That the surge sent, washingly,
    Honey up for grounds.

Ramparts rose of custard all
Where a castle muster'd all
    Forces o'er the lake;
Butter was the bridge of it,
Wheaten meal the ridge of it,
    Bacon every stake.

Strong it stood, and pleasantly
There I entered presently
   Hying to the hosts;
Dry beef was the door of it,
Bare bread was the floor of it,
   Whey-curds were the posts.

Old cheese-columns happily,
Pork that pillared sappily,
   Raised their heads aloof;
While curd-rafters mellowly
Crossing cream-beams yellowly,
   Held aloft the roof.

Wine in well rose sparklingly,
Beer was rolling darklingly,
   Bragget brimmed the pond.
Lard was oozing heavily,
Merry malt moved wavily,
   Through the floor beyond.

Lake of broth lay spicily,
Fat froze o'er it icily,
   'Tween the wall and shore;
Butter rose in hedges high,
Cloaking all its edges high
   White lard blossomed o'er.

Apple alleys bowering,
Pink-topped orchards flowering,
   Fenced off hill and wind;
Leek-tree forests loftily,
Carrots branching tuftily,
   Guarded it behind.

Ruddy warders rosily
Welcomed us right cosily
  To the fire and rest;
Seven coils of sausages,
Twined in twisted passages,
  Round each brawny breast.

Their chief I discover him,
Suet mantle over him,
  By his lady bland;
Where the cauldron boiled away,
The Dispenser toiled away,
  With his fork in hand.

Good King Cathal, royally,
Surely will enjoy a lay,
  Fair and fine as silk;
From his heart his woe I call,
When I sing, heroical,
How we rode, so stoical,
  O'er the Sea of Milk.

Aniar MacConglinne

(trans. George Sigerson)

Misquotations

✠ Almost everyone knows about certain misquotations, such as "A little knowledge is a dangerous thing," or "A poor thing, but mine own," or "Alas, poor Yorick, I knew him well," or "Tomorrow to fresh fields and pastures new." But a great many others have hardened into the better-known form with the help of the ages, some in more memorable dress, some with a change of meaning, some with no real difference, some to their detriment. In the many instances where a *the* has been substituted for an *a*, or a present tense for a past one, misquotation might be regarded as the people's right, and as only the pedant's rejection. Other changes, such as "Gather ye roses" for Herrick's "Gather ye rosebuds," are also very minor and in my opinion rather for the better. Again, such changes as "We are such stuff as dreams are made of" for Shakespeare's "made on," are inevitable, the original form being archaic today and merely odd to most people. On the other hand, "Little Latin and less Greek" won't quite do for "Small Latin and less Greek." Conversely, "When Greek meets Greek" has a distinct meaning which "When Greeks joined Greeks" does not suggest, and has a brevity which "When Greeks joined Greeks, then was the tug of war" altogether forfeits. And so on.

Hesketh Pearson once brought out a small book called *Common Misquotations*, for some of which I am very much in his debt; others of them, however, he assigns to a wrong, or at any rate not exclusive, source. Thus "A poet is born, not made" (often phrased "Poets are born, not made") seems to me clearly derived from the famous Latin saying rather than, as Mr. Pearson suggests, from Ben Jonson's "For a good poet's made as well as born." And who will insist that "Not if I know it!" descends from Charles Lamb's "Not if I know myself at all"?—Mr. Pearson must have been rather desperate the day he came up with that. With him, also, one country's misquotation may be another's completely sound one. "To the victors the spoils" may be current coin in England, a country where it was for a long time a cherished sentiment; in the United States I have always heard it "To the victors belong the spoils," which is the correct wording in Senator Marcy's more extensive quotation. Finally, shortened forms of certain quotations are inevitable and justifiable, in the very sense that phrases of this sort are called tags. "There's method in his madness" is both handier and more memorable than "Though this be madness, yet there is method in't"—even though the shorter form has become a cliché.

Herewith a selection of misquotations, some of them "justifiable," accompanied by the correct forms.

If the mountain won't come to Mahomet, Mahomet must go to the mountain.

If the hill will not come to Mahomet, Mahomet will go to the hill.

BACON, *Essays*

He who hesitates is lost.

The woman that deliberates is lost.

JOSEPH ADDISON, *Cato*

There is safety in numbers.

In the multitude of counsellors there is safety.

The Book of Proverbs

Put your house in order.

Set thine house in order.

Isaiah

Birds of a feather flock together.

Birds of a feather will gather together.

ROBERT BURTON, *The Anatomy of Melancholy*

Marriages are made in Heaven.

Matches are made in Heaven.

ROBERT BURTON, *The Anatomy of Melancholy*

There's many a slip 'twixt the cup and the lip.

Many things happen between the cup and the lip.

ROBERT BURTON, *The Anatomy of Melancholy*

Genius is an infinite capacity for taking pains.

Genius . . . means the transcendent capacity of taking trouble.

CARLYLE, *Frederick the Great*

In one ear and out the other.	One eare it heard, at the other out it went. CHAUCER, *Troilus and Criseyde*
Possession is nine points of the law.	Possession is eleven points in the law. COLLEY CIBBER, *Woman's Wit*
A snare and a delusion.	A delusion, a mockery, and a snare. LORD DENMAN, *O'Connell v. the Queen*
Accidents will happen in the best-regulated families.	Accidents will occur in the best-regulated families. DICKENS, *David Copperfield*
The even tenor of their way.	The noiseless tenor of their way. THOMAS GRAY, "Elegy Written in a Country Churchyard"
Eat your cake and have it too. [This of course is in turn misquoted, and the wit in it mangled, by the many people who say, "Have your cake and eat it too."]	Would yee both eat your cake and have your cake? JOHN HEYWOOD, *Proverbs*

Few die and none resign.

Those [vacancies] by death are few; by resignation, none.

THOMAS JEFFERSON, letter to Elias Shipman and others

There's more in this than meets the eye.

Where more is meant than meets the ear.

MILTON, "Il Penseroso"

Sleep the sleep that knows no waking.

Sleep the sleep that knows not breaking,
Morn of toil nor night of waking.

SIR WALTER SCOTT, *The Lady of the Lake*

Desperate diseases require desperate remedies.

Diseases desperate grown
By desperate appliance are relieved.

SHAKESPEARE, *Hamlet*

Death cancels all debts.

He that dies pays all debts.

SHAKESPEARE, *The Tempest*

Pure as the driven snow.

Far whiter than the driven snow.

WILLIAM SHENSTONE, "The Schoolmistress"

All men have their price. [In the U.S.: Every man has his price.]

All those men have their price.

SIR ROBERT WALPOLE

The light that never was on   The light that never was, on
land or sea.   sea or land.

WORDSWORTH,
"Elegiac Stanzas"

Music

Some to church repair
Not for the doctrine, but the music there.

ALEXANDER POPE

In an opera the poetry must be altogether the obedient daughter
of the music.

MOZART, letter to his father

Whoever studies music, let his daily bread be Haydn. Beethoven
indeed is admirable, he is incomparable, but he has not the same
usefulness as Haydn: he is not a necessity. . . . Haydn the great
musician, the first who created everything, discovered everything,
taught everything to the rest!

INGRES

I prefer late Wagner, as I prefer late Turner, to early (which I
suppose is all wrong in taste), the idiosyncrasies of each master
being more strongly shown in these strains. When a man not contented with the grounds of his success goes on and on, and tries to
achieve the impossible, then he gets profoundly interesting to me.

THOMAS HARDY

What gives Sebastian Bach and Mozart a place apart is that these
two great expressive composers never sacrificed form to expres-

sion. As high as their expression may soar, their musical form remains supreme and all-sufficient.

CAMILLE SAINT-SAËNS, letter to Camille Bellaique

In order to prevent the changes which theatres make in musical works, it is forbidden to insert anything into the above-mentioned score, to make cuts, raise or lower a key, or in general make any alteration which would entail the slightest change in instrumentation, on pain of 1000 francs fine, which I shall demand of you for every theatre where a change is made in the score.

GIUSEPPE VERDI, from a contract with Ricordi Publishers (1847)

In the course of time the distance between sources diminishes. Beethoven, for instance, did not need to study all that Mozart studied; Mozart not all that Handel; Handel not all that Palestrina, because these had already absorbed the knowledge of their predecessors. But there is one source which inexhaustibly provides new ideas—Johann Sebastian Bach.

ROBERT SCHUMANN

Only one man knew how to compose quasi-improvised music, or at least what seems such. That is Chopin. Here is a charming personality, strange, unique, inimitable.

GEORGES BIZET

Strauss remembers; Beethoven dreams.

CHARLES IVES, *Essays before a Sonata*

Two things will always be wanting at the [Paris] Opéra—rhythm and enthusiasm. They may do many things well, but they will never exhibit the fire that transports and carries one away, or at any rate not until they teach singing better at the Conservatoire . . . But it is also a little the fault of you French, putting stumbling blocks in the way of your artists with your *bon goût, comme il faut,* etc. You should leave the arts in complete liberty and tolerate defects in matters of inspiration. If you terrify the man of genius with your wretched measured criticism, he will never let himself go, and you will rob him of his naturalness and enthusiasm.

G I U S E P P E   V E R D I, letter to Léon Escudier

Our music differs from German music. Their symphonies can live in halls; their chamber music can live in the home. Our music, I say, resides principally in the theatre.

G I U S E P P E   V E R D I

How good bad music and bad reasons sound when one marches against an enemy!

N I E T Z S C H E

I cannot possibly be offended by your article in *Perseveranza* on *La Forza del Destino.* If you felt obliged, amid much praise, to add a little blame, this was wholly within your rights and you did well so to write. You must know, in any case, that I never complain of attacks, any more than I send thanks (perhaps there I am wrong) for favorable reviews. I love my own independence in all things, and I respect it in others. . . . Don't think that when I speak of my *extreme ignorance of music* I am pretending. It is the simple truth. In my house there is hardly any music to be seen; I have never stepped into a music library, nor gone to a publisher's to read a piece. I have kept up with the best contemporary operas, not by study, but by hearing them occasionally at the theatre. . . . I repeat to you that of all composers, past or present, I am the least erudite. . . . When I refer to *erudition* I do not mean musical *knowledge.* I should be lying if I pretended that in my youth I did not study long and hard. That is why I now have a hand strong enough to shape sound as I like, and sure enough to obtain, usually, the effects that I imagine. And when I write something contrary to the rules, that is because the strict rule does no give me what I want, and because I do not really believe that the rules . . . are all good.

G I U S E P P E   V E R D I, letter to Filippo Filippi

I shall never be able to say . . . "What a chorus! What an orchestra! This theatre ranks first in the whole world!" It sticks in my throat. Again and again I have heard people say one after another in Milan . . . : La Scala is the first theatre in the world. In Naples: the San Carlo is the first theatre in the world. In Venice it was: La Fenice is the first theatre in the world. In Petersburg: the first theatre in the world. In Vienna: the first theatre in the world (and that I would say too). And in Paris: the Opéra is the first theatre in two or three worlds.

G I U S E P P E   V E R D I, *Letters*

If an inhabitant of another planet should visit the earth, he would receive, on the whole, a truer notion of human life by attending an Italian opera than he would by reading Emerson's volumes. He would learn from the Italian opera that there were two sexes . . .

J O H N   J A Y   C H A P M A N, *Emerson and Other Essays*

As I looked at a portrait of Wagner, I wondered how a head which looks like that of a stingy landlord could ever have produced *Siegfried*.

J U L I E N   G R E E N, *Journal*

I do not know the Beethoven Choral Symphony "according to Wagner"; the only one I know is "according to Beethoven" and that is enough for me. . . . As a matter of principle, much as one may admire and even if one were another Beethoven . . . I do not agree that anyone has the right to correct the masters. We don't redraw or repaint Raphael and Leonardo da Vinci. . . .

But to return to the particular example of the Choral Sym-

phony, I can't see at all what this presumption of changing the
text is based on. First of all, as regards the purely instrumental
part of the work . . . Beethoven had such profound knowledge
and prodigious mastery of orchestral resources, of the tone color
and qualities of the different instruments, that I cannot understand how any one could think for a moment of offering him any
advice on this subject. For this we need Monsieur Wagner, who
gives lessons to everybody, to Beethoven just as to Mozart and
Rossini. . . .

Let us remember that it is better to let a great master retain his
own imperfections, if there are any, than to impose our own upon
him.

CHARLES GOUNOD, letter to Oscar Comettant

Berlioz was a poor, sick man who raged at everyone, was bitter
and malicious. He was greatly and subtly gifted. He had a real
feeling for instrumentation, anticipated Wagner in many instrumental effects. . . . He lacked the calm and what I may call the
balance that produce complete works of art. He always went to
extremes, even when he was doing admirable things.

His present successes in Paris are in good part justified and
deserved; but reaction is even more largely responsible. When he
was alive they treated him so miserably! Now he is dead: Ho-
sanna!

GIUSEPPE VERDI, letter to Opprandino Arrivabene

I have the number of *Ars Nova* that you sent me. I have not had
time to read it carefully; but so far as I can see it is one of the
usual screeds that do not discuss, but simply pronounce judgment
with unbelievable intolerance. On the last page I see, among
other things: "If you suppose that music is the expression of feelings of love, grief, etc., give it up. . . . It is not for you!"

And why, pray tell, must I not suppose that music is the expression of love, grief, etc.?

The fellow begins by citing as the *non plus ultra* of music

Bach's Mass, Beethoven's Ninth Symphony, and the Mass of Pope Marcellus. Personally I would not be at all surprised if somebody were to tell me, for instance, that Bach's Mass is a trifle dry; that the Ninth Symphony is badly written at some points, and that among the nine symphonies he prefers certain movements that are not in the Ninth; and that there are even better things in Palestrina than in his Mass of Pope Marcellus. . . .

Anyway, I am not going to argue. . . . But I do know that if the great man of the *Ars Nova* should be born among us, he would abjure much of the past, and disdain the pretentious utopias of the present, which do no more than substitute new faults and conventions for the faults and conventions of other days, clothing intellectual emptiness in baroque garments.

And now, keep well and cheerful, which is much more important to us than *Ars Nova*.

> G I U S E P P E   V E R D I, letter to Opprandino Arrivabene

Dear Schober:

I am ill. I have had nothing to eat or drink for eleven days now, and can only wander feebly and uncertainly between armchair and bed. Rinna is treating me. If I take any food I cannot retain it at all.

So please be so good as to come to my aid in this desperate condition with something to read. I have read Cooper's *Last of the Mohicans, The Spy,* and *The Pioneers.* If by chance you have anything else of his, I beg you to leave it for me at the coffeehouse with Frau von Bogner. My brother, who is conscientiousness itself, will bring it over without fail. Or indeed anything else.

> F R A N Z   S C H U B E R T, letter to Franz von Schober
> (1828, one week before Schubert died)

Toscanini's first rehearsal with the orchestra before the season began [at the Metropolitan Opera House in 1908] was *Götterdämmerung.*

He made a short speech and began the rehearsal with no score before him. To tell the truth, he had been unwilling to introduce himself in this fashion, but I had insisted so much that he, although far from convinced, ended by complying with my request.

The orchestra was very attentive and really admirable. But after a few measures, Toscanini stopped. Addressing the first cellist, he said, "That note should have been B-flat."

"No," replied the musician, "that's not what I have here, nor have I ever had it. In all the years that I have been playing, I have always played the note as A-natural."

"Well," said Toscanini, "you have always committed an error," and, seeing by the face of the musician that he was not convinced, Toscanini added, "It seems to me that I have not convinced you. Would you like to have me get the full orchestra score for verification?"

The cellist answered, "Yes, I'd like to see the full orchestra score."

The score was brought; it was proved that Toscanini was right and the musician wrong. A sensation! The orchestra was conquered. At the end of the rehearsal the men gave Toscanini a tremendous salute. He had won the battle decisively.

GIULIO GATTI-CASAZZA, *Memories of the Opera*

Names

✠ To the question, "What is in a name?" one alternative answer might be, "A good deal of history." Also, in the opinion of modern scholars, a good deal of false philology. In any case, for browsers in this sort of field there is a good deal of enjoyment to be had, and, disregarding linguistic derivations, I have found the oddities and ups and downs of Christian names very good reading, and, running through the Introduction of E. G. Withycombe's *Oxford Dictionary of English Christian*

Names, considerable riches in a little room. Mr. Withycombe starts us way back with a piquant sentence from that very readable if unreliable early seventeenth-century work, Camden's *Remains:* "Every person had in the beginning one only proper name, except the savages of Mount Atlas in Barbary, which were reported to be both nameless and dreamless." Himself beginning with Semitic names, Mr. Withycombe tells us the name might have a connection with the child's birth, as Isaac, i.e. laughter, because "Sarah had laughed when she heard the angel foretell his conception." In Greece "the father chose the name and could change it later at his will." Nicknames in Greece were common, and could supersede the given name: thus Aristocles, named after his grandfather, stands forth as nicknamed by his gymnastic master, Plato. Slaves in Rome had no official names, but took a form of their masters' names followed by *por* (*puer*, boy)—*Marcipor*, for example, or *Quintipor*. In the later periods of the Empire the grander families might collect a whole string of names such as, in fifth-century Gaul, C. Sallius Modestus Apollinaris Sidonius. In early England names occasionally combined the father's *and* the mother's: St. Wulfstan for example had "Æthelstanus" (in the Latin text) for a father, and "Wulfgeua" for a mother. The Norman Conquest virtually killed off Anglo-Saxon names; in a 1313–1314 list of eight hundred names of jurors and bailiffs, the only Old English names encountered are two Edmunds, one Edward, one Hereward, and one Aylwyn. What few old names survived were either saints' names (Edward, Edmund, Hilda, Mildred) or Wessex kings' names (Alfred, Edgar, Ethelbert). Actual Christian names, in the Church sense, were late in coming. William and Robert were the commonest names at the end of the twelfth century, when John appeared just once in fifty times, whereas a hundred years later John turned up once in four. By the seventeenth century John, William, and Thomas accounted, at compulsory registration of baptism, for 62.5 per cent of all men's names; and Elizabeth, Mary, and Anne for 52 per cent of all women's. Long gone were such medieval monikers as Aliena, Celestria, Hodierna, Juvenal, Melodia, and Splendor.

As late as the fifteenth century, two living children of the same parents might have the same Christian name: witness, from a famous family, the two Sir John Pastons who were brothers, and bequests in a will to "Isabel and Isabel my daughters." Pet names, nicknames, and diminutives could in such cases distinguish one sibling from the other, and in general certain names acquired all sorts of variants—Bartholomew, for example, emerging as Bat, Bate, Batty, Bartle, Bartelot, Bartelet, Batcock, Batkin, and Tolly. Into the fifteenth century girls were given men's names, baptized, and called Philip, Nicholas, James, Gilbert, Basil, Eustace, Giles, Edmund, and others; in Scotland, Nicholas was so used late in the seventeenth century. In pre-Reformation days children were often named after the date of their birth, as Christmas, Easter, Pask, Whitsun, Pentecost, or Epiphany; and were sometimes, when it was feared they might not be delivered alive, christened before birth by the midwife with such names as Vitalis and Creature. The Restoration itself became the great disseminator of Biblical names, so much so that the names of nonscriptural saints fell into disgrace and disuse (such names as Austin, Christopher, Denis, Gervase, Hilary, and Quentin almost disappeared). In their stead would soon arise the most famous of odd names, the Puritan ones: such coinages as Given and Love, as Sin-denie, Safe-on-High, and Fear-not, and such combinations as Praise-God Barebones. Some ministers refused to christen children with nonscriptural names like Richard, while others cooperated on such names as Helpless, Forsaken, Sorry-for-Sin, No-merit, and Flie-fornication; and a foundling girl was baptized in 1644 as Misericordia-adulterina. Later generations produced more secular fashions in names: the Romantic revival, and particularly the names in Sir Walter Scott's novels, reintroduced Guy, Roland, Nigel, and the like; Tennyson and the Pre-Raphaelites brought in Lancelot, Hugh, Walter, Ralph, Alice, Mabel, and Edith; and, most recently,

American films have populated England with great numbers of Garys and Shirleys, along with Maureens, Marlenes, Myrnas, and Merles.

Among the many Christian names that have become common words in the language (and eliminating compound words such as Catherine-wheel, Alice blue, Jacob's ladder, and will-o'-the-wisp) are abigail, bertha, bobby, charlotte, derrick, dickey, jack, hector, jenny, jereboam, john, jonah, robin, toby, valentine, and veronica.

The Name of Names

✠ From having a son with that name, I once bought a book called *The John Book*, written by two ladies with names as plush as John is plain: Hallie Erminie Rives and Gabrielle Eliot Forbush. The body of the book deals with the lives and careers of men whose given name, or one of whose given names, is John in one language or another, and the roll call is indeed glorious; inglorious, too, with John Wilkes Booth and the like. What I found more interesting, however, was the roll call of nations, and the equivalent of "John" in each of them. Starting very far back, we learn that the name began, in Hebrew, as Chaanach (though the *Oxford Dictionary of English Christian Names* gives the Hebrew name as *Johanan*, meaning "Jah is gracious"). Some scholars pass from Hebrew to Carthaginian, offering Hanno and Hannibal. The name came to Ireland heavily disguised as Maol-Eoin, but to Scotland as what it has always been since, Ian. We all know the equivalent of John in many European countries—Jean, Juan, Giovanni, Ivan, Hans or Johannes, Jan, Jon. But it is good to know that in Rumanian it is Ioan, in Turkish Ohannes, in Lapland Jofan or Joba, in Norwegian sometimes Jens, in Belgium sometimes Hanka, in modern Greek sometimes Giankos or Joannoulos, in Finland sometimes Juho, and "in the districts of Latvia, Lithuania and

Esthonia" there are thirteen equivalents: Ans, Ants, Ancas, Jonas, Janis, Janke, Jvo, Jvio, Jani, Johanan, Jovan, Jovica, and Jonkultis. *The John Book* cites Evan as an English variation, but surely it is Welsh; and lists Owen with the Scottish names, though I would think it Welsh also (and, according to the Oxford book, actually not of the John family, but supposedly derived from Latin, *Eugenius*).

What is also interesting, though it is something we are well aware of, is how many words and phrases John has given to the language, but most particularly in the form of its leading nickname, Jack. Thus jack the tool, jack the playing card, and jacks the girls' game; meat jack, blackjack, bootjack, jack boots, jackknife, jackscrew, jacksaw, jackpot, spinning jack, jack-o'-lantern, and many, many more. Even in the realm of persons or personifications, for every John Doe or John Bull we have a Jack-tar or a Union Jack (this last supposed to have come about because James I, in whose honor the flag and the phrase originated, signed himself *Jacques*). Which brings up the question doubtless all of us have asked, why should *John* give rise to *Jack*, when *Jacques*, which *Jack* so closely resembles, means *James?* I find in the Oxford book that this was long a puzzling problem, finally solved by a Mr. E. W. B. Nicholson in a little book published in 1892. Nicholson demonstrated that "there is no recorded instance of *Jack, Jak, Jacke* or *Jakke* ever being used to represent *Jacques* or *James*," and that the nickname came about from adding the common suffix *-kin* to *Jan* or the like, producing *Jankin* and then *Jackin*, which got shortened to *Jack*. (So from *Jon* to *Jock* in Scotland, and the process completed by the early 1300s, when *Jack* was a synonym for "man" or "boy.") Moreover, in the *Historia Monasterii S. Augustini Cantuariensis* (circa 1414) there stand revealed, in the midst of much polysyllabic Latin, these words: "ut pro *Thoma, Tomme* seu *Tomlin*, pro *Johanne Jankin* sive *Jacke*."

Just how *John*, the name, gave rise to *john*, a toilet, I can't find explained in any slang dictionaries, or in the great *Dictionary of Americanisms*. Though a genteelism, it has just a touch of something else about it; perhaps some kind reader can shed light. (Here *jack* would be much more likely; cf. *The Metamorphosis of Ajax*, by Sir John Harington, the Elizabethan who invented the water closet.) How *jack* came to mean "money" also interested me, but offers no problem: it meant, in the late seventeenth century, a farthing, and by the nineteenth century, a counter in gambling that looked like a sovereign; the next step is obvious.

Nursery Rhymes

✠ A few of the less well-known ones that I like:

When shall we be married,
Billy my pretty lad?
We'll be married tomorrow
If you think it good.

Shall we be married no sooner,
Billy my pretty lad?
Would you be married tonight?
—I think the girl is mad. . . .

ANON.

Old chairs to mend! Old chairs to mend!
I never would cry old chairs to mend,
If I'd as much money as I could spend,
I never would cry old chairs to mend.

Old clothes to sell! Old clothes to sell!
I never would cry old clothes to sell,
If I'd as much money as I could tell,
I never would cry old clothes to sell.

ANON.

Elsie Marley is grown so fine
She won't get up to feed the swine
But lies in bed till eight or nine,
    Lazy Elsie Marley.

ANON.

There was a rat, for want of stairs
Went down a rope to say his prayers.

ANON.

✠ And the rather famous rather modern rhyme:

Three young rats with black felt hats,
Three young ducks with white straw flats,
Three young dogs with curling tails,
Three young cats with demi-veils
Went out to walk with two young pigs
In satin vests and sorrel wigs.
But suddenly it chanced to rain
And so they all went home again.

ANON

✠ Herewith an old favorite and the two additional stanzas that have been written for it:

There was a little girl and she had a little curl
Right in the middle of her forehead;
When she was good she was very, very good
But when she was bad, she was horrid.

One day she went upstairs while her parents, unawares,
In the kitchen down below were occupied with meals.
And she stood upon her head on her little truckle bed
And she then began hurraying with her heels.

Her mother heard the noise and thought it was the boys
A-playing at a combat in the attic.
But when she climbed the stair, and saw Jemima there
She took and she did whip her most emphatic.

✠ Here an "updated" stanza:

The Queen was in the parlor
   Polishing the grate;
The King was in the kitchen
   Washing up a plate;
The maid was in the garden
   Eating bread and honey,
Listening to the neighbors
   Offering her more money.

✠ And here are a few rhymed riddles:

As round as an apple,
As deep as a cup,
And all the king's horses
Cannot pull it up.
[Answer: A well]

Make three-fourths of a cross,
   And a circle complete,
And let two semi-circles
   On a perpendicular meet.
Next add a triangle
   That stands on two feet;
Next two semi-circles
   And a circle complete.
[Answer: T-O-B-A-C-C-O]

Thirty white horses
Upon a red hill.

Now they tramp,
Now they champ,
Now they stand still.
[Answer: The teeth and gums]

Twelve pears hanging high,
Twelve knights riding by;
Each knight took a pear,
And yet left eleven there.
[Answer: much debated. Perhaps the best is that a knight
    named Eachknight took the pear]

Opinions

Ah Rustick! Ruder than Gothick!

C o n g r e v e, *The Way of the World*

[Shakespeare's] genius was jocular, but when disposed he could
be very serious.

J e r e m y   C o l l i e r, *Historical Dictionary* (1701)

How low and unbecoming a thing laughing is: not to mention
the disagreeable noise that it makes, and the shocking distortion
of the face.

If you love music, hear it; go to operas, concerts, and pay fiddlers
to play to you; but I insist upon your neither piping nor fiddling
yourself. It puts a gentleman in a very frivolous, contemptible
light; brings him into a great deal of bad company . . .

I love *la belle Nature;* Rembrandt paints caricatures.

L o r d   C h e s t e r f i e l d, letters to his son

We were . . . the four last [days] in crossing the Alps. Such uncouth rocks, and such uncomely inhabitants! My dear West, I
hope I shall never see them again!

HORACE WALPOLE, letter to Richard West

The giving up of witchcraft is in effect giving up the Bible.

JOHN WESLEY

A well-educated British gentleman, it may be truly said, is of no
country whatever, he unites in himself the characteristics of all
foreign nations; he talks and dresses French, and sings Italian; he
rivals the Spaniard in indolence, and the German in drinking, his
house is Grecian, his offices Gothic, and his furniture Chinese.

The Lounger (1786)

Convictions are more dangerous enemies of truth than lies.

Moral for psychologists: . . . Never to observe in order to observe! That gives a false perspective, leads to squinting and something forced and exaggerated. Experience as the *wish* to experience does not succeed. One *must* not eye oneself while having an
experience; else the eye becomes "an evil eye." A born psycholo-
gist guards instinctively against seeing in order to see; the same is
true of the born painter.

NIETZSCHE

Painters

How from age to age the art of painting continually declines and
deteriorates when painters have no other standard than work already done.

The painter will produce pictures of little merit if he takes the

works of others as his standard . . . This we see was the case with
the painters who came after the time of the Romans, for they
continually imitated each other, and from age to age their art
steadily declined.

After these came Giotto the Florentine, and he—reared in
mountain solitudes, inhabited only by goats and such like beasts
—turning straight from nature to his art, began to draw on the
rocks the movements of the goats which he was tending, and so
began to draw the figures of all the animals which were to be
found in the country, in such a way that after much study he not
only surpassed the masters of his own time but all those of many
preceding centuries. After him art again declined, because all
were imitating paintings already done; and so for centuries it
continued to decline until such time as Tommaso the Florentine,
nicknamed Masaccio, showed by the perfection of his work how
those who took as their standard anything other than nature, the
supreme guide of all the masters, were wearying themselves in
vain. Similarly I would say about these mathematical subjects,
that those who study only the authorities and not the works of
nature are in art the grandsons and not the sons of nature, which
is the supreme guide of the good authorities.

LEONARDO DA VINCI, *Notebooks*

(trans. Edward MacCurdy)

First bring me Raffael, who alone hath seen
In all her purity Heaven's virgin queen,
Alone hath felt true beauty; bring me then
Titian, ennobler of the noblest men;
And next the sweet Correggio, nor chastise
His little Cupids for those wicked eyes.
I want not Rubens's pink puffy bloom,
Nor Rembrandt's glimmer in a dusty room.
With those, and Poussin's nymph-frequented woods,
His templed heights and long-drawn solitudes

I am content, yet fain would look abroad
On one warm sunset of Ausonian Claude.

WALTER SAVAGE LANDOR

When I sit down to make a sketch from nature, the first thing I try to do is, *to forget that I have ever seen a picture.*

CONSTABLE

What is called "touch" is an abuse of execution . . . Touch, however skilful, should never be apparent; otherwise it hinders illusion and destroys movement. Instead of the object represented, it displays the process; instead of thought, it betrays the hand.

INGRES

The ballet girl is merely a pretext for the design.

DEGAS

I have seen Michael Angelo, although then sixty years old and not in robust health, strike more chips from the hardest marble in a quarter of an hour than would be carried off by three young stone-cutters in three or four times as long; a thing incredible to him who has not seen it. He would approach the marble with such impetuosity, not to say fury, that I often thought the whole work must be dashed to pieces. At one blow he would strike off morsels of three and four inches, yet with such exactitude was each stroke given, that a mere atom more would sometimes have spoiled the whole work.

BLAISE DE VIGENÈRE, *La Suite de Philostrate* (1602)

Imitators always render the defects of their model more conspicuous. Sir George Beaumont, on seeing a large picture by a modern artist, intended to be in the style of Claude, said, "I never could have believed that Claude Lorraine had so many faults, if I had not seen them all collected together on this canvas."

C O N S T A B L E

Speaking to Mr. Whistler, [Degas] said, "My dear friend, you conduct yourself in life just as if you had no talent at all."

G E O R G E   M O O R E, *Impressions and Opinions*

[The painter W. R. Sickert records a comment of Théodore Duret's:] There's one sure method of making peace. You've only got to take the Tsar, the Emperor William, the King of England, the President of the Republic, the King of Italy, and the other kings of belligerent countries, and put them in front of a bad picture. They'll all promptly unite in adoring it. They'll fall into each other's arms, and peace will reign.

[On how they do these things in France:] I myself confess to an agreeable glow on being introduced in Normandy as "the greatest painter in Neuville-lès-Dieppe."

[On painters and newspaper publicity:] The painter-pure retains, unaffected by the deaths of kings and the passing of empires, his profound belief in the impregnable rock of Romeike [the famous English clipping service]. I have seen Whistler spend mornings of precious daylight showing Nocturne after Nocturne to the football correspondent of a Fulham local paper.

We have it on the authority of his son and biographer that [Sir John Everett] Millais had "long held" that a baronetcy was "an encouragement to the pursuit of Art in its highest and noblest form."

A lady I had the honour of knowing used to say, "When I say 'religion,' I mean of course 'Christianity,' and when I say 'Christianity' I mean of course the Church of England." When Millais

said "Art" he meant British Art. And when he said "British Art"
he meant the painting of John Everett Millais.

WALTER RICHARD SICKERT,
A Free House! or The Artist as Craftsman

Pat Phrases

Achilles—Add "fleet of foot": people will think you've read Homer.

Animals—"If only dumb animals could speak! So often more intelligent than men."

Archimedes—On hearing his name, shout "Eureka!" Or else:
"Give me a fulcrum and I will move the world." . . .

Competition—The soul of trade.

Dessert—. . . Virtuous people scorn dessert: "Pastry! Good Lord,
no! I never take it."

Expire—Verb applied exclusively to newspaper subscriptions.

Food—In boarding schools, always "wholesome and plentiful."

Funeral—About the deceased: "To think that I had dinner with
him a week ago." . . .

Hangman—Trade handed down from father to son.

Inventors—All die in the poorhouse. "The wrong man profits by
their genius—it isn't fair."

Jockey Club—. . . Say simply, "The Jockey"—very swank: implies you belong.

Malediction—Always uttered by a father.

Money—Cause of all evil. . . . Politicians call it emoluments; lawyers, retainer; doctors, fee; employees, wages; workmen, pay; servants, perquisites. "Money is not happiness."

Paganini—Never tuned his violin. . . .

Pragmatic Sanction—Nobody knows what it is.

Priests—. . . Sleep with their housekeepers and give them children whom they fob off as their nephews. . . .

Republicans—"The republicans are not all scoundrels, but all scoundrels are republicans."

Science—"A little science takes your religion from you; a great deal brings you back to it."

Sneeze—After saying "God bless you!" start discussing the origin of this custom. "Sneezed": It is clever raillery to say: "Russian and Polish are not spoken, they are sneezed."

Stallion—Always "fiery." A woman is not to know the difference between a stallion and a horse. A young girl must be told it is a larger type of horse.

FLAUBERT, *Dictionary of Accepted Ideas*

(trans. Jacques Barzun)

Pills to Purge Melancholy

No man, being forbidden to do so, shall converse with the wife of another man. But this shall not apply to the wives of actors.

The Code of Manu (ancient India)

Whatever is not nailed down is mine. Whatever I can pry loose is not nailed down.

Ascribed to Collis P. Huntington

Don't trust any Englishman who speaks French with a correct accent.

French proverb

On Salvador Dali's Paintings

On the pale yellow sands
There's a pair of clasped hands
And an eyeball entangled in string,
And a bicycle seat,
And a plate of raw meat,
And a thing that is *almost* a Thing.

LORD BERNERS

The final test of fame is to have a crazy person imagine he is you.

ANON.

In converting Jews to Christians, you raise the price of pork.

SHAKESPEARE, *The Merchant of Venice*

I cannot easily buy a blankbook to write thoughts in; they are commonly ruled for dollars and cents.

THOREAU, "Life without Principle"

It is always consoling to think of suicide: in that way one gets through many a bad night.

NIETZSCHE, *Beyond Good and Evil*

I know a mother-in-law who sleeps with her glasses on, the better to see her son-in-law suffer in her dreams.

ERNEST COQUELIN

[To his other talents, Poet Harding at Oxford] added that of personification; sometimes he walked about with a scythe in his hand as Time; sometimes with an anchor, as Hope. One day I met him with a huge broken brick and some bits of thatch upon the crown of his hat; on my asking him for a solution of this prosopopœia, "Sir," said he, "today is the anniversary of the celebrated Doctor Goldsmith's death, and I am now in the character of his 'Deserted Village.' "

GEORGE COLMAN THE YOUNGER

The fourth Earl of Sandwich not only gave the English language a word for something one can bite into, but was capable of considerable bite himself. Receiving a letter that aroused his contempt, he instantly wrote back: "Sir, your letter is before me, and it will presently be behind me. I remain, Sir, etc."

Paul Louis Courier . . . when assailed by a French professor, quietly remarked: "I fancy he must be vexed. He calls me jacobin, rebel, plagiarist, thief, poisoner, forger, leper, madman, impostor, calumniator, libeller, a horrible, filthy, grimacing ragpicker. I gather what he wants to say: he means that he and I are not of the same opinion.

The Reminiscences and Recollections of Captain [R. H.] Gronow

Once—so said the tradition—[Walter Savage Landor] knocked down a man in the street, was brought before the *delegato,* as the police magistrate was called, and promptly fined one piastre, value about four and sixpence; whereupon he threw a sequin (two piastres) down upon the table and said that it was unnecessary to give him any change, inasmuch as he purposed knocking the man down again as soon as he left the court.

THOMAS ADOLPHUS TROLLOPE, *What I Remember*

Preaching before Charles II and his equally profligate courtiers, [the Rev. Robert South] perceived in the middle of his sermon that sleep had taken possession of his hearers: stopping and changing the tone of his voice, he called thrice to Lord Lauderdale, who, awakened, stood up. "My lord," says South very composedly, "I am sorry to interrupt your repose, but I must beg that you will not snore quite so loud, lest you should awaken His Majesty."

MARK NOBLE

You have very naturally, my dear Lady Ashburton, referred to me for some information respecting St. Anthony. The principal anecdotes related of him are, that he was rather careless of his diet; and that, instead of confining himself to boiled mutton and a little wine and water, he ate of side-dishes, and drank two glasses of sherry, and refused to lead a life of great care and circumspection, such as his constitution required. The consequence was, that his friends were often alarmed at his health; and the medical men of Jerusalem and Jericho were in constant requisition, taking exorbitant fees, and doing him little good.

SYDNEY SMITH, letter to Lady Ashburton

The Queen is most anxious to enlist everyone who can speak or write to join in checking this mad, wicked folly of "Woman's Rights," with all its attendant horrors, on which her poor feeble sex is bent, forgetting every sense of womanly feeling and propriety. It is a subject which makes the Queen so furious that she cannot contain herself. God created men and women different.

Memorandum from Queen Victoria

Être ou ne pas être: telle est la question.
Y a-t-il pour l'âme plus de noblesse à endurer
les coups et les revers d'une injurieuse fortune,
ou à s'armer contre elle pour mettre frein
à une marée de douleurs? Mourir; dormir;
c'est tout. Calmer enfin, dit-on, dans le sommeil
les affreux battements du coeur; quelle conclusion
des maux héréditaires serait plus dévotement
souhaitée? Mourir, dormir; dormir—
rêver peut-être. C'est là le hic! Car, échappés
des liens charnels, si, dans ce sommeil du trépas,
il nous vient des songes . . . halte-là!

ANDRÉ GIDE, translation of *Hamlet*

The children in Holland take pleasure in making
What the children in England take pleasure in breaking.

ANON.

✠ It is told of Demosthenes that in one of his speeches to the crowd, he asked in Greek "Is Æschines [his antagonist] a mercenary or a friend?" but very carefully put the wrong accent on mercenary, pronouncing it mercénary, so that the crowd roared back: "Mércenary!" Whereupon Demosthenes turned and said: "You hear, Æschines, what they say!"

Resolutions When I Come To Be Old

Not to marry a young Woman.
Not to keep young Company unless they really desire it. . . .
Not to be fond of Children.

Not to tell the same Story over and over to the same People.

Not to be covetous. . . .

Not to be influenced by, or give ear to knavish tattling servants, or others.

Not to be too free of advice, nor trouble any but those that
desire it. . . .

Not to talk much, nor of myself.

Not to boast of my former beauty, or strength, or favour with
ladies, &c.

Not to hearken to Flatteries, nor conceive I can be beloved by a
young woman . . .

Not to be positive or opiniative.

Not to set up for observing all these Rules, for fear I should
observe none.

JONATHAN SWIFT

There is one person wiser than Napoleon; *c'est tout le monde.*

TALLEYRAND

Portraits

The real Pepys sends off to his mother the meat that has grown
tainted. He is worried to see his wife's hair falling out. He is in an
ecstasy when his Mrs. Knipp sings "Barbary Allen," and he is as
pleased as Punch when his wife chooses him as her valentine. He
takes a broom to his maids, and he gives them lessons on the lute.
He likes to sing to his neighbors on moonlit nights. He prefers
The Adventures of Five Hours to *Othello, Moor of Venice.* . . .
He lies for a worthless brother; and he does not allow his sister
to eat with the family for fear she will get to thinking that she is
entitled to do so. He sings hymns before he gets out of bed in the
morning. He heartily enjoys a fine dinner to which he has been
invited, but he feels grieved to find he must foot the bill. He takes

home the silver he had planned to present to his godson when he learns that the child is to be named John instead of Samuel. He is mighty proud of an expensive cloak, and he prays God he may be able to pay for it. He dislikes to see a pretty woman eating wafers with her dog. He gives his wife £12 to spend on clothes and himself £55. He is surprised when a history of the famous families of a shire appears without noticing the Pepyses . . . He leaves a Presbyterian sermon after an hour. He likes fish stories, such as tell of Danish fish frozen stiff that leap up and down when brought into a warm room. He likes to see the King play tennis, which he does very well; but he is sickened to hear his skill flattered beyond all bounds. He is not able to enjoy *Henry V* because of a draught on his neck. He is vexed to observe his wife's hair change color in one day. He has trouble with his multiplication-table. In art he is one of the sort who can admire such a picture as Henry VIII in the midst of the four evangelists. He is troubled to be seen sitting in a shilling seat at the theatre by some of his office clerks who are enjoying seats that cost half a crown. He forces his wife into taking dancing lessons, and then he has hard work getting her to leave off. . . . He boxes a boy's ears for upsetting a glass of beer on his papers. He makes his will, leaving his money to his wife but his books to his brother. He fines himself for every kiss over one that he steals from a pretty woman. He knows the ropes with children, and so takes them to see the lions in the Tower. He cannot help carrying his new watch in his hand as he rides in the coach and looking at it to know the hour a hundred times over. Certainly he is catholic in his tastes; he can enjoy the bearded lady and *Macbeth* the same day. Snoring always makes him laugh.—This, not the Secretary of the Admiralty, is the real man.

> ROBERT P. TRISTRAM COFFIN and
> ALEXANDER M. WITHERSPOON, eds.,
> *Seventeenth-Century Prose and Poetry*

Mr. George Harvest, minister of Thames Ditton, was one of the most absent men of his time. . . . In his youth he was contracted to a daughter of the Bishop of London; but on his wedding day, being gudgeon-fishing, he overstayed the canonical hour; and the lady . . . broke off the match. . . . It is said that his maid frequently gave balls to her friends and fellow servants of the neighbourhood, and persuaded her master that the noise he heard was the effect of wind. . . .

One day Lady Onslow, being desirous of knowing the most remarkable planets and constellations, requested Mr. Harvest, on a fine starlight night, to point them out to her, which he undertook to do; but in the midst of his lecture, having occasion to make water, thought that need not interrupt it, and accordingly directing that operation with one hand, went on in his explanation, pointing out the constellations with the other.

The Olio (1796)

Once a week at least I used to go into Bath itself, to dine with my father's old friend Walter Savage Landor, who had been driven away from his Florentine home by his wife's violent temper. Mr. Landor's rooms . . . were entirely covered with pictures, the frames fitting close to one another, leaving not the smallest space of wall visible. One or two of these pictures were real works of art, but as a rule he had bought them at Bath, quite willing to imagine that the little shops of the Bath dealers could be storehouses of Titian, Giorgiones, and Vandycks. The Bath picture-dealers never had such a time; for some years almost all their wares made their way to Mr. Landor's walls. Mr. Landor lived alone with his beautiful white Spitz dog Pomero, which he allowed to do whatever it liked, and frequently to sit in the oddest way on the bald top of his head. He would talk to Pomero by the hour together, poetry, philosophy, whatever he was thinking of, all of it imbued with his own powerful personality, and would often roar with laughter till the whole house seemed to shake. I have never heard a laugh like that of Mr. Landor—"deep-mouthed Boeotian Savage Landor," as Byron called him—such a regular cannonade. He was "the sanest madman and the maddest reasonable man in the world," as Cervantes says of Don Quixote. In the evenings he would sit for hours in impassioned contemplation: in the mornings he wrote incessantly, to fling off sheet after sheet for the *Examiner*, seldom looking them over afterwards. He scarcely ever read, for he only possessed one shelf of books. If any one gave him a volume he mastered it and gave it away, and this he did because he believed that if he knew he was to keep the book and be able to refer to it, he should not be able to absorb its contents so as to retain them. When he left Florence, he had made over all he possessed to his wife, retaining only £200 a year—afterwards increased to £400—for himself, and this sufficed for his simple needs. He never bought any new clothes, and a chimney-sweep would have been ashamed to wear his coat, which was always the same as long as I knew him, though it in no way detracted from his majestic and lion-like appearance. But he was very particular about his little dinners, and it was about these that his violent explosions of passion usually took place. I have seen him take a pheasant up by the legs when it was brought to table and throw it into the back of the fire over the head of the servant in attendance. This was always a failing, and, in later days, I have heard Mr. Browning describe how in his fury at being kept waiting for dinner at Siena, he shouted: "I will not eat it now, I will not eat it if it comes," and when it came, threw it all out of the window.

AUGUSTUS HARE, *The Story of My Life*

Poverty

We see certain sullen animals spread out over the country; they are male and female, dark and leaden-looking, burned by the sun and chained to the earth which they dig and turn over with unconquerable doggedness; they have voices almost articulate, and when they raise themselves on their feet they show human faces, and in truth they are men. They retire at night into their dens, where they live on black bread, water and roots; they save other men the trouble of sowing, toiling and reaping for their livelihood, and thus do not deserve to lack the bread which they themselves have sown.

LA BRUYÈRE, *Les Caractères*

Mr. T., Margaret Place, Gascoign Place, Bethnal Green, is a bootmaker by trade. Is a good hand, and has earned three shillings and sixpence to four shillings and sixpence a day. He was taken ill last Christmas, and went to the London Hospital; was there three months. A week after he had gone Mrs. T. had rheumatic fever, and was taken to Bethnal Green Infirmary, where she remained about three months. Directly after they had been taken ill, their furniture was seized for the three weeks' rent which was owing. Consequently, on becoming convalescent, they were homeless. . . . He then had twopence and she had sixpence, which a nurse had given her. . . . Next day he had a day's work, and got two shillings and sixpence, and on the strength of this they took a furnished room at tenpence per day (payable nightly). His work lasted a few weeks, when he was again taken ill, lost his job, and spent all their money. Pawned a shirt and apron for a shilling; spent that, too. At last pawned their tools for three shillings, which got them a few days' food and lodging. He is now minus tools and cannot work at his own job, and does anything he can. Spent their last twopence on a pen'orth each of tea and sugar.

WILLIAM BOOTH, *In Darkest England and the Way Out* (1890)

Power

✠ Herewith, a superb statement in itself, is the text in which is embedded perhaps the most quoted—or slightly misquoted—pronouncement of modern times:

But in what sense is the Pope not responsible for the constitution by which he established the new tribunal? If we passed a law giving Dufferin [Governor-General of India] powers of that sort, when asked for, we should surely be responsible. No doubt, the responsibility in such a case is shared by those who ask for a thing. But if the thing is criminal, if, for instance, it is a licence to commit adultery, the person who authorises the act shares the guilt of the person who commits it. Now the Liberals think persecution a crime of a worse order than adultery, and the acts done by Ximenes considerably worse than the entertainment of Roman courtesans by Alexander VI. The responsibility exists whether the thing permitted be good or bad. If the thing be criminal, then the authority permitting it bears the guilt. Whether Sixtus is infamous or not depends on our view of persecution and absolutism. Whether he is responsible or not depends simply on the ordinary evidence of history. . . . You say that people in authority are not to be snubbed or sneezed at from our pinnacle of conscious rectitude. I really don't know whether you exempt them because of their rank, or of their success and power, or of their date. The chronological plea may have some little value in a limited sphere of instances. It does not allow of our saying that such a man did not know right from wrong, unless we are able to say that he lived before Columbus, before Copernicus, and could not know right from wrong. . . . Progress in ethics means a constant turning of white into black and burning what one has adored. . . . I cannot accept your canon that we are to judge Pope and King unlike other men, with a favourable presumption that they did no wrong. If there is any presumption it is the other way against the holders of power, increasing as the power increases. Historic responsibility has to make up for the want of legal responsibility. Power tends to corrupt and absolute power corrupts absolutely. Great men are almost always bad men, even when they exercise influence and not authority; still more when you superadd the tendency or the certainty of corruption by authority. There is no worse heresy than that the office sanctifies the holder of it. That is

the point at which the negation of Catholicism and the negation
of Liberalism meet and keep high festival, and the end learns to
justify the means. You would hang a man of no position, like
Ravaillac; but if what one hears is true, then Elizabeth asked the
gaoler to murder Mary, and William III ordered his Scots minister to extirpate a clan. Here are the greater names coupled with
the greater crimes. You would spare these criminals, for some
mysterious reason. I would hang them, higher than Haman, for
reasons of quite obvious justice; still more, still higher, for the
sake of historical science.

L o r d   A c t o n, letter to Bishop Creighton

✠ What is particularly interesting in this is that Acton,
a devout Roman Catholic, was attacking the Anglican, Creighton, for his leniency (in his *History of the Papacy*) toward the
Renaissance popes.

The Press

To appreciate the value of the *Edinburgh Review,* the state of
England at the period when that journal began should be had in
remembrance. The Catholics were not emancipated—the Corporation and Test Acts were unrepealed—the Game Laws were horribly oppressive—Steel Traps and Spring Guns were set all over
the country—Prisoners tried for their Lives could have no Counsel—Lord Eldon and the Court of Chancery pressed heavily upon
mankind—Libel was punished by the most cruel and vindictive
imprisonments—the principles of Political Economy were little
understood—the Law of Debt and of Conspiracy were upon the
worst possible footing—the enormous wickedness of the Slave
Trade was tolerated—a thousand evils were in existence, which
the talents of good and able men have since lessened or removed;

and these effects have been not a little assisted by the honest boldness of the *Edinburgh Review.*

SYDNEY SMITH, Preface to *Works*

Pronunciation of English Names

✠ How English (and sometimes Irish and Scottish) names are pronounced has long been a tollgate for foreigners, a trouble inflicted on us for no better reason than that the English *et al.* not just couldn't spell but couldn't enunciate. The way they detach and drop syllables is bad enough, but every so often they maliciously reverse the process, so that *Devereux*, which we would confidently pronounce *Devra*, turns out to be *Deverooks.* Again, Woburn, the great country house of the Dukes of Bedford, is pronounced *Woobun;* but the town of the same name, a very short distance away, is pronounced—so the townspeople told me—*Woeburn.* It's all a bit of a bore—particularly as some names are pronounced by their possessors in a variety of ways— but actually not a bad parlor game. Herewith a fair sampling, including many aristocratic samples, not, I regret to say, based upon personal acquaintance.

SPELLED	PRONOUNCED
Beauchamp	Beecham
Beaulieu	Bewly
Belvoir (Castle)	Beaver
Blount	Blunt
Bohun	Boon
Caius (College)	Keys
Cherwell	Charwell
Cholmondeley	Chumly
Cockburn	Coburn
Coke	Cook

Colquhoun	Cohoon'
Drogheda	Draw'eda
Fiennes	Fynes
Harewood	Harwood
Hervey	Harvey
Home	Hume
Ingestre	Inguestry
Iveagh	Iver
Keogh	Kō
Knollys	Nolze
Legh	Lee
Leinster	Linster
Leveson Gower	Loosen Gore
Magdalen; Magdalene (Colleges)	Maudlin
Marjoribanks	Marchbanks
Moray	Murry
Pole Carew	Pool Kayry
Romney	Rumny
Ruthven	Rivven
Sandys	Sands
Shrewsbury	Shrohzbury
Teignmouth	Tinmuth
Tredegar	Tredd-ee-gar
Tyrwhitt	Tirrit
Villiers	Villers
Wavertree	Wawtry
Wemyss	Weems

Recipes

✠ When I signed up to do this book, my wife asked me just how, in earlier days, people "kept" a commonplace book. I said that in an age when printed material, particularly for country people, was often scarce, they copied things they liked out of books they read, or cut them out of newspapers and magazines, and pasted them into their copybook "commonplace" book. "Oh," said my wife, "just the way women still do with recipes!" "What a good suggestion!" I answered. "If *you'll* cut or copy out two or three of our own special ones, I'll put them, with my thanks, into the book." And here they are, and to my mind extremely good ones.

Paradeiskraut (*Sauerkraut with Tomatoes*)

1 qt. (or 1 large can,
   drained) sauerkraut
1 large can tomatoes
2 tablespoons butter
2 tablespoons flour

1 onion, chopped fine
4 tablespoons brown sugar
1/4 lb. knackwurst, sliced
salt to taste

Cook the sauerkraut with a little water for 1 1/2 hours, or according to directions on the can. Meanwhile, rub the tomato pulp through a sieve. Melt butter, stir in flour and onion, and brown. Stew for 5 minutes, then stir in brown sugar and tomatoes. Cook 15 minutes in all. Drain the sauerkraut and add it to the sauce. Add the sliced knackwurst, salt, and more sugar if necessary. Cook slowly for 1 hour, uncovered, stirring frequently. Watch that it doesn't brown on the pan bottom.

This is particularly good for a supper party on a cold night.

Sauce for Seafood

1 tablespoon butter
1 tablespoon flour
1 tablespoon ketchup
1 teaspoon Worcestershire sauce
1 cup fish stock

salt
chopped parsley
1/4 cup sherry
1 clove garlic, minced
dash of red pepper

Melt butter, stir in flour, and add ketchup, Worcestershire sauce, fish stock, and sherry. Cook and stir until smooth and thick. Add garlic, red pepper, salt. Combine with seafood and sprinkle with parsley.

My mother first served this (without the garlic and red pepper) as a sauce for sweetbreads and mushrooms, where it proves equally good. Use it when a little tired of wine, cream, or cheese sauces.

Spinach Quiche

rich pastry for a 9-in. shell	*nutmeg*
½ cup grated Swiss cheese	*1 package frozen spinach,*
1½ cups creamed cottage cheese	*cooked, drained, and chopped*
4 eggs	*2 tablespoons chives*
⅓ cup light cream	*1 tablespoon butter*
1½ teaspoons salt	*1 small onion, sliced paper-thin*
pepper	

We once had a wonderful cold spinach tart at Demel's in Vienna, with a puzzling texture. Years later this recipe turned up in a Canadian newspaper and falls very little short.

Heat oven to 475°. Bake pastry shell for 3 minutes; remove from oven. Sprinkle grated cheese over shell. Beat cottage cheese, eggs, cream, salt, pepper, nutmeg together. Fold in spinach and chives. Pour into shell. Heat the butter, add onion, and cook until golden. Spoon over the spinach-cheese mixture and bake 45 minutes or until golden and firm.

Royalty

The King [George I] loved pleasure, and was not delicate in his choice of it. No woman came amiss of him, if they were very willing and very fat . . . the standard of His Majesty's taste made all those ladies who aspired to his favour, and who were near the statutable size, strain and swell themselves like the frogs in the fable to rival the bulk and dignity of the ox. Some succeeded, and others burst.

LORD CHESTERFIELD

✠ It was for this adjudged libel on George IV, then Prince Regent, that Leigh Hunt went to prison for two years:

What person, unacquainted with the true state of the case, would imagine, in reading these astounding eulogies, that this "Glory of the people" was the subject of millions of shrugs and reproaches! —that this "Protector of the arts" had named a wretched foreigner his historical painter, in disparagement or in ignorance of the merits of his own countrymen!—that this "Maecenus of the age" patronized not a single deserving writer!—that this "Breather of eloquence" could not say a few decent extempore words, if we are to judge, at least, from what he said to his regiment on its embarkation for Portugal!—that this "Conqueror of hearts" was the disappointer of hopes!—that this "Exciter of desire" (bravo! Messieurs of the *Post!*)—this "Adonis in loveliness," was a corpulent man of fifty!—in short, this *delightful, blissful, wise, pleasurable, honourable, virtuous, true,* and *immortal* prince, was a violator of his word, a libertine over head and ears in disgrace, a despiser of domestic ties, the companion of gamblers and demireps, a man who has just closed half a century without one single claim on the gratitude of his country, or the respect of posterity!

LEIGH HUNT, article in the Examiner (1812)

Salted Almonds

[Prince Christian of Schleswig-Holstein-Augustenburg] was unfortunate enough to lose an eye in a shooting accident. When conversation flagged at a dinner-party, as happened so often when he was the host, he would bid the footman bring him a tray containing his collection of glass eyes, which he would exhibit to his embarrassed guests, explaining at great length the peculiarities of each one—"and this one, you see, is blood-shot, I wear it when I have a cold."

GEORGINA BATTISCOMBE, *Queen Alexandra*

[Benjamin West's] Venuses looked as if they never had been naked before, and were too cold to be impassioned; his Adonises dolts, his Cupids . . . unamorous.

B. R. HAYDON

✠ Thus, said Aldous Huxley, "the last word on neo-classicism has been uttered."

I have no relish for the country; it is a sort of healthy grave.

SYDNEY SMITH

Very high and very low temperatures extinguish all human sympathy and relations. It is impossible to feel any affection beyond 78 and below 20 Fahrenheit; human nature is too solid or too liquid beyond these limits. Man only lives to shiver or to perspire.

SYDNEY SMITH, letter to Sarah Austin

From *The Jolly Beggars*

Life is all a variorum,
  We regard not how it goes;
Let them cant about decorum
  Who have characters to lose.

ROBERT BURNS

[Edward Everett, as President of Harvard, concerning the protested admission of a Negro student, 1848:] If this boy passes the examinations, he will be admitted; and if the white students choose to withdraw, all the income of the college will be devoted to his education.

One of his hostesses said Shaw was a most dangerous man, and, on being asked how and why (in the hope of eliciting some scandal), explained, "You invite him down to your place because you think he will entertain your guests with his brilliant conversation; and before you know where you are he has chosen a school for your son, made your will for you, regulated your diet, and assumed all the privileges of your family solicitor, your housekeeper, your clergyman, your doctor, your dressmaker, your hairdresser, and your estate agent. When he has finished with everybody else, he incites the children to rebellion. And when he can find nothing more to do, he goes away and forgets all about you."

FRANK HARRIS, *Bernard Shaw*

I flatter myself I shall soon . . . be in the way of becoming a *great man.* For have I not headaches, like Pope? vertigo, like Swift? grey hairs, like Homer? Do I not wear large shoes (for fear of corns), like Virgil? and sometimes complain of sore eyes (though not of *lippitude*), like Horace? Am I not at this present writing invested with a garment not less ragged than that of Socrates? Like Joseph the patriarch, I am a mighty dreamer of dreams; like Nimrod the hunter, I am an eminent builder of castles (in the air). I procrastinate, like Julius Caesar; and very lately, in imitation of Don Quixote, I rode a horse, lean, old, and lazy, like Rozinante. Sometimes, like Cicero, I write bad verses; and sometimes bad prose, like Virgil. This last instance I have on the authority of Seneca. I am of small stature, like Alexander the Great; I am somewhat inclinable to fatness, like Dr. Arbuthnot and Aristotle; and I drink brandy and water, like Mr. Boyd. I might compare myself, in relation to many other infirmities, to many other *great men;* but if fortune is not influenced in my favour by the particulars already enumerated I shall despair of ever recommending myself to her good graces.

JAMES BEATTIE, letter to Charles Boyd

[Francis Bacon] had a delicate, lively, hazel eye . . . like the eye of a viper.

Aubrey's Brief Lives

I am sorry to say the generality of women who have exceeded in wit have failed in chastity.

ELIZABETH MONTAGU, *Letters*

It is now 5 o'clock. We have our haircutter below stairs, William [Wordsworth] is reading the *Leech-gatherer* to him.

DOROTHY WORDSWORTH, letter to Mary and Sara Hutchinson

At luncheon today Emerald [Lady Cunard] remarked that she had long since ceased to be unduly depressed by the Crucifixion, in fact she had got used to it. She then went on, coyly, to read us a short note from George Moore in which he compared her to Socrates. Such was the conversation at Lady Cunard's in the third year of the Second World War.

We then drove to Kemsley House to lunch . . . Good conversation. [Deneys] Reitz told me an amusing tale how at Dunkirk time the King [George VI] had consulted the Chief Rabbi, and they had chatted. The Rabbi, whilst assuring the monarch that all would finally be well, added that "All the same, Sir, I should put some of the Colonies in your wife's name!"

I "laced" the cocktails with Benzedrine, which I find always makes a party go.

SIR HENRY CHANNON, *Diaries*

The two Grants (Charles and Robert) are always together, and both very forgetful and unpunctual. Somebody said that if you asked Charles to dine with you at six on Monday, you were very likely to have Robert at seven on Tuesday.

[Talleyrand talked] of Madame de Staël and Monti:—They met at Madame de Marescalchi's villa near Bologna, and were profuse of compliments and admiration for each other. Each brought a copy of their respective works, beautifully bound, to present to the other. After a day passed in an interchange of literary flatteries, and the most ardent expressions of delight, they separated, but each forgot to carry away the present of the other, and the books remain in Madame de Marescalchi's library to this day.

After the death of George II somebody asked if the Princess Emily, whose virtue was not thought immaculate, was to have Guards. [George Selwyn] said, "One every now and then."

CHARLES CAVENDISH FULKE GREVILLE, *Memoirs*

Twenty-two acknowledged concubines, and a library of sixty-two thousand volumes, attested the variety of his inclinations; and from the productions which he left behind him, it appears that both the one and the other were designed for use rather than ostentation.

GIBBON

To the memory of Erskine clings that deadly gibe of *The Anti-Jacobin,* which apologized for not reporting him in full because the printer had run out of capital I's.

F. L. LUCAS, *Style*

I am satisfied that Catullus, Tibullus, Propertius, and Ovid were in love with their mistresses, while they upbraid them, quarrel with them, threaten them, forswear them; but I confess that I cannot believe Petrarch in love with his, when he writes conceits upon her name, her gloves, and her place of birth.

WILLIAM WALSH

✠ Walsh—Alexander Pope's "knowing Walsh"—
thought that, ideally, you should be in love to write love poems,
and out of love to correct them.

From *Hudibras*

He could raise scruples dark and nice
And after solve 'em in a trice;
As if divinity had catched
The itch on purpose to be scratched.

. . . . . .

What makes all doctrines plain and clear?
About two hundred pounds a year.
And that which was proved true before
Prove false again? Two hundred more.

SAMUEL BUTLER

The wind came round the corner like a cab.

G. K. CHESTERTON

From *Absalom and Achitophel*

Shimei . . .
Did wisely from expensive sins refrain
And never broke the Sabbath but for gain.

DRYDEN

"O God," said God, "I've got my work cut out."

J. C. SQUIRE

Advance your pike; shoulder your pike; level your pike; slope
your pike; cheek your pike; trail your pike.

Old English manual of arms

It is only by not paying one's bills that one can hope to live in the memory of the commercial classes.

OSCAR WILDE

He in a few minutes ravaged this fair creature, or at least would have ravished her, if she had not, by a timely compliance, prevented him.

FIELDING, *Jonathan Wild*

"I have altogether lost my taste for mankind," said Monsieur de L——. "Then you haven't lost your taste," said Monsieur de N——.

CHAMFORT, *Pensées, Maximes et Anecdotes*

> Cupid among his statutes did enact
> Henceforth all lights be banished and exempt
> From bearing office in love's government.
> And in the day each should his passage mark
> Or learn to find his mistress in the dark.

SHACKERLEY MARMION, *Cupid and Psyche*

> Bow down, ye elephants, submissive bow
> To Him Who made the mite.

CHRISTOPHER SMART

Men use thought only to justify their wrongdoings, and speech only to conceal their thoughts.

VOLTAIRE, "Le Chapon et la Poularde"

[Richard Bentley] is believed to have liked port, but to have said of claret that "it would be port if it could."

R. C. JEBB, *Bentley*

Servants

[At Belvoir Castle, the home of the Duke of Rutland] the gong man was an old retainer, one of those . . . domestic servants which have completely disappeared . . . He was admittedly very old. He wore a white beard to his waist. Three times a day he rang the gong—for luncheon, for dressing-time, for dinner. He would walk down the interminable passages . . . clutching his gong with one hand and with the other feebly brandishing the padded-knobbed stick with which he struck it. Every corridor had to be warned and the towers too, so I suppose he banged on and off for ten minutes, thrice daily. . . .

The water-men are difficult to believe in today. They seemed to me to belong to another clay. They were the biggest people I had ever seen, much bigger than any of the men of the family, who were remarkable for their height. They had stubbly beards and a general Bill Sikes appearance. They wore brown clothes, no collars and thick green baize aprons from chin to knee. On their shoulders they carried a wooden yoke from which hung two gigantic cans of water. They moved on a perpetual round. Above the ground floor there was not a drop of hot water and not one bath, so their job was to keep all jugs, cans and kettles full in the bedrooms, and morning or evening to bring the hot water for the hip-baths. . . . They . . . never spoke but one word, "Water-man." . . .

Lastly there were the watchmen, who frightened many a newcomer to death. There was a little of the water-men about them, but they were dreadfully silent and they padded. All night they walked the passages, terraces and battlements, yet no one really saw them. . . . Always if one woke in the night, as the fire flickered to its death, one would hear a padded foot on the gravel

outside and a voice, not loud enough to waken but strong enough
to reassure, saying "Past twelve o'clock. All's well."

D I A N A   C O O P E R, The Rainbow Comes and Goes

Shakespeare

Grief fills the room up of my absent child,
Lies in his bed, walks up and down with me,
Puts on his pretty looks, repeats his words,
Remembers me of all his gracious parts,
Stuffs out his vacant garments with his form:
Then have I reason to be fond of grief?

King John

                       Pleasure and revenge
Have ears more deaf than adders to the voice
Of any true decision.

Troilus and Cressida

I have lived long enough: my way of life
Is fallen into the sear, the yellow leaf,
And that which should accompany old age,
As honour, love, obedience, troops of friends,
I must not look to have; but, in their stead,
Curses not loud but deep, mouth-honour, breath,
Which the poor heart would fain deny, and dare not.

Macbeth

               Come, seeling night,
Scarf up the tender eye of pitiful day;
And with thy bloody and invisible hand
Cancel and tear to pieces that great bond

Which keeps me pale! Light thickens, and the crow
Makes wing to the rooky wood . . .

Macbeth

Come not to me again, but say to Athens,
Timon hath made his everlasting mansion
Upon the beachèd verge of the salt flood;
Who once a day with his embossèd froth
The turbulent surge shall cover . . .

Timon of Athens

Is whispering nothing?
Is leaning cheek to cheek? is meeting noses?
Kissing with inside lip? stopping the career
Of laughter with a sigh?—a note infallible
Of breaking honesty?—horsing foot on foot?
Skulking in corners? wishing clocks more swift?
Hours, minutes? noon, midnight? and all eyes
Blind with the pin-and-web but theirs, theirs only,
That would unseen be wicked? is this nothing?
Why, then the world and all that's in it is nothing,
The covering sky is nothing; Bohemia nothing;
My wife is nothing; nor nothing have these nothings
If this be nothing.

The Winter's Tale

It is the cause, it is the cause, my soul:
Let me not name it to you, you chaste stars!
It is the cause. Yet I'll not shed her blood,
Nor scar that whiter skin of hers than snow,
And smooth as monumental alabaster.
Yet she must die, else she'll betray more men.
Put out the light, and then put out the light:
If I quench thee, thou flaming minister
I can again thy former light restore,

Should I repent me; but once put out thy light,
Though cunningest pattern of excelling nature,
I know not where is that Promethean heat
That can thy light relume. When I have plucked the rose
I cannot give it vital growth again,
It needs must wither. I'll smell it on the tree.
O balmy breath that dost almost persuade
Justice to break her sword! One more, one more:—
Be thus when thou art dead, and I will kill thee
And love thee after. One more, and this the last:
So sweet was ne'er so fatal. I must weep,
But they are cruel tears; this sorrow's heavenly,
It strikes where it doth love.

Othello

I am not yet of Percy's mind, the Hotspur of the north, he that
kills me some six or seven dozen of Scots at a breakfast, washes his
hands and says to his wife, "Fie upon this quiet life! I want
work."—"Oh my sweet Harry," says she, "how many hast thou
killed today?"—"Give my roan horse a drench," says he and answers, "Some fourteen," an hour after; "a trifle, a trifle."

Henry IV, Part I

ENOBARBUS: The barge she sat in, like a burnished throne
Burnt on the water: the poop was beaten gold;
Purple the sails, and so perfumed that
The winds were lovesick with them. The oars were silver,
Which to the tune of flutes kept stroke, and made
The water which they beat to follow faster,
As amorous of their strokes. For her own person,
It beggared all description: she did lie
In her pavilion—cloth-of-gold of tissue—
O'er-picturing that Venus where we see
The fancy outwork nature: on each side her
Stood pretty dimpled boys, like smiling Cupids,

With divers-coloured fans, which wind did seem
To glow the delicate cheeks which they did cool,
And what they undid, did.

AGRIPPA: O rare for Antony!

ENOBARBUS: Her gentlewomen, like the Nereides,
So many mermaids, tended her in the eyes
And made their bends adornings: at the helm
A seeming mermaid steers; the silken tackle
Swell with the touches of those flower-soft hands
That yarely frame the office. From the barge
A strange invisible perfume hits the sense
Of the adjacent wharfs. The city cast
Her people out upon her; and Antony,
Enthroned in the market place, did sit alone
Whistling to the air; which, but for vacancy,
Had gone to gaze on Cleopatra too,
And made a gap in nature.

AGRIPPA: Rare Egyptian!

ENOBARBUS: Upon her landing, Antony sent to her,
Invited her to supper. She replied
It should be better he became her guest,
Which she entreated: our courteous Antony,
Whom ne'er the word of "No" woman heard speak,
Being barbered ten times o'er, goes to the feast
And for his ordinary pays his heart
For what his eyes eat only.

AGRIPPA: Royal wench!
She made great Caesar lay his sword to bed:
He ploughed her, and she cropt.

ENOBARBUS: I saw her once
Hop forty paces through the public street,

And having lost her breath, she spoke and panted
That she did make defect perfection
And, breathless, power breathe forth.

MAECENAS: Now Antony must leave her utterly.

ENOBARBUS: Never: he will not.
Age cannot wither her, nor custom stale
Her infinite variety: other women cloy
The appetites they feed, but she makes hungry
Where most she satisfies . . .

Antony and Cleopatra

My story being done
She gave me for my pains a world of sighs:
She swore—in faith, 'twas strange, 'twas passing strange,
'Twas pitiful, 'twas wondrous pitiful.
She wished she had not heard it, yet she wished
That Heaven had made her such a man; she thanked me
And bade me, if I had a friend that loved her,
I should but teach him how to tell my story,
And that would woo her. Upon this hint I spake:
She loved me for the dangers I had passed
And I loved her that she did pity them.
This only is the witchcraft I have used;
Here comes the lady: let her witness it.

Othello

PISTOL: Bardolph, be blithe: Nym, rouse thy vaunting
    veins:
Boy, bristle thy courage up; for Falstaff he is dead,
And we must yearn therefore.

BARDOLPH: Would I were with him, wheresome'er he is, either in heaven or in hell!

HOSTESS: Nay, sure, he's not in hell: he's in Arthur's bosom, if ever man went to Arthur's bosom. 'A made a finer end and went away an it had been any christom child; 'a parted even just between twelve and one, even at the turning o' the tide: for after I saw him fumble with the sheets, and play with flowers, and smile upon his fingers' ends, I knew there was but one way; for his nose was as sharp as a pen, and 'a babbled of green fields. "How now, Sir John!" quoth I: "what, man! be o' good cheer." So 'a cried out, "God, God, God!" three or four times. Now I, to comfort him, bid him 'a should not think of God; I hoped there was no need to trouble himself with any such thoughts yet. So 'a bade me lay more clothes on his feet: I put my hand into the bed and felt them, and they were as cold as any stone; then I felt to his knees, and they were as cold as any stone, and so upward and upward, and all was as cold as any stone.

Henry V

Thou, rascal beadle, hold thy bloody hand:
Why dost thou lash that whore? Strip thine own back,
Thou hotly lusts to use her in that kind
For which thou whipst her. The usurer hangs the cozener.
Through tattered clothes small vices do appear:
Robes and furred gowns hide all. Plate sin with gold,
And the strong lance of justice hurtless breaks:
Arm it in rags, a pigmy's straw does pierce it.
None does offend, none, I say none, I'll able 'em:
Take that of me, my friend, who have the power
To seal the accuser's lips. Get thee glass eyes
And like a scurvy politician seem

To see the things thou dost not. Now, now, now, now.
Pull off my boots: harder, harder, so.

King Lear

Sins

The list [of the Seven Deadly Sins], as the Middle Ages knew it,
ran as follows: *Superbia,* Pride (always the first); *Invidia,* Envy;
Ira, translated Anger, Wrath or Hate; *Luxuria,* Lechery; *Avaritia,* Covetise or Covetousness; *Gula,* Gluttony; and *Accidia,* Accidie, Sloth . . . Characteristically, their opposites, the Seven
Cardinal Virtues, are much less known, and are more rarely and
less vividly portrayed. They are *Humilitas, Caritas, Patientia,
Castitas, Eleemosyna* (largess or bounty), *Abstinentia* (abstinence or sobriety) and *Vigilantia* . . . Many resources were
available to bring such lists alive. There were striking and singular names, witty and pithy definitions . . . Each sin came in human shape, identified and described: Wrath with the whites of
his eyes showing, snivelling with his nose, and biting his lips;
Avarice beetle-browed and bleary; Gluttony with his rumbling
guts, drinking a gallon and a gill, until he coughs up a caudle in
Clement's lap; Accidie lying in bed in Lent with his leman in his
arms till matins and Mass be done. These examples are from *Piers
Plowman,* but others as vivid might be taken from Dunbar, from
Stephen Hawes, from Marlowe or from Dekker. Not merely the
writers, but the preachers gave their imaginations rein: "Lust
consumes the body . . . It destroys the tongue of confession, the
eyes of intelligence, the ears of obedience, the nose of discretion,
the hair of good thoughts, the beard of fortitude, the eyebrows of
holy religion." The *Ancren Riwle* gives each Sin its attendant
beast: the Lion of Pride, the Adder of Envy, the Unicorn of
Wrath, the Scorpion of Lechery, the Fox of Avarice, the Sow of
Gluttony, and the Bear of Sloth. Nearly four hundred years later,
the Sins are still riding their beasts through Spenser's *Faerie*

Queene; but Avarice has now a Camel, Lechery a Goat; and Envy, riding a Wolf, carries the Serpent in his bosom.

GEOFFREY GRIGSON and
CHARLES HOWARD GIBBS-SMITH, eds.,
People, Places and Things

Slang

From the Late Seventeenth Century

Admiral of the narrow seas—One who from drunkenness vomits into the lap of the person sitting opposite to him.

Ambidexter—A lawyer who takes fees from both plaintiff and defendant . . .

Barber's chair—Said of a prostitute: she is as common as a barber's chair, in which a whole parish sit to be trimmed.

Beau-nasty—A slovenly fop; one finely dressed, but dirty.

To cascade—To vomit.

Cauliflower—A large white wig.

Cock alley—The private parts of a woman.

Cold—He caught cold by lying in bed barefoot: said of someone overcareful of himself.

Disguised—Drunk.

Finger in eye—Weeping, applied to women: "The more you cry, the less you'll piss"—a consolatory speech used by sailors to their doxies.

Gentlemen of three ins—In gaol, indicted, and in danger of being hanged in chains.

Gentlemen of three outs—Without money, without wit, and without manners; some add, without credit.

Gluepot—A parson; from joining men and women together in matrimony.

Gravy-eyed—Blear-eyed.

Hat—Old hat; a woman's privities: because frequently felt.

House to let—A widow's weeds.

Piss-proud—Having a false erection; said of any old fellow who marries a young wife.

Star gazer—A hedge whore.

Three-penny upright—A retailer of love, who, for the sum mentioned, dispenses her favors standing against a wall.

Two to one shop—A pawnbroker's; alluding perhaps to its being two to one that the goods pledged are never redeemed.

To vowel—A gamester who does not immediately pay his losings, is said to vowel the winner, by repeating the vowels, I.O.U.

F R A N C I S   G R O S E ,
A Classical Dictionary of the Vulgar Tongue (1785),
edited by Eric Partridge

Soldiers and Sailors

Marching Song

Send for the boys of the Old Brigade
To keep old England free!
Send for me father and me mother and me brother,
But for Gawd's sake don't send me!

ANON. (1914)

[Communication to Dublin Castle:] Lord Ormonde exerted himself to stop his men; he first begged and beseeched; he then upbraided and swore at them; he ran two of them through the body, and burst into tears.

EDWARD COOKE, Esq. (1798)

[Army Order, 1809:] The Soldiers are again positively prohibited to plunder bee-hives; any man found with a bee-hive in his possession will be punished.

The French and Indian War

[General Braddock's last words:] We shall know better how to deal with them next time.

[After a Boer War disaster:] Please understand that there is no depression in *this* house; we are not interested in the possibilities of defeat; they do not exist.

QUEEN VICTORIA, to A. J. Balfour

The Ironic Duke

The British public know very little of what our Army
is . . . Many of them think it is very like a fleet. One of these is
our most gracious Sovereign.

THE DUKE OF WELLINGTON (1834)

[Notation in a Diary:] [We] received orders that we were now to
go to Gibraltar directly, and not to Minorca. "What you have got
in your bag, Mr. Courier?"—"Orders, sir."—"And what in the
bag behind you, Mr. Courier?"—"Counter-orders, sir."

WILLIAM DYOTT (1801)

Dr. Barry was promoted Deputy-Inspector-General in 1851, In-
spector-General in 1858, retired in 1859, and died . . . on July
25, 1865 (born 1795)—when an official report was sent to the
War Office that Dr. James Barry was a woman.

C. H. GARDINER, *Centurions of the Century*

[Addressed to the Secretary of State:] I am determined to be
guided by your instructions so long as they are within the reach
of my comprehension.

SIR JAMES STUART to Henry Dundas (1798)

A Suggestion to Lord Nelson

His Lordship came up to me on the poop, and, after ordering
certain Signals to be made, about a quarter to noon, said, "Mr.
Pasco, I want to say to the fleet, "England confides that every man
will do his duty." He added, "You must be quick." I replied, "If
your Lordship will permit me to substitute *expects* for *confides*,
the signal will soon be completed, because the word *expects* is in
the vocabulary, and *confides* must be spelt." His Lordship replied

in haste, and with seeming satisfaction, "That will do, Pasco, make it directly."

Report by Mr. Pasco, Signal Lieutenant of H.M.S. *Victory*

Proclamations of Victory

Peccavi, I've Scinde, cried Lord Ellenborough proud;
Dalhousie, more modest, said *Vovi,* I've Oudh.

✠ In 1842, while Governor-General of India, Lord Ellenborough contrived the annexation of Scinde and communicated the fact to England with the one-word pun *Peccavi;* Lord Dalhousie, also a Governor-General of India, annexed Oudh in the 1850s (*Vovi* = I vowed).

Anglo-French Alliance

Après la guerre fini,
Tous les soldats partis,
Mademoiselle avec piccanini,
Souvenir des Anglais.

World War I song

[Spoken of a Soldier:] A good man he was, an' had his joke always. Killed in attackin' the Railway Triangle, east of Arras, an' the last thing he said was, "Get on wid ye, men! I'm makin' a separate peace."

C. E. MONTAGUE, *Fiery Particles*

✠ I know no greater example of true humor, and none more moving.

Sour Balls

Who is the greatest liar?—The man who speaks most of himself.

Chinese saying

The charge for walking on the grass is £5.

Sign at Trinity College, Oxford

[Said of Wordsworth:] He had one eye on a daffodil and the other on a canal share.

From *The Glow-Worm*

Disputes have been, and still prevail
    From whence his rays proceed.
Some give that honor to his tail
    And others to his head.

WILLIAM COWPER

My Will contains directions for my funeral, which will not be followed by mourning coaches but by herds of oxen, sheep, swine, flocks of poultry, and a small travelling aquarium of live fish, all wearing white scarves in honor of the man who perished rather than eat his fellow creatures. It will be, with the exception of the procession into Noah's Ark, the most remarkable thing of the kind ever seen.

GEORGE BERNARD SHAW

In the United States a man builds a house in which to spend his old age, and sells it before the roof is laid; he plants a garden, and rents it just as the trees are beginning to bear.

ALEXIS DE TOCQUEVILLE, *Democracy in America*

[Testimony of John Dennis, a laborer, 1729:] I asked her [his wife] to come to bed, but she would not, but said she would go into company she liked better. I told her I was sorry she should like any company better than mine—with that she upt with something to throw at me, I told her I would send it again if she did, and then I felt something hit me on the left shoulder, which by the blow I took to be a patten, but feeling for it I found it to be a knife, so I threw the knife at her again, and she cried out "Lord God, what's come to me!" With that I ran upstairs to light a candle, and when I came down again found her very bad. . . .

Leave only three wasps alive in the whole of Europe and the air of Europe will still be more crowded with wasps than space is with stars.

SIR JAMES JEANS

Mrs. Anne Pitt, Lord Chatham's sister, a very superior woman— She hated him, and they lived like dog and cat. She said he had never read but one book—*The Fairy Queen*. He could only get rid of her by leaving his house, and setting a bill upon it, "This house to let."

[The Duke of Wellington:]———, when at our head quarters in Spain, wished to see an Army, and I gave directions that he should be conducted through ours. When he returned, he said, "I have seen nothing—Nothing but here and there little clusters of men in confusion; some cooking, some washing, and some sleeping." "Then you have seen an army," I said.

SAMUEL ROGERS, *Recollections*

A child is fluent because it has no wish to substitute one word for another.

JOHN HORNE TOOKE

Art's air might be a little clearer—a little freer from certain traditional delusions: for instance, that free thought and free love always go to the same café . . .

C H A R L E S   I V E S, *Essays before a Sonata*

Things taste better in small houses.

Q U E E N   V I C T O R I A

I always put on my thickest greatcoat to go to our church in, as fungi grow in great numbers about the communion table.

E D W A R D   F I T Z G E R A L D

With great labour, he [her husband, General d'Arblay] cleared a considerable compartment of weeds, and when it looked clean and well, and he showed his work to the gardener, the man said he had demolished an asparagus bed!

The Diary and Letters of Madame d'Arblay (Fanny Burney)

Today's newspaper . . . brings to mind that placard I saw at a station in Surrey a year or two ago, advertising certain races in the neighbourhood. . . . :

"Engaged by the Executive to ensure order and comfort to the public attending this meeting:

  14 detectives (racing),
  15 detectives (Scotland Yard),
   7 police inspectors,
   9 police sergeants,
  76 police, and a supernumerary contingent of specially selected men from the Army Reserve and the Corps of Commissionaires.

The above force . . . will have the assistance also of a strong force of the Surrey Constabulary."

G E O R G E   G I S S I N G, *The Private Papers of Henry Ryecroft*

✠ In this same pseudonymous autobiographical book of Gissing's, where the passage just quoted is almost certainly factual, not fictional, there is the account of Ryecroft-Gissing very much on his uppers, and using the lavatory of the British Museum to wash up in, where he one day saw posted a sign announcing that the washbasins were "for casual ablutions only."

If a man is frequently ill and, after eating a cherry, has a cold the next day, he is sure to be consoled with the information that it is his own fault.

V A U V E N A R G U E S

Generally speaking, the theatre is the literature of society people who have no time to read.

S A I N T E - B E U V E

Degas . . . was always ready to assert that there is no arguing among the Muses. They work all day, very much on their own. In the evening, work finished, they get together and dance; *they do not talk.*

Yet he was a great arguer himself, merciless in retort, particularly excitable where politics or drawing were concerned. Unyielding, he would quickly reach the stage of shouting, using the harshest language, and then would break off abruptly. By comparison, Alceste would have seemed complaisant and easygoing. . . .

At dinner every Friday, at M. Rouart's, Degas would be the soul of the evening; a constant, brilliant, unbearable guest, spreading wit, terror, and gaiety. . . . Brilliantly unfair in his attacks, infallible in his taste, narrow-mindedly yet lucidly passionate, he was always throwing mud at . . . the artists who were bent on *getting there* . . .

P A U L V A L É R Y, *Degas, Manet, Morisot*

(trans. David Paul)

The Lord forbid that I should be out of debt, as if, indeed, I could not be trusted.

RABELAIS, *Pantagruel*

It is a very noble hypocrisy not to talk of oneself.

NIETZSCHE

If the king at noon says, "It is night," the wise man says, "Behold the stars."

Persian proverb

The prophets Isaiah and Ezekiel dined with me, and I asked them how they dared so roundly to assert that God spoke to them. . . . Isaiah answered: "I saw no God, nor heard any, in a finite organical perception; but my senses discovered the infinite in everything; and as I was then persuaded and remain confirmed, that the voice of honest indignation is the voice of God, I cared not for consequences, but wrote."

BLAKE, *The Marriage of Heaven and Hell*

To most of us the real life is the life we do not lead.

OSCAR WILDE

It is enough . . . she is willing to be married when the fifth act requires it.

DRYDEN, *Essay of Dramatic Poesy*

From *The Dispensary*

Whilst others meanly asked whole months to slay,
I oft dispatched the patient in a day.

SAMUEL GARTH

[Dr. Johnson:] Worth seeing? Yes; but not worth going to see.

BOSWELL, *Life of Johnson*

When I hear artists or authors making fun of business men I think of a regiment in which the band makes fun of the cooks.

ANON.

Speechmaking

As for the possibility of the House of Lords preventing ere long a reform of Parliament, I hold it to be the most absurd notion that ever entered into human imagination. I do not mean to be disrespectful, but the attempt of the Lords to stop the progress of reform reminds me very forcibly of the great storm of Sidmouth, and of the conduct of the excellent Mrs. Partington on that occasion. In the winter of 1824 there set in a good flood upon that town—the tide rose to an incredible height—the waves rushed in upon the houses, and everything was threatened with destruction! In the midst of this sublime and terrible storm, Dame Partington, who lived upon the beach, was seen at the door of her house, with mop and pattens, trundling her mop, squeezing out the sea-water, and vigorously pushing away the Atlantic Ocean. The Atlantic was roused. Mrs. Partington's spirit was up; but I need not tell you that the conquest was unequal. The Atlantic Ocean beat Mrs. Partington. She was excellent at a slop, or a puddle, but she should not have meddled with a tempest. Gentlemen, be at your ease—be quiet and steady. You will beat Mrs. Partington.

SYDNEY SMITH, speech after the rejection of the Reform Bill
by the House of Lords (1831)

Sport

✠ My first enthusiasm and allegiance went to the Cincinnati Reds baseball team, this in 1911 when I was six. My first job was as a sports assistant, this when I was eighteen, on the Cincinnati *Enquirer*. Yet despite such beginnings I cannot maintain that sport has, either personally or professionally, bulked large in my life. My boyhood, to be sure, was filled with baseball, and wish-fulfilled even more. In the flesh, though sometimes passable with a bat, I was notoriously butterfingered with a ball, and shall detain no one with my recollections as a player. I have happier recollections of watching the Reds play, particularly from the dugout—for a school friend of mine, Bud Bancroft, the the son of the Reds' general manager, and the team's mascot, used to take a number of us kids to games one at a time and seat us with the team. His memories, I found, were less happy than mine, for when thirty years later I saw him and told him how as boys we envied him terrifically as mascot, he said, "*You* may have envied me, but I never knew whether kids were my friends because they liked me or because I could take them to ball games."

I sat in the dugout only once or twice, but from the age of ten till the age of thirteen I played a strenuous leading role in the life of a six-team baseball league. This was known as the Snake League, and I had not only named it, I had invented it, and since Snake League games never got rained out, I had, every day from April till October, to conceive and execute three stirring contests, many of which ran to extra innings—one of them fruitlessly to thirty-two innings, when it was called, I must suppose, on account of dawn. And after typing up the scores inning by inning, I had to type up the box scores, weary though I was from having played first base on the home team, where I won many a game with a well-timed Rover Boy triple or Frank Merriwell home run. Indeed, during my worst season I hit .487, and I was being constantly pestered by bids from major league clubs. But I was loyal to my team—the Eagles—and to my league, and constantly got letters of regret but admiration from John McGraw, Connie Mack, and other famous managers of the day. And when the Snake League was disbanded in 1917 because all its players had enlisted to make the world safe for democracy, there came off my typewriter long appreciative newspaper articles, many of them about me.

But a year or two later something loomed to take the heart out of me, who might otherwise have made baseball the great love of my life. When I was nearly fifteen the Reds won the pennant—their first pennant—and went on to win the World Series. I saw all the home games against the Chicago White Sox from the bleachers, and won a quarter on the Series from an uncle. But it presently transpired that the games had been fixed, the fixing to be known forever after as the Black Sox Scandal. Like the adolescent in Sherwood Anderson's "I Want to Know Why," I felt terribly bereft and disillusioned, and, as they say, things were never again the same.

I have still a great liking for baseball, and I still, despite the Scandal and my moving away from Cincinnati, root for the Reds; but I almost never go to a game, even on television; for me, baseball is a game to read about. Tennis, on the other hand, I enjoy watching, but seldom enjoy reading about. Football I enjoyed, when young, for everything but the game itself—for the girl I was with, the liquor that went with it, the parties that came after it; but football itself bores me, perhaps because it baffles me as to fine points. Of water sports I enjoy an occasional smooth sail, though myself no sailor, and am no good at water games. Back on land, I don't shoot or hunt or ski or ride or play golf; and though the idea of mountain climbing appeals to me, I have never cared to be roped to strangers, or to freeze all night in— if you can find one—an Alpine hut. For fishing I haven't the patience to keep still or sit still, and for polo I simply haven't the money—and God knows what would happen if I did have.

As reading matter the world of sport tempts me in communicating at moderate length things hitherto unknown—the fine points of falconry, let us say, or, in seventeenth-century France, of stag hunts, or some form of *gloire*, or in setting forth clearly (as Knebworth does with boxing) certain varying techniques. Of the great early-nineteenth-century era of English sportsmen, sporting writers and humorists, and sporting pictures, I like many of Henry Alken's and Ben Marshall's pictures, but find the writings over-"technical," all too English, and quickly tedious. Hazlitt's slightly earlier "The Fight," however, still holds its own. Of what I have read on sport, culminating chronologically with Red Smith, part of almost the first thing I read gave me, by all odds, the greatest pleasure. This was a chapter in a book on baseball, published around 1912 and "written" by Johnny Evers, the middle man in the most acclaimed of baseball trios. The chapter was rather tamely entitled "Creating a Winning Team," and told how the great—the really great—Chicago Cubs, a team that included Tinker, Evers, and Chance and that won the National League pennant in 1906, 1907, and 1908, was built up player by player. I must have read that chapter a hundred times or more, till I knew it virtually by heart, and how I ever permitted it to go out of my possession I cannot imagine. Had it remained among my books, I cannot believe that part of it would not also have appeared in this one.

In Praise of the Compleat Angler

The quiet pastime of their choice
　　On Beauly rocks, in Derwent glades,
Still seems to move to Walton's voice
　　Singing of dace and dairymaids.
His water meadows still are wet,
　　His brawling trout-streams leap and glance,
And on their sunlit ripples yet
　　The flies of his disciples dance.

　　　　Aʟғʀᴇᴅ Cᴏᴄʜʀᴀɴᴇ, "The Fisherman"

Your consummate deer-stalker should not only be able to run like an antelope, and breathe like the trade-winds, but should also be enriched with various other undeniable qualifications. As, for instance, he should be able to run in a stooping position, at a greyhound pace, with his back parallel to the ground, and his face within an inch of it, for miles together. He should take a singular pleasure in threading the seams of a bog, or of gliding down a burn, *ventre à terre,* like that insinuating animal, the eel; accomplished he should be in skilfully squeezing his clothes after this operation, to make all comfortable. Strong and pliant in the ankle, he should most indubitably be; since in running swiftly down precipices, picturesquely adorned with sharp-edged, angular, vindictive stones, his feet will unadvisedly get into awkward cavities, and curious positions; thus, if his legs are devoid of the faculty of breaking, so much the better—he has an evident advantage over the fragile man. He should rejoice in wading through torrents, and be able to stand firmly on water-worn stones, unconscious of the action of the current; or if by fickle fortune the waves should be too powerful for him, when he loses his balance, and goes floating away upon his back (for if he has any . . . sense of the picturesque, it is presumed he will fall backwards), he should raise his rifle aloft in the air, Marmion fashion, lest his powder should get wet, and his day's sport come suddenly to an end. A few weeks' practice in the Tilt will make him quite *au fait* at this. We would recommend him to try the thing in a spate, during a refreshing north wind, which is adverse to deer-stalking; thus no day will be lost pending his education.

W I L L I A M   S C R O P E, The Art of Deer-Stalking (1838)

Yet well fare the gentle goose which bringeth to a man, even to his door, so many exceeding commodities. For the goose is man's comfort in war and in peace, sleeping and waking. That praise soever given to shooting, the goose may challenge the best part in it. How well doth she make a man fare at his table! How easily doth she make a man lie in his bed! How fit even as her feathers be only for shooting, so be her quills fit only for writing.

R O G E R A S C H A M, Toxophilus (1545)

We commenced the descent of the face. It was hideous work. The men looked like impersonations of Winter, with their hair all frosted, and their beards matted with ice. My hands were numbed —dead. I begged the others to stop. *"We cannot afford to stop; we must continue to move,"* was their reply. They were right; to stop was to be entirely frozen. So we went down, gripping rocks varnished with ice, which pulled skin from the fingers. Gloves were useless; they became iced, too, and the *batons* slid through them as slippery as eels. The iron of the axes stuck to the fingers— it felt red-hot; but it was useless to shrink, the rocks and the axes had to be firmly grasped—no faltering would do here.

We turned back at 4.12 P.M., and at 8.15 crossed the *Bergschrund* again, not having halted for a minute upon the entire descent. During the last two hours it was windless, but time was of such vital importance that we pressed on incessantly, and did not stop until we were fairly upon the glacier. Then we took stock of what remained of the tips of our fingers. There was not much skin left; they were perfectly raw, and for weeks afterwards I was reminded of the ascent of the *Dent Blanche* by the twinges which I felt when I pulled on my boots. The others escaped with some slight frost-bites . . .

E D W A R D W H Y M P E R, Scrambles Amongst the Alps

HIPPOLYTA: I was with Hercules and Cadmus once,
When in a wood of Crete they bayed the bear
With hounds of Sparta: never did I hear
Such gallant chiding; for, besides the groves,
The skies, the fountains, every region near
Seemed all one mutual cry. I never heard
So musical a discord, such sweet thunder.

THESEUS: My hounds are bred out of the Spartan kind,
So flewed, so sanded; and their heads are hung
With ears that sweep away the morning dew;
Crook-kneed, and dew-lapped like Thessalian bulls,
Slow in pursuit, but matched in mouth like bells,
Each under each. A cry more tuneable
Was never hollaed to, nor cheered with horn,
In Crete, in Sparta, nor in Thessaly:
Judge, when your hear.

SHAKESPEARE, *A Midsummer Night's Dream*

I believe it is very difficult to ascertain exactly what scent is: I have known it alter very often in the same day. I believe, however, that it depends chiefly on two things—*"the condition the ground is in, and the temperature of the air"*; both of which, I apprehend, should be moist, without being wet. When both are in this condition, the scent is then perfect; and vice versa, when the ground is hard and the air dry, there seldom will be any scent. It scarcely ever lies with a north or an east wind; a southerly wind without rain, and a westerly wind that is not rough, are the most favourable.

Storms in the air are great enemies to scent, and seldom fail to take it entirely away. A fine sunshiny day is not often a good hunting day; but what the French call *jours des dames,* warm without sun, is generally a perfect one: there are not many such in a whole season. In some fogs, I have known the scent lie high; in others, not at all; depending, I believe, on the quarter the wind is then in. I have known it lie very high in a mist, when not too wet; but if the wet should hang on the boughs and bushes, it will fall upon the scent, and deaden it.

PETER BECKFORD, *Thoughts on Hunting* (1781)

Young Reynard

Gracefullest leaper, the dappled fox-cub
Curves over brambles with berries and buds,

Light as a bubble that flies from the tub,
Whisked by the laundry-wife out of her suds.
Wavy he comes, woolly, all at his ease,
Elegant, fashioned to foot with the deuce;
Nature's own prince of the dance: then he sees
Me, and retires as if making excuse.

Never closed minuet courtlier! Soon
Cub-hunting troops were abroad, and a yelp
Told of sure scent; ere the stroke upon noon
Reynard the younger lay far beyond help.
Wild, my poor friend, has the fate to be chased;
Civil will conquer; were t'other 'twere worse,
Fair, by the flushed early morning embraced,
Haply you live a day longer in verse.

GEORGE MEREDITH

From *The Holcomb Song*

See the doctor in boots, with a breakfast that suits
Of strong-brewed ale and good beef;
His patients in pain say "I've called once again
To consult you in hope of relief."
To the poor he advice gives away;
To the rich he prescribes and takes pay;
But to each one he says, "You'll shortly be dead
If you don't go a-hunting today."

Then the judge sits in court, and gets wind of the sport
For the lawyers apply to adjourn:
And no witnesses come, there are none left at home,
They have followed the hounds and the horn.
Says his worship: "Great fines shall they pay,
If they will not our summons obey:
But 'tis very fine sport, so we'll break up the court,
And we'll all go a-hunting today."

> Then the village bells chime, there's a wedding at nine,
> And the parson unites the fond pair;
> But he heard the sweet sounds of the horn and the
>   hounds,
> And he knew 'twas his time to be there.
> Says he: "For your welfare I'll pray,
> And regret I no longer can stay,
> You are safely made one; I must quickly be gone:
> For I must go a-hunting today.

ANON.

There are three kinds of boxing champion, not essentially different, but varying in temperament and method. The fundamentals
are undoubtedly common to all boxers, but the aspiring champion of the future may develop his science according to one of
three different schools, the school of Corbett, the school of Fitzsimmons, or the school of Dempsey.

The first school is the school of pure, brilliant boxing, of perfect footwork, of scientific defence, of well-timed punches, of per-
fected craftsmanship. The great boxers, pure and simple, of the
past have been Corbett, Griffo, Kid McCoy, Tommy Ryan, Benny
Leonard, Jack Johnson, Jim Driscoll, and, of course, many others.
These studied boxing as a science, as an art, and they practised it
as any skilled craftsman practises his trade, with efficiency and
with pride. They studied, they thought, they calculated, they
manœuvred, they made openings, they led, feinted, ducked,
stopped, and made use of the whole paraphernalia of boxing with
such ease and precision that to them it became second nature.
They were the artists, accurate, certain of themselves, perfect in
their technique. The classical exponents of the science of self-
defence.

The second school is strategically more perfect, if tactically less
so. It is a school more of fighters than of boxers, and yet a school
of scientific fighters. It is solid where the first school is wiry, it is
sound where the other is brilliant, it is deadly where the other is
victorious. The men who belonged to this school of boxing were

such as Fitzsimmons, who is, of course, its outstanding exponent, Al Woolgast, Kid Lewis, and many of the old prize fighters. This style of boxing is, indeed, the modern adaptation of the old prize ring fighting. It calculates over a long period of time. It takes and administers punishment. It is hard and fit and dour. It is tremendously strong and endowed with immense recuperative powers. It bides its time and when the moment comes has both the strength and the art for the final blow. There is no affectation about it, no flashy brilliance, no hot-headed enthusiasm. It is the fighting spirit, controlled and held in check, cold as ice and deadly as magic. It is crafty and sinister, calm, calculating, cruel.

The third school is the school of the killer, the school of Dempsey, of Stanley Ketchell, of Terry McGovern, of Papke and of Klaus. These were fighters born and bred, with the lust of battle burning inside them from the first sound of the gong. There is no brilliant boxing here, no cold calculating strategy. There is fire, relentless energy, terrific whirlwind punching, the tenacity of the bulldog and the enthusiasm of the terrier. The exponents of this school fought all out from the beginning of each round to the end. Sustained attack was their defence, the maximum number of punches in the minimum amount of time was their goal. They wanted not only to win, but to win quickly and decisively. They were the incarnation of the fighting spirit, the tigers, the killers, the men who run gloriously amok.

V I S C O U N T   K N E B W O R T H, *Boxing*

[The Abbé Fortier was vicar of a village near Compiègne and a passionate hunter. The day before the season opened, he told his flock that if he next day said Masses at the usual time, the field would be denuded when he was able to set out. He therefore set six A.M. for Mass and "I shall take note of those of you won't show up and deal with them later."] At half-past five the Abbé Fortier began to say Mass, and it was half done when his parishioners arrived. At a quarter after six Low Mass was finished. The parishioners stirred.

"Oh, no," said the Abbé. "Since you are here, it would be fool-

ish to have you return at ten for High Mass. I shall say that now."
. . . High Mass ended, and everyone started to go.

"Now wait," said he. ". . . We're going to get through with vespers as we did with High and Low Mass. It will take fifteen minutes."

And he went through the vesper service, so that by half-past seven, a beautiful hour to start hunting, he had finished all his services. . . . Never was a human creature a better man or a worse priest.

He died at the age of ninety, and none of his flock ever forgot his last sermon.

"I'm going to leave you, my children," he said. "God gave you to me stupid, and stupid I return you. He will have nothing for which to reproach me."

ALEXANDRE DUMAS PÈRE, *Dictionary of Cuisine*

(trans. Louis Colman)

✠ Those well acquainted with English sport may figure out just what laws or traditions, and in how felonious a degree, are flouted in the following quatrain by Richard Monckton Milnes, the first Lord Houghton:

On the First of September, one Sunday morn,
I shot a hen pheasant in standing corn
Without a licence. Contrive who can
Such a cluster of crimes against God and man!

Theatre

✠ In most of its forms the theatre is much more something to see than to read. The exceptions, the things most worth reading, are good poetic drama and very good prose comedy. Prose *drama* written in English has, in my opinion—and experience—quickly become very dated and somehow overblown or

shrill or ponderous, its drama smacking of melodrama, its eloquence sunk into rhetoric, its speech gone flat or unnatural, its
slang hopelessly stale. You have only to read passages, even from
his better plays, in Eugene O'Neill, or go back to that landmark
in modern "realistic" drama, Pinero's *The Second Mrs. Tanque-
ray*, to find the evidence for this. O'Neill is of course, as a writer
of prose drama, the exception among the famous "Irish" play-
wrights, all the others having chiefly written good prose comedy,
whether Congreve or Farquhar, Goldsmith or Sheridan, Wilde
or Shaw, Synge or Sean O'Casey. Witty, worldly, urbane dialogue, however "artificial," survives from having been carefully
shaped, delicately starched; and racy, humorous, pungent dialogue survives from being brightly or boisterously amusing.
Good poetic drama we may well prefer to read rather than to see,
much of its drama being less rewarding than its poetry; and
great poetic drama—*Agamemnon, Lear, Antony and Cleopatra*
—often raises difficulties in production that make it better read
than seen.

Though *excerpts* from very good plays are not automatically
successful as reading, I have included three favorite excerpts,
one from a great poetic tragedy; one from a brilliant prose
comedy; one from a fine comedy, part prose and—as in the excerpt—part high rhetoric. Otherwise what I have chosen comes
from what might be called the comedy of the theatre itself—at
the expense, in this case, of certain Renaissance types of theatre-
goers. The comedy can be even more at the expense of the actors,
including very talented ones, from their tremendous vanity; or
of certain critics, from their great sense of self-importance. But
it must be said for the actors that they are a hive of colorful
theatre gossip and amusing, slightly malicious theatre anecdote
sufficient for all their conversational and cultural needs and for
ventilating the walled city which they inhabit; and of course,
unlike most other people, they can enrich their yarns with murderous gestures and their voices with superb mimicry.

The Gallant at the Theatre

Whether . . . the gatherers of the public or private playhouse
stand to receive the afternoon's rent, let our gallant, having paid
it, presently advance himself up to the throne of the stage: I mean
not into the lords' room [the stage box], which is now but the
stage's suburbs . . . But on the very rushes where the comedy is
to dance, yea, and under the state of Cambyses himself, must our
feathered ostrich, like a piece of ordinance, be planted valiantly,
because impudently, beating down the mews and hisses of the
opposed rascality.

For do but cast up a reckoning: what large comings-in are
pursed up by sitting on the stage. First a conspicuous eminence is
gotten, by which means the best and most essential parts of a
gallant—good clothes, a proportionable leg, white hand, the Parisian lock, and a tolerable beard, are perfectly revealed.

By sitting on the stage you have a signed patent to engross the
whole commodity of censure . . . yet no man shall once offer to
hinder you from obtaining the title of an insolent, over-weening
coxcomb.

By sitting on the stage you may, without travelling for it, at the
very next door ask whose play it is . . . if you know not the author you may rail against him and peradventure so behave yourself that you may enforce the author to know you. . . .

By sitting on the stage you may . . . have a good stool for sixpence, at any time know what particular part any of the infants
[child actors] present, get your match lighted, examine the play-
suit's lace, and perhaps win wagers upon laying 'tis copper . . .
But . . . present not yourself on the stage, especially at a new
play, until the quaking Prologue . . . is ready to give the trumpets their cue that h'is upon point to enter: for then it is time, as
though you were one of the properties, or that you dropped out of
the hangings, to creep from behind the arras with your tripos or
three-footed stool in one hand and a teston . . . in the other; for
if you should bestow your person upon the vulgar when the belly

of the house is but half full, your apparel is quite eaten up, the
fashion lost . . . It shall crown you with rich commendation to
laugh aloud in the midst of the most serious and saddest scene of
the terriblest tragedy; and to let that clapper, your tongue, be
tossed so high that all the house may ring of it; your lords use it;
your knights are apes to the lords and do so too; your inn-o'-court
man is zany to the knights and (many very scurvily) comes likewise limping after it: be thou a beagle to them all . . . for by
talking and laughing . . . you heap Pelion upon Ossa, glory
upon glory: all the eyes in the galleries will leave walking after
the players and only follow you; the simplest dolt in the house
snatches up your name and when he meets you in the streets . . .
he'll cry "He's such a gallant!" . . .

Now, sir, if the writer be a fellow that hath either epigrammed
you or hath had a flirt at your mistress, or hath brought either
your feather or your red beard or your little legs, &c. on the stage,
you shall disgrace him worse than by tossing him in a blanket, or
giving him the bastinado in a tavern, if in the middle of his play,
be it pastoral or comedy, moral or tragedy, you rise with a
screwed and discontented face from your stool to be gone: no
matter whether the scenes be good or no; the better they are, the
worse do you distaste them; and, being on your feet, sneak not
away like a coward, but salute all your gentle acquaintance, that
are spread either on the rushes or on stools about you, and draw
what troop you can from the stage after you; the mimics [actors]
are beholden to you for allowing them elbow-room . . .

Marry, if either the company, or indisposition of the weather,
bind you to sit it out, my counsel is then that you turn plain ape:
take up a rush and tickle the earnest ears of your fellow gallants,
to make other fools fall a-laughing; mew at passionate speeches,
blare at merry, find fault with the music, whew at the children's
action, whistle at the songs, and above all curse the sharers [thea-
tre proprietors] . . .

THOMAS DEKKER, *The Gull's Hornbook* (1609)

In melodrama [Charles Kean] was very effective; but nothing could be more exasperating now than to sit through his performance of a part like Richard, and hear his wooden intonation in this fashion:

> Dow is the widter of our discodtedt
> Bade glorious subber by the sud of York.

DAVID MASSON, *Memories of London in the 'Forties*

✠ The trouble here is that Richard doesn't speak these lines.

July 3 [1905]. Went to see Sarah Bernhardt in *Phèdre*. It was an extraordinary performance, at times admirable, at times odious. Duse was watching her from a box, and this led Sarah into trying to surpass herself. I think she took it rather outside her usual pitch, and roared and gurgled as she might in *La Tosca* or *La Sorcière*. She was magnificent in all the quiet scenes, almost detestable in others, indulging in horrid soundings of the last syllables and staccato effects which made one wince. Duse watched her without moving, through an opera glass. I was deeply interested.

CHARLES RICKETTS, *Self-Portrait*

MELLEFONT: But does your lordship never see comedies?
LORD FROTH: Oh yes, sometimes—But I never laugh.
MELLEFONT: No?
LORD FROTH: Oh, no—never laugh, indeed, sir.
CARELESS: No! why what d'you go there for?
LORD FROTH: To distinguish myself from the commonalty and mortify the poets; the fellows grow so conceited when any of their foolish wit prevails upon the side-boxes. I swear—he, he, he, I have often constrained my inclinations to laugh—he, he, he, to avoid giving them encouragement.

WILLIAM CONGREVE, *The Double Dealer*

In our assemblies at plays in London, you shall see such heaving and shoving, such itching and shouldering, to sit by women; such care for their garments, that they be not trod on; such eyes to their laps, that no chips light in them; such pillows to their backs, that they take no hurt; such masking in their ears, I know not what; such giving them pippins to pass the time; such playing at foot saunt without cards; such ticking, such toying, such smiling, such winking, and such manning them home, when the sports are ended, that it is a right comedy to mark their behaviour, to watch their conceits . . .

STEPHEN GOSSON, *The School of Abuse* (1579)

SIR EPICURE MAMMON: But do you hear?
I'll geld you, Lungs.
FACE: Yes, sir.
MAMMON: For I do mean
To have a list of wives and concubines
Equal with Solomon, who had the Stone
Alike with me; and I will make me a back,
With the elixir, that shall be as tough
As Hercules, to encounter fifty a night.
Th'art sure thou saw'st it blood?
FACE: Both blood and spirit, sir.
MAMMON: I will have all my beds blown up, not stuffed—
Down is too hard. And then, mine oval room
Filled with such pictures as Tiberius took
From Elephantis, and dull Aretine
But coldly imitated. Then, my glasses
Cut in more subtle angles, to disperse
And multiply the figures, as I walk
Naked between my succubae. My mists
I'll have of perfume, vapoured 'bout the room,
To lose ourselves in; and my baths, like pits
To fall into, from whence we will come forth
And roll us dry in gossamer and roses. . . .
We will be brave, Puff, now we ha' the med'cine.

My meat shall all come in, in Indian shells,
Dishes of agate, set in gold, and studded
With emeralds, sapphires, hyacinths, and rubies.
The tongues of carps, dormice, and camels' heels,
Boiled i' the spirit of Sol, and dissolved pearl,—
Apicius' diet, 'gainst the epilepsy—
And I will eat these broths with spoons of amber,
Headed with diamond and carbuncle.
My foot-boy shall eat pheasants, calvered salmons,
Knots, godwits, lampreys; I myself will have
The beards of barbels served, instead of salads;
Oiled mushrooms; and the swelling, unctuous paps
Of a fat, pregnant sow, newly cut off,
Dressed with an exquisite and poignant sauce,
For which I'll say unto my cook, "There's gold;
Go forth, and be a knight!" . . .
SURLY: And do you think to have the Stone with this?
MAMMON: No, I do think t'have all this with the Stone.

.   .   .   .   .   .

DOLL: The Prince will soon take notice, and both seize
You and your Stone, it being a wealth unfit
For any private subject.
MAMMON: If he knew it.
DOLL: Yourself do boast it, sir.
MAMMON: To thee, my life.
DOLL: O, but beware, sir! You may come to end
The remnant of your days in a loathed prison,
By speaking of it.
MAMMON: 'Tis no idle fear!
We'll therefore go withal, my girl, and live
In a free state, where we will eat our mullets
Soused in high country wines, sup pheasants' eggs,
And have our cockles boiled in silver shells;
Our shrimps to swim again, as when they lived,

In a rare butter made of dolphins' milk,
Whose cream does look like opals; and with these
Delicate meats, set ourselves high for pleasure,
And take us down again, and then renew
Our youth and strength with drinking the elixir,
And so enjoy a perpetuity
Of life and lust.

BEN JONSON, *The Alchemist*

CLERIMONT: But all women are not to be taken all ways.

TRUEWIT: 'Tis true. No more than all birds, or all fishes. If you appear learned to an ignorant wench, or jocund to a sad, or witty to a foolish, why, she presently begins to mistrust herself. You must approach them i' their own height, their own line; for the contrary makes many that fear to commit themselves to noble and worthy fellows, run into the embraces of a rascal. If she love wit, give verses, though you borrow 'em of a friend, or buy 'em, to have good. If valour, talk of your sword, and be frequent in the mention of quarrels, though you be staunch in fighting. If activity, be seen o' your barbary often, or leaping over stools, for the credit of your back. If she love good clothes or dressing, have your learned council about you every morning, your French tailor, barber, linener, &c. Let your powder, your glass, and your comb be your dearest acquaintance. Take more care for the ornament of your head, than the safety; and wish the commonwealth rather troubled, than a hair about you. That will take her. Then, if she be covetous and craving, do you promise anything, and perform sparingly; so shall you keep her in appetite still. Seem as you would give, but be like a barren field that yields little, or unlucky dice to foolish and hoping gamesters. Let your gifts be slight and dainty, rather than precious. Let cunning be above cost. Give cherries at time of year, or apricots, and say they were sent you out o' the country, though you bought 'em in Cheapside. Admire her tires; like her in all fashions; compare her in every habit to some deity; invent excellent dreams to flatter her . . . like what she likes, praise whom she praises, and fail not to make the household and servants yours. . . .

BEN JONSON, *Epicene*

A Third Round of Poetry

When thou must home to shades of underground
And there arrived, a new admired guest,
The beauteous spirits do engirt thee round:
White Iope, blithe Helen, and the rest
To hear the stories of thy finished love
From that smooth tongue whose music Hell can move,

Then wilt thou speak of banqueting delights,
Of masques and revels which sweet youth did make,
Of tourneys and great challenges of knights,
And all these triumphs for thy beauty's sake:
When thou has told these honours done to thee,
Then tell, O tell, how thou didst murder me.

THOMAS CAMPION

From *From a Stormy Night*

V I

On nights like this all cities are alike,
with cloud-flags hung.
The banners by the storm are flung,
torn out like hair
in any country anywhere
whose boundaries and rivers are uncertain.
In every garden is a pond,
the same little house sits just beyond;
the same light is in all the houses;

and all the people look alike
and hold their hands before their faces.

VIII

On nights like this my little sister grows,
who was born and died before me, very small.
There have been many such nights, gone long ago:
she must be lovely now. Soon the suitors will call.

RILKE

(trans. C. F. MacIntyre)

On Music

Many love music for music's sake,
Many because her touches can awake
Thoughts that repose within the breast half-dead,
And rise to follow where she loves to lead.
What various feelings come from days gone by!
What tears from far-off sources dim the eye!
Few, when light fingers with sweet voices play
And melodies swell, pause, and melt away,
Mind how at every touch, at every tone,
A spark of life hath glistened and hath gone.

WALTER SAVAGE LANDOR

Bewick Finzer

Time was when his half million drew
    The breath of six per cent;
But soon the worm of what-was-not
    Fed hard on his content;
And something crumbled in his brain
    When his half million went.

Time passed, and filled along with his
    The place of many more;

Time came, and hardly one of us
    Had credence to restore,
From what appeared one day, the man
    Whom we had known before.

The broken voice, the withered neck,
    The coat worn out with care,
The cleanliness of indigence,
    The brilliance of despair,
The fond imponderable dreams
    Of affluence—all were there.

Poor Finzer, with his dreams and schemes,
    Fares hard now in the race,
With heart and eye that have a task
    When he looks in the face
Of one who might so easily
    Have been in Finzer's place.

He comes unfailing for the loan
    We give and then forget;
He comes, and probably for years
    Will he be coming yet—
Familiar as an old mistake,
    And futile as regret.

                    EDWIN ARLINGTON ROBINSON

From *An Horatian Ode upon Cromwell's Return from Ireland*

That thence the royal actor borne
The tragic scaffold might adorn:
While round the armèd bands
Did clap their bloody hands.
He nothing common did or mean
Upon that memorable scene:

But with a keener eye
The ax's edge did try.
Nor called the gods with vulgar spite
To vindicate his helpless right:
But bowed his comely head
Down, as upon a bed.

ANDREW MARVELL

The Mower to the Glow-Worms

Ye living lamps, by whose dear light
The nightingale does sit so late,
And studying all the summer night
Her matchless songs does meditate;

Ye country comets, that portend
No war, nor prince's funeral,
Shining unto no higher end
Than to presage the grass's fall;

Ye glow-worms, whose officious flame
To wandering mowers shows the way,
That in the night have lost their aim,
And after foolish fires do stray:

Your courteous lights in vain you waste,
Since Juliana here is come,
For she my mind hath so displaced
That I shall never find my home.

ANDREW MARVELL

From *The Enchanted Spring*

Her pebbles all to emeralds turn,
    Her mosses fine as Nereid's hair;

Bright leaps the crystal from her urn,
As pure as dew, and twice as rare.

GEORGE DARLEY

Nature, that washed her hands in milk,
    And had forgot to dry them,
Instead of earth, took snow and silk,
    At Love's request to try them,
If she a mistress could compose
To please Love's fancy out of those.

. . . . . .

But Time, which Nature doth despise
    And rudely gives her love the lie,
Makes hope a fool, and sorrow wise,
    His hands doth neither wash nor dry;
But being made of steel and rust,
Turns snow, and silk, and milk, to dust.

. . . . . .

Oh, cruel Time, which takes in trust
    Our youth, our joys, and all we have,
And pays us but with age and dust;
    Who in the dark and silent grave
When we have wandered all our ways
Shuts up the story of our days.

SIR WALTER RALEIGH

From *The Flower*

And now in age I bud again,
After so many deaths I live and write;
    I once more smell the dew and rain,
And relish versing: Oh, my only Light,

It cannot be
That I am he
On whom Thy tempests fell all night.

GEORGE HERBERT

Hey nonny no!
Men are fools that wish to die!
Is't not fine to dance and sing
When the bells of death do ring?
Is't not fine to swim in wine
And turn upon the toe
And sing hey nonny no,
When the winds blow and the seas flow?
Hey nonny no!

ANON.

Touchés

One of the greatest horsemen of all time, Baucher, received the post of equerry at Saumur from the Second Empire when he had grown old and poor. One day his favorite pupil, a brilliant young cavalry captain, came to visit him. Baucher said to him: "I am going to ride a little for you." He was put on his horse and crossed the grounds *at a walk,* then started back. Dazzled, the captain saw coming toward him a perfect Centaur. "There!" said the master. "I am not showing off. I am at the summit of my art: walking faultlessly."

To know oneself is to foresee oneself; to foresee oneself amounts to playing a part.

In all criminal matters, the essential for the accused is to render himself infinitely more interesting than his victims.

An artist chooses even when he confesses. And perhaps above all when he confesses.

PAUL VALÉRY, *Variety: Second Series*

(trans. William A. Bradley)

[From the will of John Reed, for forty-four years employed by a Philadelphia theatre:] My head to be separated from my body immediately after my death, the latter to be buried in a grave; the former, duly macerated and prepared, to be brought to the theatre where I have served all my life, and to be employed to *represent* the skull of Yorick.

[From the will of Edmond de Goncourt:] My will is that my drawings, my prints, my curiosities, my books—in a word, those things of art which have been the joy of my life—shall not be consigned to the cold tomb of a museum, and subjected to the stupid glance of the careless passer-by; but I request that they shall all be disposed of under the hammer of the auctioneer, so that the pleasure that the acquiring of each one of them has given to me shall be given again, in each case, to some inheritor of my own tastes.

The delusive seduction of martial music.

FANNY BURNEY

When Sir Joshua Reynolds died
All Nature was degraded;
The King dropped a tear into the Queen's ear,
And all his pictures faded.

BLAKE

Art imitates art more than it imitates Nature.

JEAN CHARBONNEAUX

One always has to spoil a picture a little bit, in order to finish it. The last touches, which are given to bring about harmony among the parts, take away from the freshness. In order to appear before the public one has to cut away all the happy negligences which are the passion of the artist.

DELACROIX, *Journal*

(trans. Walter Pach)

Nothing so resembles a daub as a masterpiece.

GAUGUIN, *Intimate Journals*

In order to compose, all you need do is remember a tune that no one else has thought of.

ROBERT SCHUMANN

[On the people of Edinburgh, 1635:] Their pewter, I am confident, is never scoured; they are afraid it should too much wear and consume thereby; only sometimes, and that but seldom, they do slightly rub them over with a filthy dish-clout, dipped in most sluttish greasy water. Their pewter pots, wherein they bring wine and water, are furred within, that it would loathe you to touch any thing which comes out of them.

SIR WILLIAM BRERETON, *Travels*

How I like to be liked, and *what I do* to be liked!

CHARLES LAMB, letter to Dorothy Wordsworth

From *Epilogue to the Satires*

Yes, I am proud; I must be proud to see
Men not afraid of God, afraid of me.

ALEXANDER POPE

Insensitives are not the only lovers of horror and disgust. There is another class of men and women, often more than ordinarily sensitive, who deliberately seek out what pains and nauseates them for the sake of the extraordinary pleasure they derive from the overcoming of their repulsion. Take the case, for example, of the mystical Mme. Guyon, who felt that her repugnance for unclean and unsavoury objects was a weakness disgraceful in one who lived only for and with God. One day she determined to overcome this weakness and, seeing on the ground a particularly revolting gob of phlegm and spittle, she picked it up and, in spite of intolerable retchings of disgust, put it in her mouth. Her nauseated horror was succeeded by a sentiment of joy, of profound exultation. A similar incident may be found in the biography of St. Francis of Assisi. Almost the first act of his religious life was to kiss the pustulent hand of one of those lepers, the sight and smell of whom had, up till that time, sickened him with disgust. Like Mme. Guyon, he was rewarded for his pains with a feeling of rapturous happiness.

ALDOUS HUXLEY, *Holy Face and Other Essays*

Nine-tenths of the letters in which people speak unreservedly of their inmost feelings are written after ten at night.

An experience hard-won by an inferior mind often prompts a remark of profundity and originality not to be surpassed by one of far superior calibre.

Though a good deal is too strange to be believed, nothing is too strange to have happened.

THOMAS HARDY, *Notebooks*

Having heard that Henry Taylor was ill, Carlyle rushed off from London to Sheen with a bottle of medicine which had done Mrs. Carlyle good, without in the least knowing what was ailing Henry Taylor, or for what the medicine was useful.

Alfred Lord Tennyson: A Memoir

[Gibbon] had been staying some time with Lord Sheffield in the country; and when he was about to go away, the servants could not find his hat. "Bless me," said Gibbon, "I certainly left it in the hall on my arrival here." He had not stirred out of doors during the whole of the visit.

SAMUEL ROGERS, *Table Talk*

✠ "Chips" Channon, an American-born high-society English M.P., sat at dinner, in his youth, between Marcel Proust and Jean Cocteau:

Their manners, usually so bad, were excellent tonight . . . I felt stupid between the two wittiest men in Europe, drenched in a Niagara of epigrams. Jean is a stylist and his conversation is full of fire and rapier thrusts. . . . He is haggard at 26, and his figure and smile have something mythological, something of the cen-taur, in them.

Proust is quieter, longer-winded and more meticulous. His blood-shot eyes shine feverishly, as he pours out ceaseless spite and venom about the great. His foibles are Ruskin, genealogy and heraldry. He knows the arms and quarterings of every duke in Europe. His black hair was tidily arranged, but his linen was grubby, and the rich studs and links had been clumsily put in by dirty fingers.

Proust has always been kind to me, and I don't like to libel him in the pages of my diary, so I will boil down to the minimum all the rumours about him: that he loathes daylight and is called at tea-time, the world knows. Does the world know that he tips with thousand franc notes, and that he has prolonged evening gossips with the Figaro coiffeur at the Ritz? . . .

When I first met him long ago, he was particularly agreeable to me. A few days later, when walking with Maurice d'Astier, we met him. Maurice bowed, but I hadn't noticed him until too late, never thinking he would even remember me. The next day he wrote Maurice the letter of a madman, asking in twenty-seven pages of superb prose, for an explanation why I had cut him. Long drawn out pompous suppositions in a super-Henry James manner, as to why a young man should dare to be rude to him.

SIR HENRY CHANNON, *Diaries*

Ours is the age of the omnibus, of the third person plural, of Tammany Hall. Is it that Nature has only so much vital force, and must dilute it if it is to be multiplied into millions?

In America the geography is sublime, but the men are not: the inventions are excellent, but the inventors one is sometimes ashamed of. The agencies by which events so grand as the opening of California, of Texas, of Oregon, and the junction of the two oceans, are effected, are paltry—coarse selfishness, fraud and conspiracy; and most of the great results of history are brought about by discreditable means.

EMERSON

The ability to insinuate is more useful than the ability to persuade, for you can insinuate to everybody where you can almost never persuade anybody.

One has greater difficulty in living with one's fellow party members than in acting against one's opponents.

CARDINAL DE RETZ

Tramp Songs

He Has Gone

Close the door—across the river
    He has gone!
With an abscess on his liver
    He has gone!

Many years of rainy seasons,
And malaria's countless treasons
Are among the many reasons
    Why he's gone!

Bind the wasted jaws up lightly—
    He has gone!
Close the sunken eyelids tightly—
    He has gone!
Chinese gin from Bottle Alley
Could not give him strength to rally—
Lone to wander in Death Valley
    He has gone!

In his best clothes we've arrayed him—
    He has gone!
In a wooden box we've laid him—
    He has gone!
Bogus Hennessy and sherry
With his system both made merry:
Very hard he fought them: very!
    Yet he's gone!

Down the hill we tramp once more: friends,
    He has gone!
Once again we've seen all o'er: friends,
    He has gone!
Let us hope we may endure, or
At least our taste be surer—
Let us pray the liquor's purer
    Where he's gone!

W. S. GILBERT

✠ This Gilbert, *not* the author of *The Mikado*, left an
incomplete volume called *Panama Patchwork*, was thought to
have lived in the Panama Canal Zone, and has commemorated

here the career and collapse of a number of men who worked
on the Big Ditch.

From *Honky Tonky*

My mammy was a blushing mare,
My old man was a stallion;
The half of me is centipede
And the rest of me is hellion;
For I'm a mule, a long-eared fool,
And I aint never been to school—

My mammy was a wall-eyed goat,
My old man was an ass,
And I feed myself off leather boots
And dynamite and grass;
For I'm a mule, a long-eared fool,
And I aint never been to school.

                                        ANON.

The Dying Hobo

Beside a western water tank, one cold November day,
Sheltered in a box car a dying hobo lay.
His partner sat beside him and sadly bowed his head
As he listened to the last words his dying buddy said.

"I'm going to a better land, where everything is bright;
Where handouts grow on bushes, and you sleep-in every
    night;
Where a man don't ever have to work, or even change his
    socks,
And little streams of whisky come trickling down the
    rocks.

"I'm heading for a country where no cops are on the drag,
Where no cheap dick can shake you down, and take away
  the swag;
Where everything is lovely and the nights are two months
  long,
Where no one tries to gyp you, and no one does you
  wrong.

"Just tell my gal in Denver, whose face no more I'll view,
That I've hopped my last fast rattler, and I'm riding her
  on through."
Then his eyes grim dim, his head fell back, he'd sung his
  last refrain.
—His partner hooked his coat and shoes and flipped an
  eastbound train.

ANON.

From *The Filipino Hombre*

There once was a Filipino hombre
Who ate rice, pescado y legumbre,
His trousers were wide and his shirt hung outside,
And this, I may say, was costumbre.

He lived in a nipa bajai
Which served as a stable and sty,
And he slept on a mat with the dogs and a cat,
And the rest of the family nearby.

.   .   .   .   .

His mujer once kept a tienda
Underneath a large stone hacienda;
She chewed betel and sold for jawbone and gold
To soldados who said "No intienda."

Su hermana fue lavandera
And slapped clothes in fuerta manera
On a rock in the stream where carabaos dream,
Which gave them a perfume lifera.

. . . . . .

Of niños he had dos or tres
Good types of the tagalog race;
In dry or wet weather, in the altogether,
They'd romp and they'd race and they'd chase.

. . . . . .

When his pueblo last had a fiesta
His familia tried to digesta
Mule which had died of glanders inside—
Y ahora su familia no esta!

ANON.

pescado y legumbre—fish and vegetables; *nipa bajai*—house of nipa palm
fronds; *mujer*—woman; *tienda*—store; *"No intienda"*—"I don't understand";
Su hermana fue lavandera—His sister was a laundress; *fuerta manera*—
briskly; *carabaos*—water buffalo; *lifera*—strong-smelling; *niños*—children; *Y
ahora su familia no esta*—And now his family is no more.

Transportation

"You came by the railroad?" inquired Lord de Mowbray
mournfully, of Lady Marney.

"From Marham; about ten miles from us," replied her lady-
ship.

"A great revolution!"

"Isn't it?"

"I fear it has a very dangerous tendency to equality," said his
lordship . . . ". . . Equality, Lady Marney, equality is not our
métier. If we nobles do not make a stand against the levelling
spirit of the age, I am at a loss to know who will fight the battle.

You may depend upon it that these railroads are very dangerous things."

"I have no doubt of it. I suppose you have heard of Lady Vanilla's trip from Birmingham? Have you not, indeed? She came up with Lady Laura, and two of the most gentlemanlike men sitting opposite her; never met, she says, two more intelligent men. She begged one of them at Wolverhampton to change seats with her, and he was most politely willing to comply with her wishes, only it was necessary that his companion should move at the same time, for they were chained together! Two gentlemen, sent to town for picking a pocket at Shrewsbury races."

"A countess and a felon! So much for public conveyances," said Lord de Mowbray.

D I S R A E L I , *Sybil*

Travel

✠ Travel broadens man, but reading about it can easily bore him. For myself, if I must do armchair traveling, I prefer doing it with picture books rather than texts—for one reason because, depending on the photographer, they have an honest or a heightened vividness; for another, because the pictures are of cities or castles or lakes, where a solid text is of what the author thinks of these things, or is about the author himself. I suspect that my preference for pictures stems from some twenty volumes, in my father's library, of Stoddard's *Lectures*, Mr. Stoddard having traveled all over the world and lectured (with slides, no doubt) on what he had seen. In book form, the lectures were supplemented with countless illustrations. Volume by volume I traversed country after country, often enough to say, "I've been several times to Greece; half a dozen times to Rome; I can't tell you how often to London; and twice that often to my favorite region, the Alps." I also *read* in Mr. Stoddard's texts, most often to find out just who the subjects of all the statues—Mr. Stoddard was mad for statues—were. Today I'm not much on statues, unless by a Bernini or Donatello, but I still delight in castles, cathedrals, country houses, dungeons, and village streets.

My father had also a pleasant habit of buying picture post-cards wherever he went; and though his traveling was not far-flung or exotic, his postcard collection—begun around 1890 and continuing for some forty years—would, I imagine, have a real value as Americana today—the small-town main streets complete with shop signs, horse and buggies, and sometimes, at the end of them, statues; the tree-lined village streets; railway stations known as depots; docks, harbors, eight-story skyscrapers, early automobiles, residences of local magnates; birthplaces of the famous and forgotten; rustic front porches with "hanging baskets" and lots of wicker chairs. These I remember as most evocative, but there were also hundreds of postcards of New York, Washington, Boston, and the like; and many of Madison, Indiana —an Ohio River, Mark Twainish town where my father was born and grew up—and of Cincinnati, where he spent most of his life. I pored over the postcards, though not so often as I patronized Mr. Stoddard, and perhaps a hundred of them remain to me. I can't much object to my loss of the others, for when late in life my father was moving from Cincinnati to New York, he called all the children in the neighborhood together and told them to take their choice of his postcards, which they speedily did.

The travel pleasure I get from pictures continues, whether of places where I have been or have not been; among modern books replacing Stoddard are all those—some with very good texts—brought out over many years by Batsford's in London. These take you, inexpensively, everywhere in the British Isles, everywhere that was once the British Empire, and all over Europe, parceling out with sound judgment the landmarks, the architecture and sculpture, the scenery, and the trappings of human society. They too feature the Alps, and with their Gloucestershire or East Anglian village streets are reminiscent of the postcards.

There is, of course, a distinguished travel literature—some of it on exploration—going very far back and very far afield, and bearing such classic names as Marco Polo, Hakluyt, Purchas, and Frobisher, and such modern ones as Henry James and D. H. Lawrence. But though I admire the writing and the responsiveness of a James and a Lawrence, and profit by their observations, I am always too conscious of the man—and in James of the manner—and of looking through quite different eyes at what I like to look at through my own. There were also, in my youth, the travel books—*Cities* and *More Cities*—of Arthur Symons, written in nice, rather poetic prose, and full of color; but with Symons one reached a saturation point early.

What I find I most like to *read* travel books for is not the architecture or the scenery, but the impressions of regional and social life; less the places one visits than the people one meets; and less the sweeping panorama than the picturesque details. Here again Stoddard's *Lectures* find a parallel: I read with great interest Dickens' accounts of his traveling and lecturing all over America; and again, Matthew Arnold's. These accounts come in the letters they wrote and contain a good deal of personal comment and, in Dickens, a good many prejudices; but they make of traveling a human adventure, an anthology of discoveries and reactions, and not a branch of aesthetics. Indeed, some of Horace Walpole's, Lady Mary Wortley Montagu's, and Lord Byron's letters are, as texts, much my favorite traveling companions (and are, for that matter, good to take on one's own travels). Trollope, who wrote travel articles and books, including one about America, and who should make a third with Dickens and Arnold, is too often factual, statistical, and prosaic. It is Henry Adams who makes a nineteenth-century third, he too in the form of letters, with his accounts of life in Japan and the South Seas. There remain, often on the good side, anecdotes of travel—odd bits about places and odder ones about those who travel through them. At this level the best (which could mean worst) anecdotes treat of Americans in Europe, or the English almost anywhere.

Oh, but to travel with your family! It's just like waltzing with one's aunt . . .

MARIE BASHKIRTSEFF, *Journal*

[Of Menton, France:] A calcined, scalped, rasped, scraped, flayed, broiled, powdered, leprous, blotched, mangy, grimy, parboiled country *without* trees, water, grass, fields . . . it is infinitely liker hell than earth, and one looks for tails among the people.

SWINBURNE, letter to Lady Trevelyan

[Of the Côte d'Azur:] How contemptible and loathsome this life is . . . I love wealth and luxury, but the luxury here, the luxury of the gambling saloon, reminds one of a luxurious water closet.

CHEKHOV, letter to his brother

Cologne

In Köln, a town of monks and bones,
And pavements fanged with murderous stones,
And rags, and hags, and hideous wenches,
I counted two and seventy stenches . . .
The River Rhine, it is well known,
Doth wash your city of Cologne;
But tell me, Nymphs! what power divine
Shall henceforth wash the river Rhine?

COLERIDGE

[On leaving Holland:] *Adieu! canaux, canards, canaille.*

VOLTAIRE

On one occasion [near sunset] above Milan, over in the direction of Lake Maggiore, I saw a cloud shaped like a huge mountain made up of banks of fire . . .

This great cloud drew to itself all the little clouds which were round about it. And the great cloud remained stationary, and it retained the light of the sun on its apex for an hour and a half after sunset, so enormous was its size. And about two hours after night had fallen there arose a stupendous storm of wind.

LEONARDO DA VINCI, *Notebooks*

(trans. Edward MacCurdy)

After leaving Florence I . . . continued my journey through Sienna to Rome, where I arrived at the beginning of October. My temper is not very susceptible of enthusiasm, and the enthusiasm which I do not feel I have ever scorned to affect. But at the distance of twenty-five years I can neither forget nor express the strong emotions which agitated my mind as I first approached and entered the *eternal city*. After a sleepless night, I trod, with a lofty step, the ruins of the Forum; each memorable spot where Romulus *stood,* or Tully spoke, or Caesar fell, was at once present to my eye; and several days of intoxication were lost or enjoyed before I could descend to a cool and minute investigation.

GIBBON, *Autobiography*

[Of St. Peter's, Rome:] The fountains are magnificent. Christina, Queen of Sweden, thought they were made to play in honour of her visit, and begged they might cease—at least so says the guide —but this is the kind of story which is told of every royal head down to *Prince Le Boo;* who, when he first entered London, thought it was lighted up as a particular compliment to him.

H. MATTHEWS, *Diary of an Invalid*

England and America

1. ON A RHINE STEAMER

Republic of the West,
    Enlightened, free, sublime,

Unquestionably best
Production of our time.

The telephone is thine,
And thine the Pullman Car,
The caucus, the divine
Intense electric star.

To thee we likewise owe
The venerable names
Of Edgar Allan Poe,
And Mr Henry James.

In short it's due to thee,
Thou kind of Western star,
That we have come to be
Precisely what we are.

But every now and then,
It cannot be denied,
You breed a kind of men
Who are not dignified,

Or courteous or refined,
Benevolent or wise,
Or gifted with a mind
Beyond the common size,

Or notable for tact,
Agreeable to me,
Or anything, in fact
That people ought to be.

2. ON A PARISIAN BOULEVARD

Britannia rules the waves,
As I have heard her say;

She frees whatever slaves
      She meets upon her way.

A teeming mother she
      Of Parliaments and Laws;
Majestic, mighty, free:
      Devoid of common flaws.

For her did Shakspere write
      His admirable plays:
For her did Nelson fight
      And Wolseley win his bays.

Her sturdy common sense
      Is based on solid grounds:
By saving numerous pence
      She spends effective pounds.

.   .   .   .   .   .

But every here and there—
      Deny it if you can—
She breeds a vacant stare
      Unworthy of a man:

A look of dull surprise;
      A nerveless idle hand:
An eye which never tries
      To threaten or command:

In short, a kind of man,
      If man indeed he be,
As worthy of our ban
      As any that we see:

Unspeakably obtuse,
      Abominably vain,

Of very little use,
And execrably plain.

J. K. S T E P H E N, *Lapsus Calami*

We are seeing British Burmah, the most flourishing province of
the Indian Empire, to very great advantage, while enjoying the
society of our kind host here. We visited a large steam saw-mill on
the river to see the elephants at work. It was curious and amusing
to watch the great beasts pile up the teak-trees—curling their
trunks round a plank 40 feet long, they lift it carefully to the top
of the pile, which they insist on keeping perfectly square (people
say they shut one eye and squint along the side to see that every
log is level). By a motion of the mahout's foot behind their ear,
they understand exactly what to do—the noise is too great to hear
his voice—and threading their way through the machinery, they
lift the outsides of the teak-trees out of the way as if they were
chips; or untie a chain or rope, and bring another log into position, quite at their ease, among the whirling cog-wheels and
bands and huge steam-saws. Very handy carpenter's boys the
greatest of beasts make, to the still greater giant "steam-power."
But it does not do to annoy them. A few years ago an elephant in
this yard singled out an English overseer, who was in the habit of
teasing him, as he sauntered by with his friends one Sunday afternoon, and, catching the poor man round the waist with his trunk,
crushed him to death.

M R S. F. D. B R I D G E S, *Journal of a Lady's Travels*
Round the World (1883)

But I cannot let pass in silence the prodigious alteration [in
Italy] . . . in regard to our sex. This reformation (or, if you
please, depravation) began so lately as the year 1732, when the
French overran this part of Italy, but it has been carried on with
such fervor and success that the Italians go far beyond their pat-
terns, the Parisian ladies, in the extent of their liberty. I am not
so much surprised at the women's conduct as I am amazed at the

change in the men's sentiments. Jealousy, which was once a point of honor amongst them, is exploded to that degree, it is the most infamous and ridiculous of all characters, and you cannot more affront a gentleman than to suppose him capable of it.

Divorces are also introduced and frequent enough. They have long been in fashion in Genoa, several of the finest and greatest ladies there having two husbands alive. The constant pretext is impotency, to which the man often pleads guilty, and though he marries again and has children by another wife, the plea remains good by saying he was so in regard to his first; and when I told them that in England a complaint of that kind was esteemed so impudent, no reasonable woman would submit to make it, I was answered we lived without religion, and that their consciences obliged them rather to strain a point of modesty than live in a state of damnation. However, as this method is not without inconvenience (it being impracticable where there is children) they have taken another here: the husband deposes upon oath that he has had a commerce with his mother-in-law, on which the marriage is declared incestuous and nullified . . . You will think this hard on the old lady who is scandalized, but it is no scandal at all, nobody supposing it to be true . . .

> LADY MARY WORTLEY MONTAGU, letter to her daughter,
> the Countess of Bute

The method of treating the physician in this country [Italy], I think should be the same everywhere: they make it his interest that the whole parish should be in good health, giving him a stated pension, which is collected by a tax on every house, on condition he neither demands nor receives any fees, nor ever refuses a visit either to rich or poor. This last article would be very hard if we had as many vapourish ladies as in England, but those imaginary ills are entirely unknown here. When I recollect the vast fortunes raised by doctors amongst us, and the eager pursuit after every new piece of quackery that is introduced, I cannot help thinking there is a fund of credulity in mankind that must be employed somewhere, and the money formerly given to monks for the health of the soul is now thrown to doctors for health of the body, and generally with as little real prospect of success.

LADY MARY WORTLEY MONTAGU, letter to her husband

The Universal Man

✠ Some thoughts of Leonardo da Vinci:

There is nothing which deceives us as much as our own judgment.

Avoid the precepts of those thinkers whose reasoning is not confirmed by experience.

A natural action is accomplished in the briefest manner.

Why does the eye perceive things more clearly in dreams than with the imagination when one is awake?

The vow is born when hope dies.

He who wishes to grow rich in a day will be hanged in a year.

He who offends others is not himself secure.

When fortune comes, seize her in front firmly, because behind she is bald.

No counsel is more sincere than that given on ships which are in danger.

When beauty exists side by side with ugliness, the one seems more powerful, owing to the presence of the other.

The first picture was a single line, drawn round the shadow of a man cast by the sun on the wall.

The good painter has two principal things to depict: man and the purpose of his mind. The first is easy, the second is difficult, since

he must do it by gestures and movements of the limbs, and this is
to be learnt from the dumb, who more than all other men excel
in it.

Upstarts

✠ In "Trimalchio's Dinner," the one great chunk that
has survived from the mostly lost *Satyricon* of Petronius, we get
our first taste of the novel as we tend to think of it, and at the
same time a remarkable example of the satirical novel, by the
most modern or any other standards. In Trimalchio Petronius
offers, brilliantly, a *nouveau riche* during Rome's decadence; a
nouveau riche who is tremendously rich and lives on a scale that
even Hollywood might envy, and with a vulgarity that perhaps
only Hollywood could equal. The following passage centers on
the nature of such a host rather than on the extravagantly luxurious hospitality he dispenses, which can perhaps be inferred. A
portrait of the author by an even more distinguished author,
Tacitus, follows.

The talk was passing back and forth . . . when Trimalchio returned, and, after wiping his forehead, washed his hands in perfumed water. Then, after a moment or two of delay, he said:

"You will excuse me, my friends, but my stomach for a good
many days has been out of sorts, and the doctors don't know
where they are at. However, I have been helped by pomegranate
rind and a mixture of pitch and vinegar. I trust that my internal
economy will soon feel ashamed of itself. Moreover there is a
rumbling in my stomach so that you would imagine it to be a
bull. And so if any of you wish to go out don't be bashful. . . .
You'll find all the conveniences. Flatulence goes to the head and
kicks up a disturbance all through the body. I know of a good
many persons who have died because they were too modest to
speak the truth."

We thanked him for his kind generosity and concealed our laughter by taking numerous drinks. We had no idea, after all the rich things already eaten, that we hadn't yet, as they say, reached the top of the hill; but now, as soon as the table had been cleared off to the sound of music, three white swine were brought into the dining-room, decorated with muzzles and little bells. The slave who anounced the guests said that one of the pigs was two years old, another three years old, and a third already six years old. I thought that rope dancers were coming in and that the pigs, as is often the case in the side-shows, were going to perform some remarkable tricks. But Trimalchio, putting an end to our suspense, said:

"Which of these pigs would you like to have served up at once on the table? Country cooks can prepare a fowl or a piece of beef and other trifles of that sort, but *my* cooks are accustomed to serve up whole calves boiled!"

Immediately he had the cook summoned; and not waiting for us to make a choice, he ordered the oldest pig to be slaughtered. Then he asked the slave in a loud voice:

"Which of my slave-gangs do you belong to?"

"The fortieth," said the cook.

"Were you purchased for me," said Trimalchio, "or born on my estate?"

"Neither," replied the cook. "I was left to you in Pansa's will."

"See then," said Trimalchio, "that you set the pig before us in good style. If you don't, I shall have you transferred to the gang of running footmen."

PETRONIUS, *Satyricon*

(trans. Harry Thurston Peck)

The Suicide of Petronius

He was a man who devoted the day to sleep and spent the night in business or pleasure, and was distinguished rather for his idleness than for his thrift; one who gained the reputation, not of a glutton or of a profligate, like most spendthrifts, but of a cultured epicure, whose words and deeds were accepted all the more gladly as models of simplicity in proportion as they were unconventional and careless. As proconsul in Bithynia, and afterwards consul suffectus, he proved himself active and equal to his work; but upon returning to his evil ways, or possibly by a pretence of evil, he became one of Nero's few and most intimate friends, his authority in matters of taste, so that, fatigued with pleasures, the Emperor thought nothing charming or delicate unless Petronius had approved it. Thus Tigellinus became jealous of him as a powerful rival through his skill in entertaining, and addressing himself to that greatest of Nero's vices, his cruelty, he accused Petronius of intimacy with Scaevinus. He bribed a slave to substantiate the charge, prevented all defense, and threw a large part of the household of Petronius into prison. Nero happened at that time to be on his way to Campania, and Petronius had followed him as far as Cumae, where he was arrested. He decided not to prolong his life between hope and fear, nor to put an immediate end to it; but opening his veins and binding them repeatedly, he conversed with his friends, not on serious topics or such as might have shown his firmness of spirit. Nor did he listen to any discussion on the immortality of the soul or to the wise saws of philosophers, but only to frivolous songs and gay verses. To some of his slaves he gave largesses; others he directed to be punished. He feasted and slept, that his death, though violent, might seem due to accident. Nor, as most men do when so situated, did he in his will extol Nero or Tigellinus or any other of those in power; but, employing names of rakes and dissolute women, he described the Emperor's crimes and each new form of his license, sealed the account and sent it to Nero. He broke his ring also, lest it be used forthwith for some mischief.

T A C I T U S

(trans. William E. Waters)

Writers

[Tolstoi:] I always write in the morning. . . . Dostoevsky always wrote at night. In a writer there must always be two people—the writer and the critic. And, if one writes at night, with a cigarette in one's mouth, although the work of creation goes on briskly, the critic is for the most part in abeyance, and this is very dangerous.

[Tolstoi:] The most important thing in a work of art is that it should have some kind of focus, i.e. there should be some place where all the rays meet or from which they issue. And this focus must not be able to be completely explained in words. This indeed is one of the significant facts about a true work of art—that its content in its entirety can be expressed only by itself.

A. B. GOLDENVEIZER, *Talks with Tolstoi*

In my opinion descriptions of Nature should be very brief and have an incidental character. Commonplaces like: "The setting sun, bathing in the waves of the darkening sea, flooded with purple and gold," etc. . . . should be finished with. In descriptions of Nature one has to snatch at small details. . . .

For instance, you will get a moonlight night if you write that on the dam of the mill a fragment of broken bottle flashed like a small bright star, and there rolled by, like a ball, the black shadow of a dog, or a wolf—and so on. Nature appears animated if you do not disdain to use comparisons of its phenomena with those of human actions, etc.

CHEKHOV, letter to Alexander P. Chekhov

Lord Byron's letters are the best English I know of—perfectly simple and clear, bright and strong.

WILKIE COLLINS, in a newspaper interview

✠ The following is one of my favorite passages for what seems to me least fine in its author.

So it was, at any rate, that when my amiable friend, on the Christmas Eve, before the table that glowed safe and fair through the brown London night, spoke of such an odd matter as that a good lady of the north, always well looked on, was at daggers drawn with her only son, ever hitherto exemplary, over the ownership of the valuable furniture of a fine old house just accruing to the young man by his father's death, I instantly became aware, with my "sense for the subject," of the prick of inoculation; the *whole* of the virus, as I have called it, being infused by that single touch. There had been but ten words, yet I had recognised in them, as in a flash, all the possibilities of the little drama of my *Spoils* [*of Poynton*] . . .

HENRY JAMES, *The Art of the Novel*

✠ Here are the unnecessary reference to the table, the oddity of its glowing "safe" (the candles didn't set fire to the tablecloth?) "through the brown, London night" (the table was out of doors?); the slightly fatuous and rather condescending references to "my amiable friend" and "a good lady of the north"; the smug pomposity of "I instantly became aware, with my 'sense for the subject' "; the coy use, for perhaps the fiftieth time, of "little" in front of something or other of James's; and the fact that "There had been but ten words," which James required forty-four words to paraphrase. (The "ten words" may be viewed as a mere manner of speaking; nevertheless, the forty-four words can be reduced, by any high-school sophomore, to twenty-four.) This is not to deny how great, if in a somewhat special way, James could be, or how splendidly, in the same special way, he could write, even about himself; or how fine a critic as well as fiction writer he is at his best; only to say that on occasion he can be perhaps the most tiresome writer of great talent that one can think of. He is an absolute requirement in any course on how to write, and again in any course on how not to.

[Leigh Hunt to Joseph Severn, as a message to the dying Keats:]
Tell him he is only before us on the road, as he was in everything
else . . .

The author in his work should be like God in the universe, everywhere present and nowhere visible.

FLAUBERT

✠ We have, thanks to Caroline Spurgeon's *Shakespeare's Imagery*, a knowledge of the total number of images in
each of Shakespeare's plays, and of the dominating imagery in
many of them. Images of disease and sickness dominate *Hamlet;*
of bodily and physical movement, generally involving pain, dominate *Lear;* of animals in action, "preying upon one another,
mischievous, lascivious, cruel or suffering," dominate *Othello;*
of light, in its many forms, dominate *Romeo and Juliet;* of magnificence and vastness, dominate *Antony and Cleopatra;* of war
and weapons dominate *Love's Labour's Lost;* of food and cooking dominate *Troilus and Cressida;* and so on. The three plays
with the greatest number of images are *Troilus and Cressida*,
with 339 (3329 lines to the play); *Hamlet*, with 279 (3762 lines
to the play), and *Antony and Cleopatra*, with 266 (3016 lines to
the play). The three plays with the smallest number of images
are *The Comedy of Errors*, with 60; *Julius Caesar*, with 83; and
The Taming of the Shrew, with 92. Miss Spurgeon's investigation and documentation of Shakespeare's imagery are of notable
interest and value.

In *Hamlet* disease stands first and food second; in *Troilus*, the
other way around. But it is in our third-richest-in-images play,
Antony and Cleopatra, that food offers two great and famous
images:

> Other women cloy
> The appetites they feed, but she makes hungry
> Where most she satisfies . . .

I found you as a morsel cold upon
Dead Caesar's trencher . . .

✠ Of "magnificence and vastness" in *Antony and Cleo-patra* great images abound; great passages, one might say:

His legs bestrid the ocean; his reared arm
Crested the world; his voice was propertied
As all the tuned spheres, and that to friends;
But when he meant to quail and shake the orb
He was as rattling thunder. For his bounty
There was no winter in it, autumn 'twas
That grew the more by reaping; his delights
Were dolphin-like, they showed his back above
The element they lived in. In his livery
Walked crowns and crownets, realms and islands were
As plates dropped from his pocket.

✠ Time, curiously enough, supplies some of the most famous and best images in *Troilus and Cressida:*

Time hath, my lord, a wallet at his back
Wherein he puts alms for oblivion . . .

For time is like a fashionable host
That slightly shakes his parting guest by the hand,
And with his arms outstretched, as he would fly,
Grasps in the comer: welcome ever smiles,
And farewell goes out sighing.

If I be false, or swerve a hair from truth,
When time is old and hath forgot itself . . .

What's past and what's to come is strewed with husks
And formless ruin of oblivion . . .

The end crowns all,
And that old common arbitrator, Time,
Will one day end it.

✠ *Troilus and Cressida* also supplies what may well be
the most misunderstood line in all Shakespeare:

One touch of nature makes the whole world kin

✠ simply because most people take it as a self-contained
statement, rather than find it explained by the lines which follow.

Moonlight is sculpture; sunlight is painting.

To write a dream, which shall resemble the real course of a
dream, with all its inconsistency, its eccentricities and aimlessness
—with nevertheless a leading idea running through the whole.
Up to this old age of the world, no such thing has ever been
written.

NATHANIEL HAWTHORNE, *The American Notebooks*

On his marriage night, Byron suddenly started out of his first
sleep: a taper, which burned in the room, was casting a ruddy
glare through the crimson curtains of the bed, and he could not
help exclaiming, in a voice so loud that he wakened Lady B.,
"Good God, I am surely in hell!"

SAMUEL ROGERS, *Table Talk*

Writers on Writers

I never saw the man [Dostoevski], had no sort of direct relations
with him; but when he died, I suddenly realized that he had been
to me the most precious, the dearest, and the most necessary of
beings.

TOLSTOI

Thackeray sees his characters, both men and women, with a man's eye and with a woman's. He dissects with a knife and also with a needle.

The sale of his [Dickens'] books . . . is so great as almost to induce a belief that Pickwicks and Oliver Twists are consumed in families like legs of mutton.

ANTHONY TROLLOPE, *Four Lectures*

Pride and Prejudice . . . tends toward the vase rather than the washtub, which is rare in English novels.

[Tolstoi's] eyesight exceeds all eyesight before or since.

GEORGE MOORE

Can one imagine anything more terrible than the story of *Romeo and Juliet* rewritten in prose by D. H. Lawrence?

WILLA CATHER

Cheer up, old fellow! After all, you are Flaubert!

TURGENEV, letter to Flaubert

Writers on Writing

My opinion is that a poet should express the emotion of all the ages and the thought of his own.

THOMAS HARDY

I wrote today to Laura Riding . . . that her school was too thoughtful, reasonable and truthful, that poets were good liars who never forgot that the Muses were women who liked the embrace of gay warty lads.

W. B. YEATS

The objections to Sterne's wild way of telling *Tristram Shandy*
lie more solidly in the quality of the interrupting matter than in
the fact of interruption.

GEORGE ELIOT

[Tolstoi:] If you ask someone: "Can you play the violin?" and he
says: "I don't know, I haven't tried, perhaps I can," you laugh at
him. Whereas about writing, people always say: "I don't know, I
have not tried," as though one had only to try and one would
become a writer.

A. B. GOLDENVEIZER, *Talks with Tolstoi*

It was with many misgivings that I killed my old friend Mrs.
Proudie . . . It was thus that it came about. I was sitting one
morning at work upon the novel at the end of the long drawing-
room of the Athenaeum Club. Two clergymen, each with a magazine in his hand, seated themselves . . . close to me. They soon
began to abuse what they were reading, and each was reading
some part of some novel of mine. The gravamen of their complaint lay in the fact that I reintroduced the same characters so
often! "Here," said one, "is that archdeacon whom we have had in
every novel he has written." "And here," said the other, "is the
old duke whom he has talked about till everybody is tired of him.
If I could not invent new characters, I would not write novels at
all." Then one of them fell foul of Mrs. Proudie. It was impossible for me not to hear their words, and almost impossible to
hear them and be quiet. I got up, and standing between them, I
acknowledged myself to be the culprit. "As to Mrs. Proudie," I
said, "I will go home and kill her before the week is over." And so
I did. The two gentlemen were utterly confounded, and one of
them begged me to forget his frivolous observations.

ANTHONY TROLLOPE

My impossible ones. Seneca: or the toreador of virtue. *Rousseau:*
or the return to nature *in impuris naturalibus. Schiller:* or

the Moral-Trumpeter of Säckingen. *Dante:* or the hyena who *writes poetry* in tombs. *Kant:* or cant as an intelligible character. *Victor Hugo:* or the pharos at the sea of nonsense. *Liszt:* or the school of smoothness—with women. *George Sand:* or *lactea ubertas*—in translation, the milk cow with "a beautiful style." *Michelet:* or the enthusiasm which takes off its coat. *Carlyle:* or pessimism as a poorly digested dinner. *John Stuart Mill:* or insulting clarity. *Les frères de Goncourt:* or the two Ajaxes in battle with Homer—music by Offenbach. *Zola:* or "the delight in stinking."

N I E T Z S C H E

Acknowledgments

(continued from copyright page)

Acknowledgment is made to the following for permission to use material owned by them. Every reasonable effort has been made to clear the use of the material in this volume with copyright owners. If notified of any omissions, the editor and publisher will gladly make the proper corrections in future editions.

George Allen & Unwin Ltd.: From *The Years with Mother* by Augustus Hare (abridged by Malcolm Barne).

The American Academy of Political and Social Science and John E. Burchard: *The Urban Aesthetic* by John E. Burchard.

Atheneum Publishers, Inc.: "The Deserted Poet" from *Pretending to Be Asleep* by Peter Davison. Copyright © 1970 by Peter Davison. Reprinted by permission of Atheneum Publishers.

Barnes & Noble, Publishers, and Routledge & Kegan Paul Ltd.: Adapted from Champion: *Racial Proverbs.*

Brandt & Brandt, Sonia Brownell, and Secker & Warburg: From *Down and Out in Paris and London* (Harcourt, Brace and World, Inc., N.Y.). Copyright, 1933 by George Orwell. Copyright renewed © 1960 by Sonia Pett-Rivers. Reprinted by permission.

Cambridge University Press: From *Life in the Middle Ages* by G. G. Coulton.

Jonathan Cape Ltd. From *A Peck of Troubles,* edited by Daniel George.

Chatto and Windus Ltd.: From *The Babees Book* by John Russell, translated by Edith Rickert. Reprinted by permission of Chatto and Windus Ltd. and the Estate of Edith Rickert.

Collins Publishers: From *Autobiography* by Sir Neville Cardus.

Columbia University Press: From *The Art of Courtly Love,* translated by J. J. Parry; Columbia University Press, 1941.

Constable & Co. Ltd.: Anthony Trollope, *Four Lectures* (1938). Published for Morris Parish.

Crown Publishers, Inc.: From *The Journal of Eugène Delacroix,* translated by Walter Pach. © 1937, by Covici Friede; renewal © 1965 by Crown Publishers, Inc. Used by permission of Crown Publishers, Inc.

Curtis Brown, Ltd.: From *Intimate Journals* by Charles Baudelaire, translated by Christopher Isherwood. Copyright © 1947 by Christopher Isherwood. Reprinted by permission of Curtis Brown, Ltd.

Farrar, Straus & Giroux, Inc.: From *The Selected Letters of Flaubert,* translated by Francis Steegmuller, copyright 1953 by Francis Steegmuller. Reprinted by permission of Farrar, Straus & Giroux, Inc.

Harcourt Brace Jovanovich, Inc.: From *Poems 1923–1954* by E. E. Cummings. Copyright, 1931, 1959, by E. E. Cummings. From *A Book of Seventeenth Cen-*

tury Prose, edited by Robert P. Tristram Coffin and Alexander M. Witherspoon. Copyright, 1929, by Harcourt Brace Jovanovich, Inc.; renewed, 1957 by Alexander Witherspoon. From *The Notebooks of Leonardo Da Vinci* by Edward MacCurdy. All reprinted by permission of Harcourt Brace Jovanovich, Inc.

Harper & Row, Publishers, Chatto & Windus Ltd., and Mrs. Laura Huxley: "Swift" by Aldous Huxley.

Rupert Hart-Davis: From *The Rainbow Comes and Goes* by Lady Diana Cooper.

Harvard University Press: Letter to Paul Rosenfeld from *i: Six Nonlectures* by E. E. Cummings.

P. K. Hitti: From *Memoirs of Usamah*, translated by P. K. Hitti, Columbia University Press, 1929, reprinted Beirut 1964.

Hawthorn Books Inc.: From *The Seven Sins*, edited by Geoffrey Grigson and Charles Harvard Gibbs-Smith.

Holiday magazine and *Le Nouveau Guide:* From *The Red King, the White Queen* by Henri Gault and Christian Millau. © 1968 The Curtis Publishing Co. Reprinted by permission of *Holiday* and Henri Gault.

Houghton Mifflin Company: From *John Jay Chapman and His Letters* by M. A. De Wolfe Howe.

The Lonsdale Library: From *The Fisherman* by Alfred Cochrane. From *Boxing* by Viscount Knebworth.

Mrs. F. L. Lucas: From *Studies in French and English* by F. L. Lucas.

Macmillan & Co. Ltd.: From *A Free House* by Osbert Sitwell.

Macmillan & Co. Ltd. (London and Basingstoke) and The Macmillan Company (New York): From *Letters of Sir Walter Raleigh.*

The Macmillan Company, Macmillan London & Basingstoke; and The Macmillan Company of Canada Limited: "A Glass of Beer" from *Collected Poems* by James Stephens. Copyright 1918 by The Macmillan Company, renewed 1946 by James Stephens. By permission of Mrs. Iris Wise.

The Macmillan Company: "Bewick Finzer" from *Collected Poems* by Edwin Arlington Robinson. Copyright 1916 by Edwin Arlington Robinson, renewed 1944 by Ruth Nivison.

John Murray: From *The Ascent of the Matterhorn* by Edward Whymper.

New Directions Publishing Corp.: From *The Dictionary of Accepted Ideas* by Gustave Flaubert, translated by Jacques Barzun. Copyright 1954, © 1968 by Jacques Barzun. Reprinted by permission of New Directions Publishing Corporation.

The Duke of Portland: From *Men, Women and Things.*

Random House, Inc., and Faber and Faber Limited: "Musée des Beaux Arts." Copyright 1940 and renewed 1968 by W. H. Auden. Reprinted from *Collected Shorter Poems 1927–1957*, by W. H. Auden.

Random House, Inc., and Editions Gallimard: *Hamlet*, translated by André Gide. Copyright 1945 by André Gide. Reprinted by permission of Random House, Inc., and Editions Gallimard.

Random House, Inc.: From *My Diaries*, by Wilfrid S. Blunt. Copyright 1921 by Wilfrid S. Blunt and renewed 1949 by Margaret T. Carleton. Reprinted by permission of Alfred A. Knopf, Inc. From *The American Credo*, by George Jean Nathan and H. L. Mencken. Copyright 1920 by Alfred A. Knopf, Inc., and renewed 1948 by George Jean Nathan and H. L. Mencken. Reprinted by permission of the publisher.

Routledge & Kegan Paul Ltd.: From *Passing English of the Victorian Era* by J. Redding Ware.

St. Martin's Press, Inc., and Macmillan & Co., Ltd.: From *Letters of Mozart and His Family* by Emily Anderson.

Charles Scribner's Sons: From *Memories of Opera* by Giulio Gatti Casazza.

Simon & Schuster, Inc.: From *Alexandre Dumas Père Dictionary of Cuisine*, translated by Louis Colman. Copyright © 1958 by Louis Colman. Reprinted by permission of Simon and Schuster.

Tudor Publishing Company: From *The Great Fables*, edited by Manuel Komroff.

University of California Press: From *Moral Scolarium of John of Garland*, "On Table Manners," University of California 1927, edited by Louis John Paetow. From *Translations from Rilke*, "From a Stormy Night" by Rainer Maria Rilke, translated by C. F. MacIntyre, University of California Press, 1940. Reprinted by permission of The Regents of the University of California.

Vanguard Press, Inc.: From *English Eccentrics* by Edith Sitwell. Copyright 1957, by Edith Sitwell. Reprinted by permission of the publishers, The Vanguard Press.

The Viking Press, Inc.: From *The Portable Roman Reader* edited by Basil Davenport. Copyright 1951 by The Viking Press, Inc. Reprinted by permission of The Viking Press, Inc.

Weidenfeld & Nicolson Limited: From *The Chips Channon Diaries* by Sir Henry Channon.

Index

of Authors, Translators, and Other Sources